WAR CRIMES
AND
ATROCITIES

WAR CRIMES
AND
ATROCITIES

by

JANICE ANDERSON,
ANNE WILLIAMS
and
VIVIAN HEAD

Futura

A *Futura* Book

First published by Futura in 2007

Copyright © Omnipress 2007

ISBN 13: 978-0-7088-0784-2

Produced by Omnipress, Eastbourne

Printed in the EU

Futura
An imprint of Little, Brown Book Group
Brettenham House
Lancaster Place
London WC2E 7EN

Photo credits: Getty images

CONTENTS

PART THREE:
WAR CRIMES AND ATROCITIES
1600–1930

PART FOUR:
WAR CRIMES AND ATROCITIES
OF WORLD WAR II

PART FIVE:
WAR CRIMES TRIALS

PART SIX:
WAR CRIMES 1950–2000

PART SEVEN:
21ST CENTURY – THE WAR CRIMES CONTINUE

Introduction

What is a war crime? To most people, war itself is a crime, a total breakdown of the civilized process of negotiation, compromise and conciliation that normally takes place between nations or opposing parties to settle a dispute. Thus, war is by its nature a resort to brute force, to armed violence, in which ordinary, innocent people are killed, injured and have their lives disrupted. So how can it be anything but a crime?

This is a persuasive moral point, but there is also a pragmatic argument to be made: in a situation where a dispute has not been settled, and nations, states or opposing groups have already become involved in conflict, surely there is a need to lay down some rules that everyone will abide by – a need, in short, for damage limitation. And surely there are some actions that occur in times of war – such as massacres of prisoners of war and atrocities perpetrated on civilians, including children – that serve no real political purpose at all, but appear to be purely sadistic in nature and are simply an affront to human decency and dignity.

MASS MURDER AND GENOCIDE

These are the terrible crimes of mass murder, torture,

9

rape and brutality, such as the Holocaust of World War II, the genocide of the Rwandan people, and the abuses of Saddam Hussein's regime, that shame all of humanity. Crimes that are hard for most of us living in peacetime to explain or imagine, but that we all recognize as expressing the darkest, most destructive side of human nature. In most cases, such horrifying crimes take place in times of war, when chaos reigns and the normal, civilizing structures of social life are removed. Because of this, wars can – must – be waged in such a way as to protect human beings, both soldiers and civilians, from the worst excesses of human violence, so that war can become an exercise in disciplined military strategy, keeping casualties to a minimum, rather than an excuse for the unleashing of random acts of barbaric cruelty on a grand scale.

In modern history, each time there has been a major world conflict, there have been a series of protocols, conventions, and agreements laid down to try to learn some lessons from the situation, so as to achieve the goal of minimizing human suffering for future generations. Some might argue that this is a hopeless task, that war in itself is bound to create suffering, and to try to create laws for such a lawless situation is absurd. However, it can also be argued that the process of laying down rules for the pursuance of war is extremely important, and it is an essentially civilizing development that has done much to protect individuals in recent years. Moreover, even if nations fail, time and time again, to abide by the rules laid down, surely it is an inspiring ideal to expect all humanity to reach certain standards of basic conduct in times of war as well as times of peace?

CHEMICAL WEAPONS

The first treaty to lay down international laws of war and to establish the nature of war crimes was the 1899 First Peace Conference at The Hague in The Netherlands. Subsequently, there was another peace conference at The Hague in 1907, which expanded on the first. The Hague Convention, as the rules became known, focused on the banning of certain types of weapons that were considered particularly destructive and harmful, for example bombing from air balloons, chemical warfare (in particular the releasing of noxious gases), and hollow point bullets (that expand or flatten once in the human body). The second convention focused on how naval warfare should be conducted, and tried to establish rules at sea – for example, how mines should be laid from submarines, how prisoners of war should be treated at sea and so on.

In 1925, the Geneva Protocol augmented the Hague Convention's list of rules by putting forward a protocol 'for the prohibition of the use in war of asphyxiating, poisonous or other gases, and of bacteriological methods of warfare'. The protocol established a total ban on all types of chemical and biological warfare, as

11

a response to public protests about the use of mustard gas in World War I. This noxious gas was widely used in this and other wars; exposure to it produces no immediate symptoms, but after four or more hours, the skin develops burning blisters all over the body. In high concentrations, these blisters can cause death. In addition, mustard gas can cause blindness and fatal damage to the respiratory system, as well as serious long-term effects, including cancer.

Mustard gas was first used by the Germans in World War I, and then by the British during the war. It has been used at various times since then, in contravention of the protocol, for example by Saddam Hussein against the Kurds in 1988. In 1972, the protocol was augmented by the Biological Weapons Convention, and again in 1993 by the Chemical Weapons Convention. All these amendments were designed to try to rid the world of the terrifying consequences of chemical warfare in general, not only for human beings but for the environment; sadly, in many cases, the conventions have been broken, mainly because of lack of international monitoring or effective international sanctions.

CRIMES AGAINST PEACE

A further important step in the establishing of war crimes was the Kellog-Briand Pact, also called the Pact of Paris, which was an international treaty 'providing for the renunciation of war as an instrument of national policy'. This ambitious treaty had the aim of stopping nations from using warfare as a means of settling disputes. It was named after the American secretary of state, Frank B. Kellog, and the French foreign minister, Aristide Briand. It was initially drafted as an agreement between the USA and France, but it later became a multilateral pact, and was signed by 11 states, including the UK, Germany, Italy and others, in 1928.

However, as became clear during World War II, with the German invasion of Poland, the Italian invasion of Ethiopia (Abyssinia as it was then called) and other acts of aggression, the pact was ineffectual. Even so, many argue that it was a significant initiative, and provided a legal basis for later war crimes trials, in particular the Nuremberg Trials that took place after World War II. This was because the Kellog-Briand Pact identified the concept of the 'crime against peace' for the first time – that is, the act of military invasion – as a war crime. In terms of international law, the waging of a war against the integrity, independence or sovereignty of a state now became an illegal act, punishable in various ways.

This definition of state aggression as a war crime became part of the Nuremberg Principles, drafted as a set of guidelines to help prosecutors in the trials of Nazi war criminals after the war. The principles set out a relatively new idea, that a political figure acting within the legal framework of his own country could, in actual fact, violate international law through acts of aggression and violence, either towards other sovereign nations or towards political, ethnic or religious groups in his own country. In this way, the international courts were pointing out that functionaries of a totalitarian regime, such as the Nazi Third Reich, however much their actions were sanctioned by the regime at the time, and however important their position, were ultimately answerable to the international community and must be judged by absolute standards of humanitarian morality. Even in cases where an individual was ordered by superiors to pursue a particular act of aggression, if it could be proved that a person had the possibility of a moral choice, he or she could be prosecuted under international law.

CRIMES AGAINST HUMANITY

The crimes listed under the Nuremberg Principles included, firstly, crimes against peace – that is, 'planning, preparation, initiation or waging of a war of aggression or a war in violation of international treaties, agreements or assurances' and 'participation in a common plan or conspiracy for the accomplishment of any of the acts mentioned above'. (Most importantly, in the wake of this legislation, which was later incorporated into the United Nations Charter, nations have had to invoke the principle of self-defence to justify aggression into foreign territories.) Secondly, war crimes were listed as: 'violations of the laws or customs of war, which include murder, ill treatment or deportation of slave labour or for any other purpose of the civilian population in occupied territory; murder or ill treatment of prisoners of war or persons on the seas; killing of hostages, plunder of public or private property; wanton destruction of cities, towns or villages, or devastation not justified by military necessity.' Thirdly, there were crimes against humanity that included 'murder, extermination, enslavement, deportation and other inhumane acts done against any civilian population, or persecutions on political, racial or religious grounds, when such acts are done or such persecutions are carried on in execution of or in connection with any crime against peace or any war crime.'

In addition to this legislation, which over the years has been amended, expanded and ratified by the United Nations, there are also a series of treaties known as the Geneva Conventions that focus on the conduct of war. These conventions were initiated by Henri Dunant, a Swiss businessman who witnessed the carnage at the Battle of Solferino in 1859, while on a business trip there. Dunant recorded his experiences in a book entitled, *A Memory at Solferino*, which helped to inspire the creation of the Red Cross, a private humanitarian organization set up to protect and aid victims of war, whether prisoners, refugees or ordinary civilians.

Today, the Geneva Conventions have been signed by 194 countries across the world. The Conventions make certain inhuman acts punishable as criminal offences under a court of law. Of course, the countries who have signed the agreement do not always abide by the rules, but at least the legislation now exists to take nations that break the conventions to task; moreover, they provide a firm basis to ensure that humanitarian treatment of prisoners and civilians in war time remains an achievable goal, rather than an impossible dream.

HUMANITARIAN TREATMENT

The Conventions and their various protocols, amendments and revisions, are wide-ranging and extremely detailed, but in essence they focus on humanitarian treatment of all those caught up in warfare and conflict throughout the world, in an attempt to improve general standards and ban inhuman acts. They cover, for example, the treatment of sick and wounded prisoners, the prohibition of certain methods of warfare and the political status of refugees. In addition, they set out 'laws of war', that is, rules for the conduct of warfare: for example, under the conventions, it is illegal for soldiers to attack enemy troops displaying a flag of truce, thus avoiding needless casualties.

As well as this extensive legislation, in 2002 a further body, the International Criminal Court, was set up to prosecute contemporary war crimes. This court has identified various acts as illegal, including 'grave breaches' of the Geneva Conventions: wilful killing, torture and inhumane treatment, wanton destruction of property, forcing a prisoner of war to serve in the forces of a hostile power, depriving prisoners of war of a fair trial, unlawful deportations and the taking of hostages. It further bans attacks directed against civilians and humanitarian workers, killing surrendered combatants, using civilians as human shields and employing child soldiers. It also outlaws summary executions, rape and pillage, sexual slavery and forced prostitution.

The court only has jurisdiction over these crimes where they are part of a large-scale initiative, as for example when the government of a country, or a prominent political group within it, pursues or condones such acts. To date, the court has indicted such figures as former Iraqi president Saddam Hussein and the former Yugoslav president Slobodan Milosevic.

CONTROVERSY

Some important nations, such as the USA and China, have refused to become signatories to the International Court. (This does not, of course, make individuals from those countries exempt from the court's rulings.) Moreover, many nations have criticized the Geneva Conventions and other international legislative rulings as being unfair and historically based in a way that favours certain countries over others.

It is, indeed, true to say that in the aftermath of World War II, the war crimes and atrocities of the

Allied countries were never prosecuted, whereas those of the Germans and other Axis powers were heavily punished. For example, certain appalling attacks that would certainly have been classified as war crimes under the terms of the Geneva Conventions were never punished: the atomic destruction by the USA of the cities of Hiroshima and Nakasaki, for instance, or the mass firebombing of Dresden by Allied Forces. In addition, firebomb attacks by Allied forces on Tokyo and Kobe were not ruled as war crimes by the international courts. In more recent times, the excesses of the Indonesian occupation of East Timor, between 1976 and 1999, have been pointed out as having been tacitly condoned for political reasons, as well as a host of other conflicts, both international and internal, in the new millennium.

WAR CRIMES IN HISTORY

In this book, we take a look at some of the major war crimes that have been committed throughout history. In Part I, we cover ancient atrocities described in biblical and classical literature, as well as other historical sources: for example, the brutal campaigns of Alexander the Great. Next, we move on to the invasion of Britain by William the Conqueror in 1066, and to the Holy Land battles during the Crusades of Richard the Lionheart. We tell the story of the fifteenth-century tyrant Vlad the Impaler, on whom the legend of

Dracula was based; and, from the same period, of the deranged despot Ivan the Terrible, as well as the conquistador Francisco Pizarro, and his attack on the Incas of Peru.

In Part III we explore some of the most notorious war crimes in history, such as the brutal colonization of the Congo by King Leopold of Belgium in the late nineteenth and early twentieth century; the sinking of the *Lusitania*, the ocean liner torpedoed by a German submarine in 1906, which helped persuade the USA to enter World War I; and the Armenian genocide, the persecution, deportation and killing of up to two million Armenians by the Ottoman Empire from 1915 to 1923. We also cover the Amritsar Massacre of 1919 (also known as the Jallianwala Bagh Massacre), in which British Indian Army troops opened fire on an unarmed gathering of what is now estimated to be more than 1,000 men, women and children.

THE HOLOCAUST

Part IV brings us to World War II, to what is perhaps the greatest war crime of all time: The Holocaust, in which up to six million Jews were persecuted, tortured and brutally murdered by Adolf Hitler and his henchmen of the Third Reich. Our history of war crimes in this period not only encompasses the horrifying experiences of Jews in the extermination camps, but also looks at the treatment of prisoners of war, mentally and physically disabled people and Poles, Serbians, Russian and other ethnic communities. As well as systematic, state-sanctioned killings of these groups, German soldiers also committed hundreds of unlawful bloody reprisals on civilians and prisoners of war, especially towards the end of the conflict, when it was clear that Germany would be defeated. In addition, there were reprisals by Communist partisan troops, especially in Yugoslavia, as well as by Allied soldiers. We also include here some of the war crimes committed by the Allied powers, which were never prosecuted in courts of law, but which, in recent years, have been the subject of much controversy: the fire-bombing of Dresden and the atomic bombing of Hiroshima and Nagasaki.

In Part V, we look at the great War Crimes Trials of history: in particular, the Nuremburg and Tokyo Trials that took place in the aftermath of World War II, in which Nazi leaders of the Third Reich and important officials of Japanese government were convicted. We also investigate the high profile trials of individuals such as Dusko Tadic, the Bosnian Serb convicted of crimes against humanity, and Slobodan Milosevic, the former president of Serbia and Yugoslavia, who died before his trial came to an end in 2006.

TWENTIETH-CENTURY WAR CRIMES

Part VI continues with a look at twentieth-century war

crimes and atrocities between 1950 and the year 2000, starting in 1950 with the No Gun Ri Tragedy, in which US troops gunned down inhabitants of a village in the early days of the Korean War, and ending with the nightmare of Rwanda, in which over one million people were massacred by Hutu militia groups over a period of about four months in 1994. Other notorious crimes of the period include the massacre at My Lai of unarmed Vietnamese civilians, mostly women and children, by US soldiers in 1968; the Bloody Sunday massacre of 1972, in which British soldiers shot down a group of Irish civil rights protesters; atrocities committed during the Indonesian occupation of East Timor from 1975 until 1999; and the massacres of hundreds of Arab refugees at Sabra and Shatila, carried out in September 1982 by Lebanese militias, with the support of the Israeli armed forces.

War crimes and atrocities continue, sadly, in great numbers into the twenty-first century, with the evil regime of Saddam Hussein in Iraq; the subsequent invasion of Iraq led by the USA; the treatment of detainees at Guantanamo Bay; the war in Kosovo; and ethnic cleansing, also described as genocide, at Darfur in Western Sudan.

Today, it seems that war crimes and atrocities continue day by day, despite the mass of legislation aimed to prevent and limit such tragedies. However, the fact that the legislation is now in place to identify such crimes and charge the perpetrators is significant:

for example, on 5 November, 2006, former Iraqi president Saddam Hussein was sentenced to death by hanging for his crimes against humanity. Whether or not such convictions will help to stem the tide of tyranny and terrorism of the twenty-first century, in which innocent people continue to suffer, remains to be seen; but at least in modern times, war crimes have been identified as such, so that – whether committed by heads of state or by terrorist groups – we can begin to regard such crimes as having no rightful place in our modern global society.

PART ONE

ANCIENT ATROCITIES

The Sword of David Carves Out the Kingdom of Israel

——————— *c.*10th Century BC ———————

*T*he Bible's Old Testament books of I and II Samuel, I Chronicles and I Kings are full of the deeds of David, a farmer of Bethlehem who created and was the first ruler of the kingdom of Israel and Judah. In the Bible, David is a strong and extraordinarily successful warrior, a gifted poet and musician – he is invariably depicted in Christian iconography with a harp – and, in startling contrast, a murderous adulterer. David slew the landowner Nabal so that he could make Nabal's wife, Abigail, his own wife. She was one of many, as David was both promiscuous and fecund. He also sent a gallant soldier, Uriah the Hittite, to certain death by putting him in 'the forefront of the battle' so that David could gain Bathsheba, Uriah's wife.

David is a much more shadowy figure in the historical records of the period in which it is generally agreed that he lived – that is, ten centuries before the birth of Christ, with his death occurring, at the earliest, in 1018 BC but no later than *c.*970 BC. As many records from this period do not mention him at all, it is impossible to assign any more definite dates than these to him. Modern historians agree that around 1003 BC, a strong and warlike man called David did combine the states of Israel and Judah to create a kingdom whose size was unmatched by anything else in the history of Israel. He seems to have built the kingdom by using ferocious military energy to overcome the states and tribes that surrounded and threatened Israel.

King David entered biblical history as a simple shepherd boy, whom God directed the prophet Samuel to seek out and anoint as the Lord's chosen one. He was taken into the court of Saul, the first king of Israel, initially as a musician. David became the beloved of Saul's son Jonathan and was raised to a position of military command after his spectacular slaying of the giant Philistine champion Goliath.

David married Saul's daughter, Michal, whose wedding gift from her husband was the foreskins of 200 Philistines David had slaughtered in an encounter with Israel's foremost enemy at the time. However, David's increasing power and popularity in Israel attracted Saul's jealous displeasure, so much so that David fled Saul's court and became an outlaw.

With a force of 400 warriors at his command, David established himself as a free-ranging warrior, moving from valley to valley and camp to camp in the wilderness of Judah, where he acted with murderous cruelty when occasion demanded. A base in this early period of his wanderings was the cave of Adullam, near Gath, a city-state whose king was a Philistine vassal. David thus operated as an ally of the Philistines, whose confederation of city-states on the coastal land of Canaan lay to the west of Israel, and who were perpetually at war with Saul and Israel. Eventually, David established himself and his forces in the city of Ziklag.

DAVID'S REVENGE

It was the destruction of Ziklag by the Amalekites that first allowed David to demonstrate just how ruthless he could be. Amalek and his descendents had long been an unrelenting enemy of Israel, and Saul had recently made an unsuccessful attempt to deal with them. David was away from Ziklag, intending to ally himself alongside the Philistines in their last struggle with Saul. However, the Philistines, apparently considered David to be a treacherous ally and refused his help. Returning to Ziklag, David and his men found the city reduced to smouldering ruins, and their wives, including two of David's, their daughters and their sons taken away as captives of the Amalekites.

At first, the distraught people of Ziklag threatened to stone David, but he persuaded them to visit their vengence on the Amalekites instead and to accompany him in pursuit of their lost wives and children. Eventually David caught up with the Amalekites, 'spread abroad upon all the earth, eating and drinking, and dancing, because of all the great spoil they had taken out of the land of the Philistines and out of the land of Judah'.

David descended on this drunken hoard and slaughtered them, the work lasting from twilight on the day he caught up with them until the evening of the next day. David rescued his wives and the wives and children of his followers, and everything else that had been looted from Ziklag by the Amalekites. He also took all their flocks and herds and drove them back to Ziklag. The Amalekites were wiped out, except for 'four hundred young men, which rode upon camels and fled', and the Amalekite state was never again a threat to Israel.

THE CONQUERING KING

Saul and his three sons, including Jonathan, were killed in battle with the Philistines, and their bodies, stripped of their armour and their heads cut off, were fastened to the wall of Beth-shan. 'The beauty of Israel is slain upon thy high places: how are the mighty fallen . . . and the weapons of war perished,' mourned the poetical David. At the same time, according to Samuel, David taught the children of Judah the use of the bow: the practicalities of warfare would always come before poetry to David. (He had also slain the messenger who brought the news of the deaths of Saul and Jonathan.)

After the death of Saul, David first became king over Judah in the south, then over Israel in the north. Thus, he became king over 'all Israel'. He did not stop there. A series of aggressive wars against neighbouring states and tribes, all of which involved the massacre of thousands of men, women and children, as well as looting and pillaging in a grand scale, extended the boundaries of Israel far to the north and south.

One of David's earliest moves was the conquest of the city of Jerusalem, wrested from the Jebusites and made the capital of his kingdom. David brought the sacred Ark of the Covenant to Jerusalem, and, at God's command, built a temple there to house it. (Jerusalem's great Temple was built by Solomon, David's son by Bathsheba.) It seems that David neither killed nor drove out all the Jebusite inhabitants of Jerusalem, as the Bible records that he bought land from a local landowner to build an altar in Jerusalem.

David did not treat his later conquests so lightly. Philistines, Syrians, Moabites and Ammonites were slaughtered in great numbers, their lands were pillaged and their wealth looted. Most of the gold that adorned the Temple in Jerusalem was looted from neighbouring states.

The tribal state of Ammon and the kingdom of Edom were both overcome by David and incorporated into his kingdom. The people of Edom suffered particularly dreadfully at David's hands: 18,000 of them were slaughtered in the Valley of Salt (the valley of the Dead Sea) and the rest of them enslaved. David ensured his position by installing garrisons throughout the conquered kingdom.

Hadadezer, king of Zobah, was smote by David as he tried to recover his borderland on the Euphrates. David took from him 1,000 chariots, 700 horsemen and 20,000 men on foot but generously left Hadadezer the horses for 100 chariots. He was not so forgiving towards the Syrians who came from Damascus to aid Hadadezer; David slew 22,000 of them. According to the Bible, 47,000 Syrians were slaughtered in all by King David of Israel, who extended his kingdom almost to the gates of Damascus.

As for the Moabites, the Second Book of Samuel does not give numbers of those slaughtered, telling us only that David used three lines to measure the Moabites, put to death those measured with two lines and chose 'one full line to keep alive'. David subjugated Moab and turned it into a vassal state of his kingdom.

David's great 'empire' did not last long after the death of his son, Solomon. Never again would Israel be so large or so powerful. And never again would Israel have a leader so strong and so contradictory in his nature. Most of our 'knowledge' of King David comes from the Bible, and most of what we know is myth and legend. However, the mythical story was built on fact. Israel did indeed have a strong leader in the tenth century, a man of forceful, contradictory character and undoubted abilities that put him head and shoulders above his contemporaries and ensured him such an enduring place in the history of Israel.

Alexander the Great Destroys Thebes

————— 336 BC —————

The origins of the Greek city of Thebes, which was capital of the district of Boeotia, form a thick strand in the web of myths and legends woven by the Ancient Greeks to explain their early history. Cadmus was the hero of the Thebes legends. He was the son of Agenor, king of Phoenicia and the brother of Europa, the princess carried off by Zeus to Crete.

As Cadmus searched for his sister involved seeking advice from the Oracle at Delphi, following a cow into Boeotia and building the Cadmea (the citadel of Thebes) on the spot where the cow sank to the ground. Near the Cadmea was a well guarded by a dragon. On the advice of the goddess Athena, Cadmus slew the dragon, and sowed its teeth in the ground. From these teeth grew fierce, armed men, five of whom became the ancestors of the Thebans. Thebes was reputed to be the birthplace of two great divinities,

Dionysus and Heracles, the setting for the tragedy of Oedipus, and at the heart of the legendary wars of Adrastus. In two separate wars, Adrastus fought Thebes, and during the second series of attacks Thebes was razed. All this was to provide plenty of material for later Greek epic and tragic poets, including the Theban Pindar, who was born in 518 BC in the village of Cynoscephalae in the district of Thebes.

By the time Thebes appeared in recorded history, it was a flourishing city on the fertile plains of Boeotia, large enough to require seven gates in the wall that surrounded it. The Thebans had acquired a reputation for being dull-witted – despite the fact that, according to Herodotus, they were the first use of written letters in Western Europe, which were introduced from Phoenicia (by Cadmus). In classical times, the city was the leading state among the 14 independent states of Boeotia that came together in a league.

EARLY BATTLES

From the earliest years of the founding of their city, the Thebans lived up to their legendary origins in those fighting men sprung from dragon's teeth. They were constantly at war with their near neighbours, the Athenians, and sided with the Spartans in the Peloponnesian War, where they played a sizable part in the downfall of Athens. Later, the Thebans, like other Greek states, became anti-Spartan, and scored a great victory against them at the battle of Leuctra in 371 BC. For a time after this Thebes was the major power in Greece.

Within 40 years of this great victory, the story of Thebes had taken a dark turn indeed. The kingdom of Macedonia was north of Thebes, and it had been quietly flexing its muscles for centuries. It had acquired a new and ambitious king, known as Philip of Macedon. Philip, born in 382 BC, instilled a new sense of ambition and discipline into Macedonia and its army. Soon, Macedonia's modest ambitions to exercise sovereignty over the Greek coastal states nearest to them had turned into an ambition to gain supremacy over the whole of Greece.

Faced with a common danger, Thebes set aside its centuries-old animosity towards Athens, and joined the Athenians in a league against Philip of Macedon. However, their combined forces proved no match for Philip and his reorganized army, and they were comprehensively defeated at the battle of Chaeronea in Boeotia in 338bc. The broken pieces of a marble lion that adorned the sepulchre built for the Thebans who fell in the battle can still be seen among the remains of this once-great Theban city. As for Thebes itself, just as Greece had lost its independence, so the city had lost its liberty.

ALEXANDER THE GREAT

In 336 BC, the 46-year-old Philip of Macedon was

murdered by poisoning during his daughter's wedding feast, possibly as the result of a plot in which his wife was implicated. The Thebans thought they saw the chance of regaining their liberty and rose up in revolt. Unfortunately for the Thebans, they did not understand the calibre of the young prince, Alexander, who succeeded Philip.

The 20-year-old Alexander was as unlikely as his father to allow any show of independence from the cities and states under his control. Showing all the ruthless strength and determination that was to gain him the title 'Great', Alexander descended on Thebes and destroyed the city. The city wall was part of the fortifications that legend said had been built by Amphion and Zethus, twin sons of Zeus. During Alexander's attack, the wall was flattened.

Within the walls, Alexander destroyed houses, theatres, shops and the Acropolis, or Cadmea, and almost everything else. He left standing only the temples and the house in which the poet Pindar had lived. Pindar's great fame had grown out of his ability to compose fine choral songs for special occasions, a skill that had given him employment by princes all over the Hellenic world. Alexander the Great is believed to have spared the house that Pindar had lived in at Thebes because of the fine poems he had written in praise of Alexander's ancestor, King Alexander of Macedonia.

Alexander may also have had spared the temples of

Thebes because of their historical associations, perhaps picked up in his reading of the work of the sixth-century historian Herodotus. Herodotus mentioned in his *Histories* the oracle of Ismenian Apollo at Thebes and the great temple dedicated to Ismenian Apollo, where he recalled seeing the solid gold shield and spear that Croesus had dedicated to the Argos hero Amphiaraus and examples engraved on three tripods of the Cadmean writing that the Phoenicians had brought to Greece.

Determined that no Thebans would ever rise in revolt against him again and, no doubt, wanting to make an example of Thebes to the rest of Greece, Alexander slew 6,000 of the inhabitants and sold 30,000 of them as slaves. The once-great city was subdued indeed. At the same time, the four centuries-long era of the classic, Hellenistic city state was ended; from this time on mainland Greece became very much a political backwater.

Thebes was rebuilt 20 years later by the Macedonian prince, Cassander, with the help of the Athenians, but it later suffered considerable damage again during the wars for possession of Greece and Macedonia that were fought among the successors of Alexander the Great. Thebes never regained its former greatness and power, and its death blow was finally dealt by the Roman dictator Sulla, who handed over half its territory to the Delphinians.

SUCCESSFUL FORMATIONS

There is a historical irony in the fact that Alexander the Great's amazing success as a warrior king owed much to the great Theban statesman and general Epaminondas, who scored a decisive success over the Spartans in the battle of Leuctra in 371 BC. The general was helped to victory by the way in which he changed the battle formation of his army. Instead of deploying his heavily armed soldiers (hoplites) in the usual long even lines, Epaminondas formed some of them into a wedge, 50 men deep, on one wing, in which he included the Theban 'Sacred Band'. Alexander's father, Philip of Macedon, improved on this 'strength-in-depth' principle demonstrated so effectively by Epaminondas by creating the more open and freer-moving phalanx. When Alexandra the Great added a large cavalry force on the wings of his father's phalanx at the outset of his Persian campaign his army became virtually unbeatable.

PART TWO

MEDIEVAL WAR
CRIMES

William the Conqueror and 'the Harrying of the North'

─────── 1069–70 ───────

*D*ictionaries define 'to harry' as 'to ravage', 'torment', 'harass by forced exactions', 'make rapacious demands' and, in warfare, 'to devastate'. William the Conqueror did all these things in the north of England when, within three years of his victory at the Battle of Hastings in October 1066, he found himself having to put down serious rebellions in the northern parts of his new kingdom.

William had fought at Hastings to gain the English crown from Harold, the last Anglo-Saxon king. William claimed it had been promised to him by Edward the Confessor, who had spent many years at the court of William's father in Normandy before mounting the throne of England in 1042. However, by the time Edward died in 1065, his realm was in disarray. He was not a forceful ruler and the kingdom's great men, or thanes, had everything their own way, while at the same time they quarrelled among themselves.

England looked as if it would fall back into the hands of the Scandinavians, so the thanes buried their differences. Ignoring William of Normandy's claims and those of Edward's nearest blood relative, the youthful Edgar the Atheling, they elected the strongest among themselves as their new king. He was Harold Godwineson, the son of the Earl of Wessex. The thanes were prompted to this decision by two strong northern lords, Morcar, Earl of Northumberland, and his brother Edwin. Harold had worked hard to placate these two, even siding with them in a quarrel with his own brother, Tostig. However, this may have led to Harold's defeat at Hastings. His army had been weakened by having to fight off a Scandinavian invasion, led by Harold Hardraada and Tostig, at Stamford Bridge, before marching rapidly south to deal with William's invasion from Normandy. During the battle, Harold was killed by an arrow shot in the eye.

Although there was some bitter fighting against William of Normandy in the north and west of England, he did not respond too harshly – there were no burnings and hangings at the time – and by the time he was crowned king in Westminster Abbey at Christmastide 1066, rebellious thanes, including Morcar and Edwin of Northumberland, had submitted. William could be reasonably sure that his success was complete and he felt no need to be particularly harsh in his dealings with his new subjects and their leading men. He tried initially to rule England with the support of a nobility that was a mixture of Anglo-Saxons and Normans, but no genuine trust developed between the two groups and it was soon clear that William's policy was doomed to failure. It was to take William and his Norman followers six years of often brutal campaigning in many parts of the country before his will was firmly imposed on his new kingdom.

QUELLING THE NORTH

The most brutal of all William's responses to rebellion took place in the north of the country. In 1069, Morcar and Edwin of Northumberland took up the sword again on behalf of Edwin the Atheling, arguing that with Harold dead, Edgar was the legitimate heir of Edward the Confessor. Edgar had been proclaimed king in London immediately after the Battle of Hastings, but his claim had been easily brushed aside. Now Morcar and Edwin were raising armies in the former kingdom of Mercia, the heartland of which was in counties centred on the river Trent, while their northern neighbour, Gospatric, Earl of Bernica (who had actually bought his earldom from William), was trying to persuade the great men of Northumbria to rise on behalf of Edgar.

William led an army north to quell this latest

rebellion. As he approached in force, the rebels retreated, Edgar the Atheling fleeing to Scotland and Morcar and Edwin submitting themselves to William's mercy. Once again, he pardoned the leaders of this latest rebellion. However, he did not treat the ordinary people of the north so lightly. Perhaps he had been angered by the news of the Norman castle that the rebels had razed at York. More likely, he decided that now was the time to show his iron fist and make sure that never again would rebels have the resources to wage war against him.

Whatever the thinking that impelled him, William acted with extraordinary savagery against the north in the winter of 1069–70. He ordered the destruction of whole villages, the burning of crops and the killing of domestic animals over an area of northern England that stretched from York to Durham in the north and from York down to the county of Derby, and to Stafford and Chester in the south and west. There was wholesale destruction and burnings of much cultivated land and property between the rivers Humber and Tees. Starvation stalked the land.

The excessive force of William's 'harrying of the north', as his campaign soon came to be called, deeply shocked Anglo-Saxon England. As the monk Simeon of Durham wrote, 'It was horrible to see human bodies rotting in their houses and on the roads, and there was a terrible smell. And a great silence fell over the land.' Oderic Vitalis, author of a contemporary *Ecclesiastical*

History, said that he could not commend William 'for an act which levelled both the bad and the good in one common ruin by a consuming famine.'

With much of the north now devastated and acquiescent, William began a process of breaking up the great estates of the Anglo-Saxon thanes, distributing smaller parcels of land among his Norman followers. He was careful never to give any one lord so much land in one place that it could be used as a power base from which to stir up trouble against the king. He emphasized the fact that the land came from the king, its ultimate owner, and that lords held it in trust from him. Thus the land-owning system of Anglo-Saxon England disappeared and was replaced by the system that came to be called feudalism.

After the northern rebellions of 1069-70, William's rule in England became much harsher. To ensure his power, he began a major programme of building forts and castles the length and breadth of his realm. He brought from Normandy a style of castle-building that resulted in fortifications much more impregnable than anything the Anglo-Saxons built. The Norman castle, later built of stone but in William's time mostly of wood, were based on the 'motte and bailey' castle, erected on a high mound so that they rose threateningly above the surrounding countryside. Norman lords occupied these castles, which were built by English serf labourers. Once William was assured that England was quiet, he returned to Normandy after 1072 and seldom visited his English possessions thereafter.

Oderic Vitalis had asserted that William should be punished for the 'barbarous homicide' he had carried out during the harrying of the north. Of course, he never was punished – except, perhaps, in his own mind. On his deathbed in 1087, William the Conqueror is said to have admitted that he had persecuted the native inhabitants of England beyond all reason. 'I am stained with the rivers of blood I have shed,' he said. Perhaps it was partly contrition that led him to leave his English lands to his second son, William Rufus, a man thought to be less hard and ruthless than his elder brother, Robert, who became Duke of Normandy on the death of his father.

As for other participants, Edwin of Northumberland was killed by his own men during another, abortive, rising in 1071, after which Morcar was imprisoned by William. Although he outlived William, Morcar was returned to prison by the new king, William Rufus, and disappeared from history. Edgar the Atheling, who had never been much more than a hook on which to hang rebellious thanes' ambitions, was reconciled with William in 1074 and spent the rest of his life as a minor courtier. He took part in the First Crusade.

The First Crusaders Take Jerusalem from the Infidel

──────── 1099 ────────

*F*rom the time of its founding by the prophet Muhammad in the 7th century, Islam was remarkably successful in its waging of jihad, or holy war, to convert the peoples of Arabia and the eastern Mediterranean to what they saw as the true faith. Within a few years of the death of Muhammad in 632, the three greatest cities in the Christian Eastern Roman (or Byzantine) Empire – Alexandria, Antioch and Jerusalem – had all fallen to Islam. Syria and Egypt, also parts of the Byzantine Empire, and the Persian Empire had all been overwhelmed.

Largely because the Holy Places of Christendom were in the Byzantine Empire, the capital of which was Constantinople (now Istanbul), Western Christianity long ignored events in the area. It was not until the 11th century that Western Christianity awoke to the danger of complete annihilation that faced the Christian Church in the eastern Mediterranean and chose to do something about it.

Medieval religious enthusiasm was at its height in Western Europe when, in 1095 at the Council of Clermont, Pope Urban II called on the Christian laity to take up arms for the reconquest of Jerusalem, which had been in Muslim hands since 638. The pope was answering a call for help from the Byzantine emperor Alexius I Comnenus, in despair that his once mighty and far-reaching power over the lands of the Near East had been reduced to little more than over the land around the walls of his capital.

At the end of the Council, the pope preached a sermon on the suffering of the Christians in the East to an immense crowd gathered outside the city of Clermont. He ended with a passionately worded appeal for men to enlist under the sign of the Cross of Christ. His call was answered with huge enthusiasm by hundreds in the crowd, many of whom began there and then to mark their clothes with the sign of the cross. Within weeks, they were joined and in a more professional manner by Frankish, German and Italian counts, dukes, and other rulers from many parts of Western Christianity. Thus the First Crusade began.

The enormous enthusiasm shown by the common people for Pope Urban's call to arms under the banner of the cross turned into a huge pilgrimage across Europe and into Turkey, which came to be called the People's Crusade. Leaving behind families, homes and livelihoods, about 20,000 men, women and children – most of them simple, poor folk from Germany,

Flanders and France – set out from Cologne for Constantinople after the Easter celebrations of 1096.

The People's Crusade was made up opf a motley and unruly vanguard, which was led by a preacher of great charisma, Peter the Hermit and included a few knights and fighting men. However, there was no leading soldier in their midst. They made the arduous, 3,000-km (2,000-mile) journey across Europe only to be ambushed and virtually annihilated by the Seljuk Turks near Nicaea (modern-day Iznik in Turkey) in October 1096. A contemporary account of the battle recorded how the Turks swept into the peasants' camps and 'destroyed with the sword whomever they found, the weak and feeble, clerics, monks, old women, nursing children, persons of every age'. The remnants either made their way back home or joined up with the contingents of crusaders who were by now arriving in Constantinople, no doubt spreading graphic accounts of what the Turks had done at Nicaea.

THE FIRST CRUSADE

The military crusaders took more time over their preparations. Great lords began assembling armies in France and Italy, while Godfrey of Bouillon, Duke of Lower Lorraine, gathered together a large force from Germany and the Low Countries. Although the kings of England and France were not directly involved, both were represented: William II of England by his brother, Robert of Normandy, and Philip of France by his brother, Hugh of Vermondais.

Eventually, there were to be four main contingents making up the crusading force, each of which took its own route across Europe to their meeting point at Constantinople, where they joined into one vast force.

The first contingent set off in August 1096 and the fourth, led by Robert of Normandy and his brother-in-law Stephen of Blois, in October. Duke Godfrey, lauded by medieval bards as the perfect crusader, was to be the most prominent of the knights on the First Crusade, even being offered the crown of Jerusalem by fellow crusaders. About 4,000 to 5,000 mounted knights and squires, 30,000 foot soldiers and many thousands of non-combatants took part in the First Crusade.

With the average distance covered by a medieval army on the march being only approximately 24 or 25 km (15 or 16 miles) a day, it was clearly going to take the various armies descending on the Holy Land from across Europe many months of arduous marching to get there. For this First Crusade, the Christians could not get to Palestine by sea, as the forces of the Third Crusade were able to do in the following century, for they had no friendly ports at which to land.

It was not until May 1097 that the first of the crusaders, a force about 30,000 strong, came within sight of the city of Nicaea, which they successfully besieged. In early July, they were involved in their first battle of the First Crusade. They were attacked by the

47

same Seljuk Turks who had had such an easy victory over the People's Crusade – and who were expecting another one now. However, the Battle of Dorylaeum was a complete victory for the crusaders.

Considerably heartened by this success against a foe whose style of warfare was so different from their own, the crusaders moved on towards the distant Holy Land. Had they known that, in all, they were to endure three years of battles, sieges (including a year-long siege of Antioch, about 640 km [400 miles] from Jerusalem), disease and near-starvation before they reached their goal, Jerusalem, they would almost certainly still have continued, so strong was their fervent belief in the cause.

They were also strengthened by signs that God was on their side. The crusaders had won at Antioch, for instance, because of the miraculous discovery in the city of the Holy Lance, which was said to have pierced Christ's side when he was on the Cross. The final march on Jerusalem, from January to June 1099, was also marked by a series of visions and miracles that indicated the rightness of their cause.

The crusaders sighted the wall of Jerusalem on 7 June, 1099. Many of them stood with tears running down their faces, others fell to their knees and kissed the dusty ground. So uplifted were they by the sight that many among them wanted to attack the city at once. An assault was launched on the walls a few days later, but it failed through a lack of scaling ladders. It was not until 15 July, when two enormous siege engines had been completed, that the crusaders' assault on Jerusalem began.

Duke Godfrey began the attack, riding on one of the siege engines to the weakest point in the city wall. Beams were run out from it at rampart height to make a bridge, and the first crusader knights charged across it into Jerusalem. What followed was the sacking of Jerusalem and a bloody massacre of its citizens. The Jewish population of the city – men, women and children – were cut down in the chief synagogue, where they had taken sanctuary. A group of Muslim defenders made a formal capitulation to a leading crusader, having agreed to pay a large ransom. The agreement was honoured and they were escorted out of the city. Few, if any, other Muslims survived.

The blood-crazed crusader soldiers, oblivious to the orders of their knight commanders, went on the rampage. For two days, they slaughtered the citizens of Jerusalem, 'wading in blood up their ankles,' according to a medieval account of the sack of Jerusalem. 'Almost the whole city was full of their dead bodies,' recalled one knight, noting that the temple where the Muslims made their last stand was 'streaming with their blood'.

The slaughter ended at last, and the crusade leaders processed solemnly to the Church of the Holy Sepulchre, where they gave thanks to God for their great victory. The next day, they chose Duke Godfrey as the first leader of the new crusader kingdom of Jerusalem.

Godfrey, who died in Jerusalem, never took the title of king. His brother, Baldwin, who had accompanied him on the crusade, did, ruling as Baldwin I.

The scale of the slaughter, huge even in an age when massacres were a regular part of warfare, while it caused great rejoicing in the West. However, many Church leaders were horrified, and it deeply shocked the Muslim and Jewish worlds and undoubtedly helped fuel the warlike response of Islam to the Christian presence in the East in the next century.

The Battle of Hattin

——————— July 1187 ———————

During the half century between the first two crusades mounted by Catholic Christianity to wrest the Holy Land back from the Infidel, from about 1096 to 1149, the crusaders established a hold over a sizeable part of Syria and Palestine, with its frontiers the mountains of Lebanon and the river Jordan. There were four main Christian-ruled areas: the Kingdom of Jerusalem, the principality of Antioch, the County of Tripoli and the County of Edessa (lost again to Islam in 1144).

The main problem with this Christian presence in the Holy Land was that it was never much more than a token. Once a crusade was over, most of the knights and the fighting men returned to Europe, leaving small contingents to hold on in castles built to defend weak points. Some of these, such as Krak des Chevaliers, were massive, and virtually impregnable. The Christian fighting men, most of them belonging to two military orders, the Knights Hospitallers and the Knights Templars, stayed within them and made little attempt to persuade the local Muslim townsfolk and peasantry to convert to Christianity.

The crusaders had been lucky when they first arrived in Syria and Palestine at the end of the 11th century because the Muslim leadership had been disunited and at loggerheads with one another. Encounters between crusaders and Muslims, although called battles, were usually quite small affairs, involving just half a dozen knights and their attendant soldiers on the Christian side. By the 1170s, however, things were very different. The Muslim powers in the region were reorganizing themselves and providing a much more united opposition to the crusaders. From the mid-1170s, this opposition was led by the formidable figure of Salah al-Din Yusuf, sultan of Egypt and Syria, and known as Saladin.

Saladin was one of the most remarkable men of his age. Although untiring in his preaching of the jihad against the Christians, he was a patient, clever and far-sighted statesman and a humane, chivalrous warrior. 'Abstain from the shedding of blood, for blood that is spilt never slumbers,' he once said – this in an age when massacres were seen as just another element of warfare, or acceptable 'collateral damage', in modern terms.

Saladin's outwardly attractive personality led the Christian barons in Palestine to think that this was a man whom they could trust and come to terms with. They decided on a policy of appeasement, partly because it was obvious that Saladin was the most powerful Muslim leader they had faced, but also because his possessions surrounded them. On land, Saladin could attack them from the south and the east, while his Egyptian fleets could blockade their Mediterranean ports.

The leader of the crusaders who advocated appeasement was Raymond, Count of Tripoli, who was regent for the king of Jerusalem, Baldwin the Leper, from 1174 to 1185. When Baldwin the Leper died without a son and heir in 1185, Count Raymond III expected to be made king in Baldwin's place. However, his policies in the kingdom had been unpopular. He had made enemies, and a group of war-supporting barons chose Guy of Lusignan as king instead. Thus the first steps on the road to war with Saladin and his Muslim forces were taken.

A BROKEN TRUCE

In 1187, Raymond, Count of Tripoli, made some sort of agreement with Saladin, the precise terms of which have never been established. In giving Saladin's army permission to cross the river Jordan into the district of Tiberias, Raymond said that he – and Saladin – had intended only that the Muslim peasantry was to be the object of Saladin's attentions. The crusaders in their towns and castles were to be left wholly alone and certainly not attacked. But Gerard de Ridfort, Grand Master of the Templars, was in the area with some 130 Knights Templar. He had long been Raymond's enemy, and chose to ignore the order to remain inside the crusaders' castles and instead engaged the infidel intruders in battle. Saladin claimed that the truce, or whatever his agreement with Raymond had been, was broken and he laid siege to Tiberias. The crusaders, including Raymond, were forced into action.

At this time, the crusader army of the kingdom of Jerusalem, one of the largest ever gathered together in Palestine, was established at al-Saffuriyah, about 32 km (20 miles) from Tiberias. Raymond advised the army not to make the long day's march to Tiberias – along a road where Saladin had blocked the few wells and springs and on which they could easily be ambushed. Instead they should wait until Saladin moved to country more suitable for fighting a cavalry battle. However, his advice was ignored. The crusader army, led by King Guy of Jerusalem and including the 130 Knights Templar, their attendant fighting men and their grand master, set off at dawn on 3 July, 1187. Saladin, given this news, was jubilant. He had noted just weeks before, if this crusader army could be destroyed, then Jerusalem would be his for the taking.

It was a hot march, and the crusader army, with throats parched and eyes and noses full of the dust raised by their own feet and their horses' hooves – was being harried in the rear by Saracen archers on horseback. Saladin's intention was to cut the crusader column in half. A battle on the move was a well understood tactic in crusader warfare; provided the column of armoured knights and men-at-arms could stay together and march steadily to their objective, losses would be acceptably small. But Saladin's tactic meant that the rear, marching under a near constant rain of arrows, was in danger of being left behind. To prevent this, the army chose to make camp for the night near low twin peaks known as the Horns of Hattin, having covered less than half the distance to Tiberias.

Early the next day, battle began between the closely surrounded Christian army and Saladin's forces. The fighting was fierce. The Christian army was exhausted, outnumbered, lacked water and was fighting on unsuitable ground – the dry grass was torched by a Muslim soldier so that the Christian infantry gasped for breath. It was decisively beaten, though only after a last, heroic stand round a relic of the True Cross, which was brought to Palestine by the Franks and always carried into battle by the Christians.

King Guy, Gérard de Ridfort, Grand Master of the Templars, and Count Raynald of Chatillon were among the nobles captured. Only the contingent of men-at-arms led by Raymond of Tripoli escaped, retiring from the battle in good order. Their departure was actually aided by a wily tactic from the Muslim army, which instead of engaging the charging Christian soldiers, opened their ranks to allow them to pass through unopposed, then closed up again, thus cutting them off from the main army. Seeing that the battle was lost, Raymond led his force back to Tripoli.

Except for Raynald of Chatillon, whom Saladin regarded as a truce breaker, the lives of King Guy, the grand master and other nobles were spared. The rank and file of the kingdom of Jerusalem's army, most of them highly trained and fanatically Christian Hospitallers and Templars, were not. Saladin ordered a mass killing of all the captured knights and fighting men, which he watched from a dais set up in front of the army, and which he forced the Grand Master of the Templars to watch, too. The killings were particularly ghastly, for they were assigned, not to professional fighting men well able to use a weapon, but to the many scholars, holy men and jihad enthusiasts who had flocked to Saladin's standard. More often then not, it took such men several blows to sever the heads from their victims' bodies.

This atrociously bloodthirsty annihilation of the army of Jerusalem, with its attendant loss of the relic of the True Cross, deeply shocked the Christian West. One of the best-known depictions of the Battle of Hattin was drawn by the 13th-century English monk, Matthew Paris of St Albans for his *Chronica Majora*. He illustrated the (fictional) moment when Saladin seizes the relic from the desperately clutching hands of King Guy, despite the efforts of the knights at the king's side. Beneath the trampling hooves of the horses, the ground is strewn with the bodies, limbs and heads of the slain.

The city of Jerusalem capitulated on 2 October,

1187; Saladin had achieved his long-held goal, setting free 'the mosque of al-Aqsa, to which Allah once led in the night his servant Muhammad'. Within a year the Christians had either lost or surrendered almost all their ports and castles in the kingdom of Jerusalem. As for the relic of the True Cross, tradition has it that Saladin ordered it to be buried under the entrance to the great mosque at Damascus, so that the feet of the faithful could tread on it as they went in to pray.

Richard the Lionheart Massacres the Hostages at Acre

————— 22 August, 1191 —————

News of the Battle of Hattin and the capitulation of the city of Jerusalem to Saladin in 1187 reached the Christian West within weeks. The shock of the dreadful news is said to have hastened the death of Pope Urban III. It galvanized the new popes, Gregory VIII (who lived only two months after his investiture) and Clement III into calling for the leaders of Western Christianity to set aside their differences and come together to save Christianity in the East from 'the barbarians who thirst for Christian blood'.

In the Holy Roman Empire, Emperor Frederick Barbarossa began gathering together an army for the relief of the Holy Land that eventually numbered over 200,000 men. Henry II of England, who was also overlord of half France, and Philip II Augustus of France both began levying taxes in their countries to finance this third crusade mounted by Catholic Christianity in the past century.

Henry II died in October 1189, before his 'Saladin tithe', drawn from every subject, including the clergy, had been collected. It was left to his son, the tall, red-blonde, handsome and lionhearted Richard I, to collect the English contribution to the Third Crusade. Although Richard I was considered 'a bad king, a bad son, a bad husband and a bad father', he was a great soldier, and the main object of his life was a heartfelt desire to recover Jerusalem, the city of Christ's Passion for Christendom. Among Europe's Christian princes, Richard, while still Prince of Aquitaine, had been the first to fall to his knees and take the cross.

Once he became king of England, at the time the wealthiest and strongest nation in Europe, Richard carried out his father's crusading intentions with ruthless vigour, turning all his tax-raising efforts to financing the crusade. He sold high church offices, earldoms and lordships, castles and manors, even whole towns to finance his crusade. Richard's remark that he would have sold London if he could have found a buyer was not a joke. As for the Saladin tithe, it was levied for three years, and any parish that did not collect its full due was excommunicated.

Of the three most important rulers involved in the Third Crusade, Richard was the last to arrive in Palestine. Frederick Barbarossa, leading his huge army down through eastern Europe and into Turkey, died of a chill in Armenia in mid-1190 after bathing in the River Saleph. More than half his army turned back to Europe. Frederick of Swabia led a remnant of Barbarossa's army down into Palestine, reaching there after Philip II Augustus of France, who had arrived in March 1191. After numerous adventures on land on the way, Richard went to the Middle East by sea, meeting up with Philip II Augustus at Messina in Sicily. There, the two kings completed the building up of the great fleet that would carry the crusaders to Palestine.

Philip II Augustus set off first, leaving Richard to get the main body of the fleet to the eastern Mediterranean. Unfortunately, a great storm scattered the mighty fleet and it took weeks to find all the ships and gather them together again. The three largest ships, carrying Richard's betrothed, the Princess Berengeria, his sister Joanna and his English gold and treasure that were to finance the crusade, ended up on the island of Cyprus. When he caught up with them, Richard found that his gold and treasure had been snatched and his ships held in custody by the governor of the island, the son of the Byzantine emperor. Diplomacy availing him nothing, Richard, stormed ashore, rescued his betrothed and his sister, got back all his gold and treasure and, for good measure, wrested the island of Cyprus from the Byzantine Empire. This immensely useful bridgehead to Palestine remained in Latin Christian hands until 1571.

ENDING A STALEMATE

Once in the Holy Land, Richard and Philip found that the Christian position was not good. However, the fortress and port enclave of Tyre had remained firmly in the hands of the able Conrad of Montferrat. King Guy of Jerusalem, who was released from captivity by Saladin in the summer of 1188 – in the belief that he was a spent force – had managed to gather together the remnants of the army of the destroyed kingdom of Jerusalem and meld it into a force large enough to besiege the great city of Acre, eight leagues from Tyre. Acre had been one of the most prosperous merchant cities in the kingdom of Jerusalem and Saladin had made a point of taking it within days of the Battle of Hattin, setting up his court and celebrating Friday prayers in the city for the first time in 80 years.

When Philip II Augustus and Richard the Lionheart arrived in Palestine in 1191 the siege of Acre, which had been going on for nearly a year and a half, had reached a stalemate. The Christian army was not strong enough to storm Acre, and Saladin, himself in difficulties with rebellious Muslim leaders, was unable to gather together a force great enough to dislodge the Christians from their entrenched position in front of the city.

By early June 1191, Philip II Augustus and Richard, having agreed months before to divide between them any plunder won in Palestine, were with the Christian army at Acre, deeply involved in bringing the siege to a victorious conclusion. Richard personally directed the design, building and placement of new siege engines, including one that was said to be able to lob stones large enough to kill 12 men at a blow into the heart of Acre. At the same time, the walls of the town were mined; once tunnels were dug, the crusaders would fill them with combustible materials and set alight to them.

The Muslim garrison commanders in Acre knew they could not hold out much longer, unless Saladin could bring up many more fighting men to take on the by now greatly enlarged Christian army – which he could not do. Nor could he supply them with food and arms, for his ships could not get into the ports now that the Christian fleet had arrived and was guarding them.

Peace negotiations ended on 12 July, when the city's leaders agreed terms with Conrad of Tyre that were favourable for the crusaders. In return for the lives of the citizens and garrison of Acre, the Christians were to receive the city and its contents, the harbour and its ships, several hundred prisoners, a large ransom and the relic of True Cross lost at the Battle of Hattin. Some 3,000 of Acre's defenders were to remain as hostages to ensure these terms were met.

Philip II, desperate to leave the Holy Land and ignoring the pleas of his own military leaders and of Richard, set off for home at the end of July, escorted as far as Tyre by Conrad of Montferrat, to whom Philip gave his share of the plunder from the capture of Jerusalem, plus the prisoners he had been allotted.

Richard the Lionheart was now in sole charge of affairs in Acre.

A MASSIVE SLAUGHTER

Saladin did not hand over the first part of the ransom payment and some prisoners until 11 August. By now, Richard had had plenty of time to consider the Christian position. The importance of maintaining the military advantage far outweighed, in his eyes, the size of the ransom the Christians might eventually get. Those 3,000 hostages were too many to be guarded and could not be allowed to be reabsorbed into Saladin's forces. Richard decided to kill them.

He warned Saladin of his intentions, threatening to execute the hostages if the ransom, the relic of the True Cross, and those of Saladin's warriors specifically named in the surrender terms were not produced immediately. Saladin stalled. On 22 August, Richard had 2,700 of the hostages tied together, brought out of the city and ranged alongside a large stage set up below the city walls. One by one, the hostages were taken up onto the stage, blindfolded and ordered to kneel. Men from Richard's army beheaded them all, in full view of Saladin's army, powerless to do anything to stop the slaughter.

According to the Norman minstrel, Ambroise, who accompanied the crusaders, the Christian soldiers delighted in butchery, for they saw it as revenge for the killing of so many Christian soldiers during the siege of Acre. Another chronicler relates how the bodies were disembowelled and a great many gold and silver coins were found in the entrails. The massacre at Acre was a reminder to Richard's contemporaries that 'lionheart' could signify ferocity as well as bravery.

By the time Richard left the Holy Land in 1193, the standard of the cross flew over Acre and several stronghold towns along the coast to the south, largely through his efforts. Although the kingdom of Jerusalem was lost, those towns could have been a bridgehead for the recovery of Jerusalem from the infidel. They were not so used and Jerusalem was never regained by the Crusaders.

Richard the Lionheart and Saladin remain heroic figures to this day. A statue of Richard on horseback, sword raised high in the air, stands proudly in front of the Houses of Parliament in London. As recently as 1992 a statue of Saladin as victor of Hattin was erected in Damascus, capital of modern Syria and site of Saladin's tomb. And because Saladin was born in Tikrit, where the Iraqi dictator Saddam Hussein was also born, Hussein portrayed himself side by side with Saladin (despite Saladin's Kurdish ancestry) on propaganda posters in the 1980s.

Edward III, Victorious at Crécy, Takes Calais from the French

-----------1346-47-----------

Almost from the day he became king of England at the age of 15 in 1337, Edward III began planning how he would wrest back from France the rich lands of Flanders that had been lost from England so soon after the death of William the Conqueror. He also began looking for ways of claiming his right to the throne of France, partly because this would ease the task of finding allies for his cause in northern Europe.

Before he sent his first troops across the English Channel to northern France in 1337, starting the Hundred Years War, Edward III had been carefully building up England's fighting strength. He increased the output of his armoury in the Tower of London and encouraged archery and the use of the longbow, a weapon that his grandfather, Edward I, had first used in significant numbers. Later in Edward III's reign, an Act of Parliament decreed that all able-bodied men between the ages of 16 and 60 must 'learn and practise the art of shooting' at the butts every Sunday and feast day.

Edward's fame as a leader of men grew enormously in 1340 when he put himself in command of a 150-strong English fleet – the first true naval fleet created in England. It attacked and comprehensively destroyed a considerably larger French fleet at anchor in the harbour of Sluys. The longbowmen on the English ships caused havoc among the French crews, emphasizing their value as fighting men. This first, brilliant sea victory for England greatly impressed Europe, and Edward was even offered the title of Holy Roman emperor. He refused it.

BATTLE AT CRECY

By 1346, with the French fleet in the Channel much weakened, Edward III was ready personally to lead his army into battle in France. Accompanied by his 17-year-old son, Edward, the Black Prince, and many of the nobles of England, Edward crossed to France in July 1346 with a force of between 12,000 and 20,000 men (probably nearer the lesser than the greater number, historians believe).

In their march across northern France to Paris, in the early stages of which they captured the large Normandy town of Caen, Edward and his army had to fight many minor skirmishes and battles. By the time they eventually neared Paris, the army had been considerably weakened by heavy losses from disease as well as from fighting. With a large French army massing in front of them, Edward decided he must retreat northwards to the coast. Having crossed the Somme quite near its mouth, he halted in Ponthieu, near a village and forest called Crécy, where he turned to face his enemy.

The French army, made up mostly of heavily-armoured and beautifully caparisoned knights, mounted cavalry and Genoese crossbowmen, caught up with Edward and his depleted force on 25 August, 1346. The French should have won the ensuing battle. However, Edward III was too good an army commander, and his men were experienced. He drew up his army in two forward arrays of dismounted men and archers, with the Black Prince in charge of one of them, and with a third array slightly to the rear, which he himself commanded. Edward, mounted on his war horse and with the commander's white staff in his hand, ordered the battle from the mound of a windmill overlooking the field of battle.

The French, confused by conflicting orders from King Philippe VI, went into battle late in the afternoon, virtually blinded by a heavy thunderstorm. Their crossbowmen, the strings of their bows so drenched by the rain that they could not be stretched to the bow, hardly shot a single bolt. They and the French infantry fell in their hundreds under the arrows from the

English longbows. (Well used to rain, English long-bowmen kept their bow strings dry under their helmets until needed, a habit that is supposed to be the origin of the expression 'keep it under your hat'.)

During the rest of the day and long into the night that followed, the French made charge after charge against the English, only to be met by a hailstorm of arrows, and in each charge losing many men to the English archers. Many times, the English were desperately hard-pressed, the Black Prince himself often dangerously in the thick of the battle. Edward is famous for refusing to send aid to his son.

> *Send no more to me as long as my son is alive . . .*
> *suffer him this day to win his spurs; for if God be*
> *pleased I wish this day to be his, the honour thereof,*
> *and for them that be about him.*

The day, and the Battle of Crécy, did belong to the English, and the honour of it to the Black Prince, who won his knight's spurs at Crécy (they are still on his feet on his tomb in Canterbury Cathedral). Contemporary British reports claim that the French lost 11 princes, 1,200 knights and more than 10,000 foot soldiers at Crécy. However, the English dead totalled just 40. Edward III's great victory at Crécy resounded through Europe.

Departing from the usual practice of medieval warfare, the English took few prisoners at Crécy. This may have been because they felt themselves to be too small in numbers to be able to oversee a large number of prisoners adequately, but it is surprising, given the ransom value of many of the French and the enormous cost of the war. Edward had already defaulted on his war loans in 1340, bankrupting two major Florentine banking houses in the process. Edward's mild treatment of his enemy after Crécy stands in stark contrast to the actions he threatened to take against the town of Calais just a year later.

PLEAS FOR CLEMENCY

After Crécy, Edward led his army north to Calais, where his fleet was blockading the port, so that they could embark for England. But Calais was strongly fortified and well defended and Edward had to lay siege to the town until July 1347, before near-starvation caused its governor, Jean Vienne, to offer to surrender if Edward would spare the lives of Calais' people.

Edward, enraged at having been hindered in France so long by the common people of a town, replied that he would accept the town's surrender on condition that six of the town's leading citizens, or burghers, came before him, heads and feet bared and with halters round their necks, and present to him the keys of the town on their knees. He would then take the keys and hang the burghers by the ropes around their necks.

Pleas for clemency from many English knights were

brushed aside by Edward and it seemed as if the six burghers of Calais, who had offered themselves to save their town and its citizens, were doomed. Suddenly, Edward's wife, Queen Phillipa, intervened. She knelt before her fierce husband and begged him, 'in all humility, in the name of the Son of the Blessed Virgin Mary and by the love you have for me,' to show mercy towards the men. Edward hesitated, then said that the men could live.

Had Edward III executed the burghers of Calais, men who in themselves posed no threat to the king or his army, it would have been an atrocious act indeed. The fact that it was a woman's intervention that prevented the atrocity taking place gives added piquancy to the story.

As for the struggle between the English and the French, something far more dreadful than warfare put an end to their immediate differences. The bubonic plague, or the Black Death, hit southern France in 1347. By 1348, spreading like wildfire, the Black Death had reached England, possibly on a ship coming back to England after supplying Calais. It would be years before France and England, their populations dreadfully depleted, could think about making full-scale war again.

In 1350, Edward officially laid claim to the throne of France through his mother, Isabella, daughter of Philippe IV of France. It was a flimsy claim, since Salic Law banned women from inheriting the throne of France, but

Edward gave it weight by quartering the arms of the king of France with the three golden lions on the arms of England, and by adopting his motto, 'Dieu et mon droit'. Adopting St George as the patron saint of England was another clever move, since St George was the patron saint of all European knighthood.

The importance of the English victory at the Battle of Crécy lay much less in the fact that a large French army had been defeated than in the fact that victory at Crécy enabled Edward to secure Calais for the English. This gave England an opening to the rich manufacturing towns of Flanders, which were ready markets for English wool and cloth exports. No wonder that when England lost Calais, its last possession in France, two centuries later, Queen Mary Tudor said that, when she died, the word 'Calais' would be found engraved on her heart.

Vlad the Impaler

—————— 1400s ——————

*H*istory can show many examples of men and women who have committed appalling acts of cruelty against their fellow men, not a few of them in the name of religion. But there are few whose actions can match those of Vlad III, ruler of the central European state of Wallachia in the mid-15th century. Not that Vlad stayed quietly and untroubled in his castle, Tirgoviste, during the 20 years of his reign. As with other states in this seldom peaceful region of central Europe, where Islam and Christianity had fought bloody battles for control for centuries, Wallachia was pulled to and fro between rival factions. Vlad, turned out of his castle and his country in the 1460s, spent almost as many years off his throne as on it.

Vlad was born about 1431 in the Danube principality of Transylvania, where his father, Vlad Dracul, was the military governor put in charge of the region by Holy Roman Emperor Sigismund, at a time when Turkish control was strengthening. In 1387, the young Sigismund had founded an order of knights, called the Order of the Dragon ('Dracul' in Romanian), which, like the much older Knights Templars and Knights Hospitallers, was a Christian order, devoted to turning back the Islamic tide: the Ottoman Turks had been expanding their influence into eastern Europe for much of the past century. Vlad was a knight of the Order of the Dragon, hence his name, Vlad Dracul.

In 1436, Vlad Dracul was promoted to the throne of the neighbouring state of Wallachia, taking the title Vlad II and installing his family, including Vlad and his younger brothers Mircea and Radu, in the castle of Tirgoviste. Within two years, Vlad II Dracul, probably with an eye to securing his position as a ruler in his own right rather than as a nominee of the Holy Roman emperor, had changed sides. He formed an alliance with the Turks and sent two of his sons, Vlad and Radu, to the court of the Sultan Murad II as insurance for his own good behaviour and future loyalty.

Vlad II's alliance with the Ottoman Turks was disliked by many of the leading men ('boyars') of Wallachia, including the statesman and warrior Janos Hunyadi, who had expelled the Turks from Transylvania in 1442. In 1447, Hunyadi led a revolt of the boyars against Vlad II. Vlad was assassinated and his son Mirea was buried alive after his eyes were gouged out. Sultan Murad granted Vlad II's other two sons their freedom, and Vlad returned at once to his homeland. Radu chose to stay in Turkey.

The young Vlad, called Vlad Dracula ('son of Dracul'), was not turning his back on the Turks. With the help of the Turkish cavalry, he wrested his father's throne from the boyars and proclaimed himself Vlad III of Wallachia. This first period of occupation of the throne was short-lived, for Janos Hunyadi soon ousted him and put his own man in Vlad's place.

THE CRUEL RULER

Whether it was that dreadful killing of his father and his brother, plus the ensuing homeless years of conspiring and building up connections and relationships in the tangled, dangerous politics of the Christian-versus-Ottoman Turk world that turned Vlad Dracula into a ruthless killer, apparently enjoying the spilling of blood for its own sake, or whether he was born with a mind attuned to bloodlust, history does not tell us. What we do know is that when he eventually got his throne back in 1456, Vlad Dracula treated the boyars who had opposed him and his father with quite extraordinary cruelty.

He started off by handing out to the boyars a punishment meted many times throughout history: inviting one's enemies to dinner, then murdering them all. Vlad's version, carried out after a feast celebrating Easter Sunday, involved long-term torture rather than simple death for most of those at the feast. The healthy among them were put to work on building him a new castle, Poenari, on the river Arges. They were treated like animals: beaten and tortured for the slightest reason, ill-fed and ill-clothed. Many worked naked in the harshest weather as their clothes wore into shreds. And, of course, many died.

What happened to the old, weak and infirm among the boyars invited to that Easter Sunday feast was an even greater pointer to the way in which Vlad was to operate in the coming years. He impaled them on stakes, setting them up in a public place so that his subjects could watch them die, slowly and in hideous pain. This was the start of a career that would have future generations calling him Vlad the Impaler.

Over the years, Vlad's methods became more and more twisted and psychopathic. A near-contemporary etching shows Vlad's victims impaled on stakes pushed through their bodies, from front to back and through the neck. Other accounts of his impalements describe how the stakes were pushed up through the body, through the anus in the case of men, or the vagina in the case of women. He impaled large numbers at a time, often setting the stakes in circles and other patterns in the ground. He is said to have impaled 30,000 merchants outside the Tirgoviste city walls because they transgressed trade laws.

Vlad delighted in all forms of torture. His victims had their eyes gouged out, were eviscerated, decapitated, dismembered, boiled in oil and burnt. He once had a mistress disembowelled in public for having – perhaps mistakenly, perhaps dishonestly – told him that she was pregnant. Rumour had it that Vlad ate the bodies and drank the blood of his victims. The etching that showed men and women impaled on stakes, also depicted men hacking up and boiling body parts while Vlad, hands outstretched, sat waiting at a table covered with a white cloth for the cooked flesh to be set in front of him.

In his own kingdom, Vlad imposed his dreadful catalogue of punishments on the sick, the poor, the dishonest, the lazy and the work-shy. His aim, he said, was to make Wallachia a well-ordered, crime-free society where only the healthy, happy and prosperous had a place.

A FAILED ATTACK

When Vlad took his methods beyond his own borders into the valley of the river Danube in 1461, he came unstuck, partly because he had not taken into account the full measure of Mehemmed II, who had succeeded his father as sultan of Turkey in 1451. When Vlad attacked but failed to subdue the Turks along the Danube, largely because the sultan's army there was too strong, he made an abortive attempt at murdering the sultan in his tent. He succeeded only in enraging Mehemmed, a man whose actions, including the conquest of Constantinople in 1453, were to earn him the title of Conqueror. Mehemmed ordered the invasion of Wallachia.

Vlad retreated into the heart of his kingdom, razing villages and poisoning wells as he went so that the

Turks could find no forage. Those Turkish soldiers he captured were impaled. Sultan Mehemmed is said to have found at one place in Wallachia a veritable forest of stakes, each with its dead, decomposing and stinking Turkish soldier impaled on it. Sultan Mehemmed chose to make a tactical withdrawal from Wallachia. Soon, he had sent in another force, this one led by Vlad's brother, Radu. As this force neared Vlad's castle of Poenari, his wife chose suicide over capture by the Turks and leaped to her death from the castle battlements. Vlad escaped into the mountains and made his way into Transylvania, leaving his throne for Radu to mount.

Years of exile now followed for Vlad Dracula. In Transylvania, he fell into the hands of King Matthias Corvinus of Hungary, who had been remarkably successful in driving the Turks out of his land. Matthias Corvinus took Vlad to Hungary and imprisoned him. After a time, 'imprisonment' turned into guest status, with the occasional reporting back to the king. Vlad Dracula even married the king's cousin. And in exile he continued his habit of impaling living creatures on stakes, though now he was reduced to small animals and large insects.

In the end, fortune once again favoured Vlad Dracula. His brother Radu in Wallachia had been making too many concessions to the Ottoman Turks and had turned the Order of the Dragon out of Wallachia. In 1467, King Matthias Corvinus gathered together a Christian force, led by him and Prince Stefan Bathory of Transylvania. With Vlad Dracula in its train, they drove the Turks out of Wallachia (now ruled by a prince called Basarab the Old, Radu having died of syphilis) and Moldavia. As was only to be expected, Vlad Dracula's path back to his throne was marked by burnt and subdued villages and thousands of stakes on which were impaled the bodies of Turkish soldiers. Because he was a Christian destroying the infidel, Vlad's favourite method of execution was this time officially approved by the pope in Rome.

Vlad Dracula died fighting the Ottoman Turks. Sultan Mehemmed, never likely to acquiesce in the Christian takeover of Wallachia, soon sent a huge force against him. Vlad could not count on the support of Wallachia's boyars, and when his final battle came in 1476 he was greatly outnumbered. No one knows the manner of Vlad Dracula's death, only that he died fighting fiercely for his throne.

Vlad Dracula was resurrected in spectacular style in the 19th century. It was a time when interest in the Gothic merged with Romanticism to create a feverish interest in the occult, in bloodsucking vampires, in devil-worship and much else. When Bram Stoker wrote *Dracula*, his classic vampire horror story, it is not surprising that one of his main inspirations was Vlad Dracula. Vlad was not a vampire, and he had not worshipped the devil. But his name – another meaning of 'dracul' in Romanian was 'devil' – and his habit of impaling people on stakes, then eating their bodies and drinking their blood, certainly made him a prime candidate for the lead in a story about vampires, which could only be destroyed by driving a stake through their body.

Henry V at Agincourt

──────── 25 October 1415 ────────

*H*enry V's destruction of the military strength French nobility at the Battle of Agincourt in 1415 was the high point of English success in the Hundred Years War. Edward III, Henry's great-grandfather, had begun the campaign 80 years earlier to wrest back from France territories that the English king laid claim to through his French ancestry.

When Henry V succeeded to the throne in 1413 he was already planning to consolidate the work begun by his ancestor. He wanted to win back lands lost and to gain possession of other lands that the French had never handed over. He planned to first take possession of Normandy, which he claimed to have been a domain of the English crown since the time of William the Conquer. From this power base, he would be in a strong position to make the French acknowledge and honour his claim to the French crown.

Henry V's invasion of Normandy was no quick raid across the Channel. On 11 August, 1415, a pleasant Sunday afternoon on Southampton Water, the king gave the signal that sent on its way to France an armada of 1,500 ships – 12 times the number of ships that Spain sent against England in 1588 – carrying an army of 12,000 men and the huge tonnage of arms and equipment needed to support them in the months ahead. Three days later the little ships, most of which were merchant ships and coastal traders, were unloading their cargoes near Harfleur, on the south bank of the mouth of the river Seine in Normandy.

Henry had originally intended to cross the Seine from Harfleur and push north to the English possession of Calais, gathering in the lands of Normandy as he went and relying on speed to get him to Calais before the French could muster a response. Unfortunately, the town of Harfleur was well garrisoned and Henry had to besiege it. It was a month before Harfleur capitulated, and Henry eventually set off north early in October. By this time, his army had been depleted in both men and resources, with much having to be left behind to garrison and defend Harfleur.

At the same time, the French were organizing their forces into an increasingly formidable, well-organized army. The English found themselves constantly harried, short on rations, and again and again having to turn away from their chosen line of march because bridges and fords were now held by the French. Much of the way was through wooded country or marshy land on either side of rivers, and when the weather broke, heavy rain turned the country into a muddy quagmire. Much of this land, the valley of the Somme, was to be fought over again by French and British forces during World War I, now on the same side, in equally dreadful conditions in 1916.

On 20 October, the French sent heralds to the English camp, with a formal challenge for Henry V from the dukes of Orléans and Bourbon. Henry rejected it, sending back a message to the French that he intended to continue his march to Calais and would fight them if they opposed him. For the next four days the English and French armies marched virtually in parallel north towards Calais. Late in the day on 24 October, the two armies came together in a gorge between Agincourt and Tramecourt, with the French army blocking Henry's way to Calais. Both armies made camp within sight and sound of each other. Clearly, there would be a battle between the two the next day, the Feast of Saints Crispin and Crispinian.

Of the two armies, the English was undoubtedly in the worse condition and the less prepared for a major encounter. It was much smaller than the French force. Henry is generally thought to have had about 900 lightly armed men-at-arms and 5,000 archers, all armed with the English longbow, at his disposal. Many of these men were suffering from dysentery, they had all been underfed for weeks and they were all tired: one military historian has calculated that they had marched about 420 km (260 miles) in 17 days. Nearly 200 years later the playwright William Shakespeare turned this ragged army into an heroically romantic 'happy few, a band of brothers' whose actions on 'Crispin Crispian day' would be remembered from that day onwards.

French numbers have been less easy to calculate. A generally accepted number is somewhere between 20,000 and 30,000, with the probable total being nearer the former number than the latter. Half the French army was made up of dismounted men-at-arms and the other half consisted of roughly two-thirds mounted knights (cavalry) and one-third crossbowmen and archers.

During the night heavy rain fell on both armies and the ground on which they would be fighting the next day. The English army made its preparations quietly; the French, full of confidence, could be heard eating and drinking, dicing and gambling, the knights resting on bales of straw to keep them above the mud, and their servants bustling to and fro and shouting cheerfully at each other. A rumour went about among the English that there was a brightly painted wagon at the back of the French camp and that in a few days' time the English king was going to be paraded through Paris in it.

THE BATTLE BEGINS

Next day, 25 October, 1415, both the English and French were up at dawn, moving their armies into position about 914 m (1,000 yds) apart. The French had decided on a battle plan that involved sending their troops into the fight in three waves. To this end, they formed their army into three lines, or 'battles', each battle consisting of two ranks of dismounted men, five or six men deep, and a line of horsemen – about 6,000 men in all in each battle. Bodies of 600 cavalry were stationed on each flank. There were well-disposed crossbowmen and gunners among the lines.

Henry, with far fewer fighting men at his disposal, had a single line of men-at-arms, four men deep. The line was divided into three divisions, with wedges of bowmen between them and more archers on the wings, standing behind well-sharpened stakes set in the ground in front of them at an angle carefully calculated to make the enemy turn aside or risk being impaled.

To ensure that no one would forget that his invasion was being carried out in the name of God, Henry had his priests well to the fore before battle was joined, praying continually. He himself received the sacrament before donning his gold-plated helmet, surmounted by a gold, jewel-studded crown, and mounting his horse. Late in the morning, after addressing his troops and reminding them of the justice of his cause and of those back home in England awaiting their return, Henry ordered his army to advance. Once in the centre of the field, the line stopped. The archers hammered their stakes into the ground, and let fly a storm of arrows at the enemy.

The longbow, used by the English much more suc-cessfully than other European states, helped Henry V win the Battle of Agincourt so comprehensively. It has been said that, not until the American Civil War, would a weapon with the range and accuracy of the longbow appear on a battlefield. The first French battle into the attack was led by the flanking cavalry, advancing so tightly packed that the knights could not wield their weapons. Their charge broke apart under the hail of arrows, which a well-trained archer could loose off every ten seconds. Many of the horses and riders that did get as far as the English line were impaled on the stakes in front of the archers. The remnants of the cavalry, retreating, plunged back into the heavily-armed and armoured foot soldiers, slowly lumbering into action behind them. The same thing happened to the second French battle.

Within four hours, the whole thing seemed to be over. The field was covered with dead and dying French; the French are calculated to have lost more than 6,000 men at Agincourt, while the English dead numbered less than 250. Many slightly wounded or unhorsed knights became so bogged down by their armour in the deep mud that they had become completely ineffective as fighting men. As one commentator noted, 'Great people of [the French] were slain without any stroke'. There was a perceptible lull in the fighting, and it looked as if the third French battle would not continue. The English began gathering up prisoners who could be ransomed and searching for booty among the dead.

Then came what looked like a serious attack on the English from the rear. A French knight and a troop of men-at-arms made a sally from Agincourt Castle and seized Henry's baggage train and the 1,000 peasants that looked after it. Thinking that he would have to repel an attack from his rear as well as cope with renewed fighting on his front, and seeing that many of the French prisoners and wounded still had their weapons, Henry ordered the slaughter of all French prisoners in English hands. He also warned that any Englishman who disobeyed his order would be hanged.

Although many of the English nobles and senior officers, thinking of the fortunes in ransom money to be made from the prisoners, refused to follow the order, the common soldiers did, and many hundreds, perhaps thousands, of French prisoners were slaughtered before the order was rescinded.

Modern historians have condemned Henry V for his order, forgetting that he was acting within the codes of an age much harsher and more cruel than our own. Then, too, it is probable that the number actually butchered was considerably less than suggested in accounts of the battle in the years after 1415. It is a matter of record that nearly 2,000 prisoners, still alive, were in Henry's train when he moved on to Calais. One of them, Charles, Duke of Orléans, was to spend 35 years in captivity in England while his ransom money was raised.

Like many war crimes, Henry V's 'crime' was the

result of a decision taken in the heat of battle in response to his realization that certain specific actions by the enemy could, if not checked, turn victory into defeat. His action was not condemned by his contemporaries, English or French: indeed, French commentators blamed the leaders of the French army for not withdrawing when they could see that the battle was lost. Despite his 'crime', Henry V remains England's most heroic king and Shakespeare's 'star of England', whose sword was made by Fortune [– and, Henry would have added, by God].

Pizarro Destroys the Inca State

———— 1532 ————

Christopher Columbus returned to Europe from his first voyage of discovery across the Atlantic in 1493. His enthusiastic report to Ferdinand and Isabella of Spain of his findings and his assessment that the New World had vast riches ready for the taking could not have come at a better time. Spain had recently ended several centuries of struggle to rid their country of the infidel Moo. It was full of religious fervour and had a good supply of soldiers and fighting men willing to risk their lives for the sake of those riches in gold and silver that Columbus had described.

In Central and South America, the Spanish conquistadors found two great, rich empires. Although they had witnessed years of burnings in the name of religion in their own country – Torquemada's years as Inquisitor General in Castile and Aragon had seen some 10,000 people sentenced to death by the dreadful *auto de fe* – the Spanish used their shock and horror at the Aztecs' practice of human sacrifice in the name of religion in

Mexico as an excuse for their ruthless suppression of the Aztecs and the looting of the empire's wealth.

Two decades later, the Spanish conquistador Francisco Pizarro's conquest of the Inca Empire of Peru was every bit as rapacious and murderous as that of his fellow Spaniard, Hernan Cortés, in Mexico. However, unlike Cortés, Francisco Pizarro was a rough, uneducated man, unable to read or write and totally unversed in the social graces or the ways of diplomacy. He was nearly 40 years old when he arrived in the New World in 1509. He helped Balboa found a colony on the Darien isthmus, and in 1515 he crossed the isthmus to the Pacific side of America, to trade with the native Americans there.

Pizarro made three great voyages of discovery down the Pacific coast of South America, setting out each time from or near the little colonial capital of Panama. On each, he put in at various points on the coast, exploring a little inland and getting to know something of the nature of the vast Inca empire, most of which lay hidden on the high plateaux of the Andes.

THE INCA EMPIRE

Although the Inca empire had reached peaked only about 100 years before Pizarro arrived on the scene, it had been in existence for several centuries, built on much older civilizations about which little is now known. This is partly because the earlier peoples of

Peru had not developed any form of writing or picture writing and partly because the Spaniards' indoctrination of the Indians they conquered was so thorough.

Archaeologists and historians have discovered that the states of South America that preceded the Incas, who pulled them all together into one vast empire, were as advanced as anything in Mexico. They had highly bureaucratic societies, well-developed agricultural techniques, including the use of irrigation, and rich cultural bases, as demonstrated by their finely woven and designed textiles, fine pottery and metalwork, and jewellery. They had also developed a sophisticated building technique that allowed their stone buildings, made without mortar, to withstand the strong earthquakes regularly experienced in the Andes. All this, the Inca Empire inherited and built upon.

The first Inca, or emperor, appeared in Peru some time in the 13th century. He and his successors gradually melded together the various states and peoples in that part of South America, creating a vast empire that stretched for 3,200 km (2,000 miles) down one of South America's coasts, contained one of the world's greatest mountain chains and reached inland as far as the rain forests of the Amazon. It was ruled by the absolute Inca, aided by a highly organized governing bureaucracy, many of whose members were his blood relatives and children. The capital of the Inca Empire was Cuzco, in the central highlands. The empire's huge army, whose officers, like the government bureaucrats, came from the Inca's extended family, expanded its operations through the empire by using an amazing network of roads which, by the time the Spaniards arrived, stretched 5,230 km (3,250 miles) from Quito in the north to Talca in central Chile. This road network was to make the Spanish conquest of Peru relatively simple and speedy.

The Inca was the divine symbol on earth of the sun god whom the Peruvians worshipped. Unlike the Aztecs in Mexico, the Incas were not bloodthirsty in their religious observance. Captives were sometimes sacrificed and in times of difficulty, such as drought, parents might sacrifice a child, but the usual sacrifice was a llama or an alpaca. Offerings to the gods were often as simple as a cone of spun wool, set down on the temple steps. Pizarro and his men did not know this when they arrived in Peru and expected to deal with people as bloodthirsty as the Aztecs. This perhaps explains the cold-blooded violence with which Pizarro conducted his first meeting with the Inca.

FALL OF AN EMPIRE

Pizarro's third expedition to the Andes sailed out of Panama in January 1531. He had under his command three small ships carrying 180 men, 27 horses, arms, ammunition and stores. By September 1532, Pizarro had established a garrison settlement at a place he called San Miguel on the river Chira.

Far away in the heart of Peru, the last Inca, Atahualpa, had just concluded the victory over his brother that gave him control of the whole Inca Empire, not just the northern part of it bequeathed to him in 1527 by his father, Huayna Capac. Historians have puzzled over the question of why this Inca should have divided and thus weakened his kingdom. They have come to the conclusion that Huayna Capac, hearing about the tall, bearded strangers from across the sea who were becoming such a strong presence in the north, while mounted on strange and enormous animals the South American people had never seen, decided to put the more vulnerable part of his country in the hands of his son Atahualpa, a strong and ruthless warrior. Whatever the reason, the fact was that the great Inca Empire was not as fully united and strong as it needed to be to meet this unprecedented crisis in its history.

At San Miguel, Pizarro heard that the Inca was not in his capital, Cuzco, but resting at Cajamarca, a town with hot springs much nearer than Cuzco. The way across the Andes to Cajamarca was difficult and dangerous, but on 24 September, 1532 Pizarro marched his small force out of San Miguel into the mountains to the heart of the Inca Empire. The march took seven terrible weeks, during which Atahualpa sent two embassies to welcome Pizarro to his kingdom and try to judge his intentions. These embassies threatened no violence and, indeed, seemed ready to treat the Spaniards with correct formality and hospitality.

When Pizarro and his men finally emerged from the high Andes on 15 November and made the relatively easy descent to Cajamarca, they found the town deserted. Atahualpa, his attendants and his army were a couple of leagues away in a tented settlement set up by the hot springs that had brought the Inca to the town in the first place. The town, a neat and orderly place with its steets and alleys laid out in straight, intersecting lines and with a triangular courtyard at its heart, had been handed over to Pizarro as a place for him and his men to stay in comfortably. Once settled in, Pizarro, having waited long enough for word from the Inca, sent a messenger with 20 horses to ask that the Inca visit him in the town.

Next day, Saturday, 16 November, 1532, Atahualpa told Pizarro that he would visit the Spaniard in the town. He said that he would come armed because the Spaniards had come armed to him the previous day. It was not until late in the afternoon that the Inca's state procession appeared in front of the town. It was an impressive sight. First came a squadron of men in col- oured livery, who swept the road in front of Atahualpa. Then came men in different costumes, some singing and dancing, others bearing large metal plates and crowns of gold and silver. Atahualpa's litter was born by 80 officers, all richly dressed. The litter was lined with plumes and macaws' feathers, and Atahualpa was seated on a gold throne covered with a feather-lined palanquin, richly clothed and adorned with gold and turquoise, as befitted the [divine] symbol of the sun god on earth.

This procession entered Cajamarca and proceeded to the central courtyard. There was no sign of the Spanish force. A priest holding a bible and crucifix confronted the Inca and made a long speech about the Christian faith. When this man had the effrontery to thrust the bible at Atahualpa, he rejected it.

It is possible that, as he sat on his litter high above the crowd of his people, the Inca actually saw the handkerchief dropped by Pizarro as a sign that his men should open fire. Their cannon, dragged across the Andes, began cutting swathes through the crowd in the courtyard, while the sharp sound of firing from the soldiers' arequebuses combined with the pounding of the hooves of the charging cavalry raised a hellish storm of choking smoke and noise over the scene.

The ceremonial weapons carried by a few of the Inca's men into Cajamarca were useless against the Spanish arms. The Inca's men were butchered as they fought with their bare hands to save the Inca. Soon, every way of escape from the courtyard was blocked by the bodies of the fallen. Those remaining inside were hacked to bits by the Spanish soldiers, in the grip of a terrible bloodlust. Only the intervention of Pizarro and several of his officers saved the Inca. As the sun set and darkness fell, the Inca was led away in chains.

The Inca Empire collapsed. No effort was made to save the Inca, for there was no one with the authority to make the attempt. In the months that followed, while Atahualpa remained a prisoner of Pizarro, his empire was looted of its gold, silver and precious stones. Eventually, after a 'trial' that was in reality a farce, Atahualpa was sentenced to death by burning: his fate was to be a true *auto de fe*. When Atahualpa saw the stake and realized that his body was to be consumed by fire, which would damn him completely in his life after death, he agreed to become a Christian in return for being garrotted. The sentence was carried out on 16 July, 1533.

Ivan the Terrible Destroys Novgorod
—————— 1570 ——————

*I*van IV, the first ruler of Russia to take the title 'Tsar of all the Russias', was only three years old when he became ruler of the Russian state in 1533. Ivan was the grandson of Ivan III, called 'the Great' because he had rid Russia of the Mongols, united all the Russian principalities and states under his own rule and laid the foundations for the great state of Russia.

Ivan IV, who was born in 1530, came to the throne less than 30 years after Ivan III's death. He inherited a country that was geographically ill-defined and racially disunited and was still a state in the making. Most of its influences – cultural, religious and social – as well as its most likely enemies, came from the Asiatic east and Byzantine south, not from Europe. So irregular, distant and ill-defined (and tinged with suspicion) was Russia's relationship with Europe, that a 17th-century king of France wrote to a tsar of Russia not knowing that the man had been dead for ten years. Even the title 'tsar', was an Asiatic word, and the great Imperial double-headed eagle that Ivan III included in his emblem came from Byzantium.

Ivan IV spent most of his reign building on his grand-father's work, establishing the Russian state on a more firm administrative footing, and subduing surrounding states, such as Astrakhan and Kazan, where 60,000 died during the siege and capitulation of the city of Kazan in 1552. He contributed much to his country's cultural and commercial development. However, Ivan carried out much of this work, especially later in his reign, with such a savage, ferocious cruelty that even in his own time he was called 'Terrible', and it is as Ivan the Terrible that he still figures in Russia's history.

Ivan's childhood had not been a happy one. His mother, who acted as regent during his babyhood, was poisoned when he was eight years old, and respon-sibility for his care was taken over by a group of men from the ruling class, or nobility, called 'boyars', of whom Ivan lived in constant fear. From the time he grew to manhood and began his personal rule, Ivan the Terrible seems to have constantly suspected conspira-cies against him everywhere. He always carried a long wooden stave, which he would lash out with when enraged, killing many people in his entourage.

THE OPRICHNINA

To control the Russian people, Ivan established a sort

of secret police, or military force, called the Oprich-nina, which he founded early in the years of his personal rule in a determined effort to eliminate all villains and traitors from his land. The Oprichnina operated through a corps of 6,000 *oprichniki*. These men, above the law, tortured, raped, murdered and looted from the people of Russia in their ferocious loyalty to the tsar.

Ivan was fanatically religious, spending hours on his knees in church (always after he had killed someone), and he saw the Oprichnina as something akin to the Spanish Inquisition. The *oprichniki* wore black garments like a monk's robe and rode black horses, carrying a broom and a severed dog's head on their saddles as symbols of their role as purifiers of the state.

A CITY MASSACRE

Among Ivan the Terrible's many appalling actions, often ordered by him in fits of destructive rage and carried out by the *oprichniki*, the destruction of Novgorod and the massacre of the city's citizens in 1570 stands out for its sustained cruelty.

In the centuries before Ivan III subjugated Novgorod territory in 1478, the city of Novgorod had grown from a trading post, dealing in furs, and an Orthodox Christian city into the overlord of a great state stretching across northern Russia as far as the Urals and as far north as the White Sea and the Arctic Circle. In the 15th and early 16th centuries, the Peterhof in Novgorod was one of the four great, and most distant, trading posts, or kontore, of the Hanseatic League. Thus, Novgorod had stronger connections with Europe and the West than most parts of Russia. Although Ivan III deprived Novgorod of its independence, of its wealth and of its links with Europe, the city was still the third largest in Russia, after Moscow and Kiev, in the time of Ivan the Terrible.

Ivan's increasingly paranoic attention was drawn to the city in the far north-west of his territory in the late 1460s, after General Kurbsky, the hero of Russia's war against Kazan and a leading counsellor of the tsar, fled the country. Kurbsky was escaping from the escalating horrors of Ivan's bloodthirsty ten-year reign of terror against the boyars, which saw many boyars and their families either murdered or ordered by the Oprichnina to be deported to Siberia. But when General Kurbsky became a commander in the Polish army, Ivan began to see Polish conspiracies everywhere, not least in Novgorod, with its long history of dealings with Europe.

Believing that Novgorod was a hotbed of conspiracy and intended defection to Poland, Ivan the Terrible sentenced the whole population of the city to death. With a large force of *oprichniki*, Ivan marched north to Novgorod, arriving outside the city on 2 January, 1570. The *oprichniki* immediately began throwing a cordon round the city, building a great wall to prevent its citizens escaping.

When the wall was complete, Ivan and his entourage, which included his son, Tsarevitch Ivan, attended a great banquet in the house of the Archbishop of Novgorod. The next day, 9 January, the massacre began. Every day for five weeks, up to 1,000 men and women of Novgorod were gathered up by Ivan's men and paraded before him and the tsarevitch in the city's main square. With their own children looking on, the men and women were tortured and then killed, many by being pushed under the ice of the frozen river Neva and drowned. Every day, after Ivan and his son had witnessed this dreadful spectacle, Ivan, clad in a monk's robe, went into church and prayed to god – not for forgiveness, but to give thanks.

About 60,000 people were killed during the Novgorod massacre. Many thousands more were deported. When the killings ceased, the *oprichniki* sacked the city and then laid waste to the surrounding countryside. Novgorod never regained its former greatness.

Ivan the Terrible followed the destruction of Novgorod with more bloodletting during a 'Great Festival of Blood' in Moscow, in which the main event was more murdering of 'traitors'. However, the reign of the Oprichnina was soon to be over. Its fighting men failed so utterly to protect Moscow from an invading force of Tartars from Crimea in 1571 that the city, like Novgorod, was reduced to ashes, with only the Kremlin still standing. The following year, Ivan disbanded the Oprichnina and the reign of terror it had overseen came to an end.

Not that Ivan the Terrible's own actions became any less terrible or his rages less murderous. He killed his son Ivan, whom he loved and admired – and with whom he shared a delight in torturing animals – in the course of an argument with him. This was one killing that *even* Ivan the Terrible could not forget, and when he died three years later, in 1584, it was said that sorrow for his dead son had caused his own death.

PART THREE

WAR CRIMES AND ATROCITIES 1600–1930

Black Hole
of Calcutta

1756

The Black Hole of Calcutta is memorable for being a singular atrocity, and little in either history or fiction can compare to the horrors that the survivors of that night described. The incident got its name from a small, airless dungeon at Fort William in Calcutta, which was led by the British East India Company.

ENGLISH PRESENCE IN INDIA

The British established their first trading post in India in 1614, and since then their presence has grown steadily. The East India Company was established by the British to consolidate their trading posts in India. It was an early example of privatization and was possibly the single, most powerful economic force of its time. It had been founded by the Royal Charter of Queen Elizabeth I, and it was given a group of knights and merchants from London to try to take over some of the East Indies spice trade from the Dutch. Although the company failed in this mission, it was successful in setting up trading posts in both Madras and Calcutta. Troops were hired by the company to protect their employees from the agitated natives and from other European powers. It wasn't long before the East India Company was extremely rich and powerful, with branches all around the world and with its own private army.

INDIAN HATRED

The Nawab of Bengal, Siraj-Ud-Daulah, was not happy with the British interference, seeing them as a direct threat to his own rule. The 27-year-old ruler had a reputation for his harsh tactics and had been been described by Robert Clive, the young English warrior, as 'a monster of vice, cruelty and depravity'.

When Dauley heard about the new fortifications being erected at Fort William, he demanded that they be demolished. His demands were ignored and the young Indian grew more and more angry at the British intervention and organized an army to lay siege to the fort. The fort's commander got wind of the siege and decided to leave with the majority of his army. In their place, he left just a token force under the command of John Zephaniah Holwell, who was a civil servant with the East India Company. With further desertions, and so few people to hold Fort William, Dauley and his army quickly overcame the stronghold and indeed

Calcutta itself, which was the centre of power for the East India Company.

At Fort William, Dauley's warriors quickly gathered together the remaining group of 146 Europeans who had not managed to escape. He ordered his soldiers to march them into a cell, which was nicknamed the 'Black Hole'. The cell itself was only 7.3 m (24 ft) wide by 5.4 m (18 ft long) and in the blazing heat of the Indian summer this was indeed a hellhole for one person, let alone 146. The prisoners were packed into the dungeon with no food or water, and little air came through the two small, barred windows. The room was packed so tightly, that the guards had a difficult job to shut he door, and fires in the courtyard outside made the air even more oppressive. It was Monday 21 June, 1756, and it was going to be a long and horrifying night for the captives.

The prisoners tried to bribe one of the guards stationed on the verandah outside the cell, offering him 1,000 rupees if he would move them to a larger room. He went away to ask permission, but came back and said it was impossible because the nawab was asleep and he was not allowed to wake him. The captives doubled their bribe, and the guard made another attempt at getting them moved, but again no one dared to wake the nawab.

By 9.00 p.m. several of the prisoners had died due to heat exhaustion, and many more were becoming delirious. Those strong enough to speak, pleaded desperately for water and a few water-skins were brought to the gratings. However, in their mad struggle to reach the water, many of the inmates were trampled to death, while the heartless guards simply held torches up to the gratings and mocked them for their frantic struggles. As the hours went by the screams and struggles died down, and all that could be heard were faint moans from those who were still conscious.

As the sun rose the next morning and the nawab awoke, he ordered the guards to open the door to the tiny cell. They were horrified at what they saw. The majority of the captives were dead, however, they were still standing, due to the crowded conditions of the room. Only 23 faint and weak people actually staggered out into the daylight. Although some were revived by being taken into the fresh air, others remained delirious and incoherent. Holwell, who was one of the survivors, and three others were taken as prisoners to Murshidabad, while the corpses were simply thrown into a ditch to rot.

ROBERT CLIVE

Britain was horrified by what had taken place at Fort William and wanted revenge. They sent in Robert Clive, an ex-civil servant of the East India Company, who now worked for their military. Clive and his mighty army marched on Calcutta and by January 1757 they had taken control, flying the British flag proudly over the city.

Some 150 km (96 miles) away, the Nawab was waiting for Clive at Plassey with an army at least 20 times the size of the British. However, luck was on the side of Clive and his army because the majority the nawab's army had deserted him, led by his own great-uncle, Mir Jafar. Clive and his army crossed the river and set up camp for the night. Unaware that the Indian army was now considerably depleted, Clive had a restless night, knowing too well the fearful odds that his army would have to face the next morning.

The battle started as soon as the dawn broke, but it had barely started when it was all over, with the nawab taking flight on the back of his camel. The remainder of what was once the great native army retreated in wild disorder. Clive stood triumphant in the middle of the battlefield at Plessey, with a loss of only 22 men. He had succeeded in defeating an army of almost 60,000 men. Not only was Clive the conqueror of Plassey, but far more importantly he had set the footings of a brand new empire for Great Britain.

For the nawab, the fact that India now found itself completely under the administration of the triumphant East India Company was too much for him to bear. A few days later, his lifeless body was found floating down the river.

King Leopold and the Congo Atrocities

1880–1908

King Leopold II succeeded his father Leopold I to the Belgian throne in 1865, and he occupied this position until his death in 1909. Leopold II has been described as a man with exceptional greed who became obsessed with the idea of owning a colony. He believed that the key to a country's greatness lay with the overseas colonies, and he strived hard to obtain a colonial territory for Belgian at any cost. Even though he didn't have the backing of the Belgian people or government, Leopold eventually acquired the Congo Free State as his own private venture, which turned into one of the most infamous international scandals at the turn of the 19th century.

LEOPOLD AND SIR HENRY STANLEY

During the late 19th and early 20th century, Europe started to branch out and became aware of less developed countries. In these countries, they saw the perfect opportunity to colonize – that is to spread European civilization to native people in exchange for cheap labour and natural resources. Africa at this time was still called the 'Dark Continent' and the western districts had been virtually unexplored due to the difficulties of negotiating the massive system of rapids on the Congo River.

In 1876, Leopold set up a private holding company called the International African Society, which he camouflaged as an international scientific and philanthropic association. Under the auspices of this company, which strove for colonization and exploration of Africa, Leopold hired the already famous explorer, Sir Henry Stanley to try and acquire as much land as possible for him in the Congo Basin.

Stanley was able to gain control of an enormous region of the Congo – 2.344 million km^2 (905,000 square miles) – by trading with the local chiefs through illicit treaties. The chiefs, who believed that they were signing friendship treaties, were in fact selling their land to Leopold II, and Stanley managed to get over 450 treaties over the next five years.

In 1884–85, the Berlin Conference took place for representatives of both Europe and the USA to discuss the even distribution of Africa. However, with the treaties that Stanley had been able to obtain, it meant that Leopold was legally able to lay claim to an exceptionally large region of Central African rainforest. Leopold became sole ruler to a population of over

30 million people and, without international intervention, he was left to do exactly as he pleased with his newly acquired colony.

REIGN OF TERROR

Pronouncing himself as sovereign of the Congo Free State, Leopold continued to use and finance the services of Stanley. Leopold wanted to develop the area due to the high concentration of natural resources, such as rubber, ivory, copper, diamonds and gold. He started to make plans to improve transport in the area so that he would be able to freely export these valuable goods. In fact, Leopold did anything he could to gain wealth out of the Congo, even if this meant the use of slave labour.

Leopold continued to strengthen his new realm with the construction of a new railway, which took a total of eight years to build, with the loss of many native lives. However, this was just a minor obstacle. The main hurdle Leopold had to overcome was the dissipation of Arab slave traders living along the Lualaba River, who also considered the Congo to be their rightful claim. Having lived in the area since the 1860s, the slavers were firmly established in the region and were unprepared to accept Leopold as their new sovereign. The slavers already felt threatened by the proposed abolition of Africa's interior slave trade as laid down by the Berlin Conference, and the situation became tense.

To try and appease the predicament he found himself in, Leopold once again sent Stanley to approach the slavers. Stanley met with their leader, Tippu Tip, in an effort to try and get him to confine his activities to a smaller area upstream of Stanley Falls. Tippu, who had previously helped Stanley on one of his explorations, was outraged by the betrayal of an old associate. The result was that in 1886 the Arab slavers attacked Stanley Falls and killed the entire garrison stationed there.

Leopold, who knew that he did not have enough forces to overcome the slavers, relented and sent Stanley to meet Tippu again with a new proposition. This time Stanley offered the leader a compromise by taking control of the region under the protection of Leopold's company. Tippu agreed to his new arrangement and three years later he was able to retire in comfort from the considerable profits he had acquired. However, this caused new problems for Leopold as the remaining slavers were not happy with the liaison with the king's company.

Leopold knew that he would no longer be able to cooperate with the natives peaceably, and in 1889 called for an antislave congress. Despite the fact that the Berlin Conference was in favour of keeping the Congo as a free trade zone, Leopold was able to win enough support to enable him to start charging import taxes on any goods coming into the Congo. Using the income from these taxes, Leopold planned a campaign to end slave trading in the area and, by 1895, the Arab slavers had largely been driven out of the area.

Between the years 1885 and 1890, Leopold had spent an enormous amount of his own money on his project, totalling almost 20 million francs. As the problems rose, so did the cost of dealing with them, and Leopold was now desperate to start making a profit from his African colony. In 1889, he convinced the Belgian government to loan him 25 million francs, and with these new funds Leopold started to squeeze every bit of money he could out of his project, determined to recoup his losses at all costs.

CRIMES AGAINST HUMANITY

Under the reign of Leopold II, the Congo Free State became the subject of a terror regime that included a long list of atrocities, the vindictiveness of which are almost too much to believe. Leopold's prime interest in the Congo was its natural resources, and he relied heavily on the indigenous labour. Natives were required to provide State officials with a set amount of rubber and ivory at a fixed government-set price, provide food to the local outposts, and also to provide at least ten per cent of their men as full-time labourers.

To make sure that the officials received their full quota of rubber, the *Force Publique* (FP) was formed. The FP was an army whose sole purpose was to terrorize the local natives. The officers were white agents of the State, while the soldiers were local black natives, many of whom were cannibals from the fiercest tribes in the Upper Congo. Many of them had been kidnapped as children from their own villages and raised by Catholoc missions, where they received harsh military training in appalling conditions.

The soldiers were armed with modern weapons and the *chicotte*, which was a bull whip made out of hippopotamus hide. This whip was frequently used as a means of punishing anyone who violated the State, and it quickly became a feared symbol of Leopold's administration. It was quite usual for workers to literally be beaten to death with this whip, with 90 lashes being considered the normal punishment.

The *Force Publique* frequently took and tortured hostages, mainly women, who were flogged and raped. Whole villages were burnt without warning, and its people were rounded off. The men were sent off into the forests, while their women were tied up and used as helpless targets of abuse until their husbands returned with the required amount of rubber to satisfy the agents. Men who failed to bring enough rubber to the agents were killed, but perhaps the most atrocious activity of all was the mutilation, which became common practise. It was quite normal for the soldiers to take trophies of human hands or ears back to their white officers to prove that they had not been wasting their time. The severed hands became a sort of currency, and it is purported that the soldiers of the

Force Publique were paid their bonuses on how many trophies they had collected.

One soldier described a raid to punish a village:

> ... *ordered us to cut of the heads of the men and hang them on the village palisades, also their sexual members, and to hang the women and the children on the palisade in the form of a cross.*

John Harris, a missionary who had travelled to the Congo, was so shocked by what he had encountered, that he felt compelled to write a letter to Leopold's chief agent:

> ... *I have just returned from a journey inland to the village of Insongo Mboyo. The abject misery and utter abandon is positively indescribable. I was so moved, your Excellency, by the people's stories that I took the liberty of promising them that in future you will only kill them for the crimes they commit ...*

Some of the brave survivors of this period said they had managed to live through the massacre by pretending that they were dead. Unbelievably, they did not dare to move even when their hand was severed. They had to lay motionless until the soldiers left, at which time they could cry for help. Estimates of the death toll range from 5 million to 15 million and historians have compared the atrocities to actual genocide.

THE SECRET WAS OUT

Leopold managed to suppress the rumours of the atrocities for more than a decade, and in this period he managed to reap fantastic personal gains from the exploitation of the natives of the Congo. The horrors of what was happening remained a secret for so long because the country was difficult to visit. Even missionaries were only allowed there on sufferance, and mostly only if they were Belgian Catholics who Leopold had vowed to silence.

Eventually, the most damning evidence came from an unexpected source – the secret was out – but few were prepared to believe it. Edmund Dene Morel, a clerk for a major shipping office based in Liverpool, became curious when ships carrying large loads of rubber from the Congo returned to the country full of guns and ammunition for the *Force Publique*. In an effort to gain more information, Morel left his job and became a full-time journalist.

With the support of merchants who wanted to break Leopold's monopoly, and the financial support of the chocolate millionaire, William Cadbury, Morel started to publish details of the atrocities. In 1902, Joseph Conrad's novel *Heart of Darkness* was published, which was based on his own experiences as a steamer captain on the Congo River a few years before. The book confirmed the public's suspicions of what was happening under Leopold's reign of the Congo. The following year, Morel, with the support of the House of Commons, succeeded in passing a resolution that called for the British government to carry out a full-scale inquiry. In 1904, the British Consul, Roger Casement, delivered a long and detailed eye-witness account, which was made available to the public. Morel, with Casement's support, founded the British Congo Reform Association, who immediately demanded action. The USA and other European nations quickly followed suit and the Belgian Parliament forced Leopold to set up an independent inquiry. Despite the king's efforts to cover up, Casement's earlier report was soon confirmed in all its incriminating detail.

Even though Leopold promised to implement reform to his regime, the public were unprepared to take his word seriously, and every nation was in agreement that his reign must be terminated as early as possible.

THE AFTERMATH

After much debate as to who would take over control of the Congo, finally on 15 November, 1908, four years after the Casement Report, the Belgian Parliament annexed the Congo Free State and took over its administration. A debt of around 250 million francs was transferred from Leopold to the Belgian government, who in turn offset the debt against the population of the Congo. Having been squeezed of every bit of its wealth for the past decade, the Congo now found itself shackled even further by this enormous debt.

The Congo continued to remain under Belgian rule and their recovery was incredibly slow. The State took over Leopold's private colony, but the rubber boom was past its peak, and the natives relied on the influences of the missionaries to improve their way of life. In the 1950s, a more modern-thinking world started to urge for a free Congolese republic, which was created in the 1960s following an intense period of civil war.

Right up to the present day the country has been hampered by civil wars, and even now there is no stable government to improve the state of the Congo. It would be fair to say that much of the instability of the present country can be traced back to the atrocities of Leopold II.

Balangiga Massacre

——————1901——————

*T*he Balangiga Massacre, which took place in a small seaside village on the island of Samar in the Philippines, personified the brutality of the Philippine–American War. The 9th Infantry Regiment of the US Army sailed into Balangiga on 11 August, 1901. The batallion consisted of 74 veterans, led by Captain Thomas Connell and was in response to the mayor's request for protection from rebel forces. When they arrived in the town, the US soldiers took over the affairs of the town and forcibly took occupation of some the local's huts. Although relations between the soldiers and the villagers were friendly when they first arrived, things started to deteriorate rapidly. The soldiers issued an order that all male residents from the age of 18 were to clean up the town in preparation for an official visit by their superior officers. While these men were busy, the soldiers allegedly abused one of their women, which led to retaliation by the villagers. On top of this, Captain Connell ordered the destruction of all food stores in the town for fear of it falling into the hands of the Filipino guerilla forces.

119

VILLAGERS FIGHT BACK

The already angry people of Balangiga, feared that they would starve in the coming rainy season without their food stores, and decided to attack the US garrison. At 6.45 a.m. on 28 September, 1901, the villagers made their move. Having killed the few armed sentries, the chief of police, Valeriano Abanador, ordered his people to attack. The US soldiers, who were having breakfast at the time, were taken completely by surprise as men rushed into their camp armed with axes and *bolos* (Filipino knives), many of them disguised as women. Most of the soldiers were simply hacked to death, while Captain Connell managed to lead a few of his men out onto the street, but they didn't survive for long. The soldiers fought back as best they could, using anything they could get their hands on, including knives from the kitchen and chair legs. One private even used a baseball bat to fight off his attackers.

A few of the soldiers who managed to escape feared for their lives and fled the island by boat to a nearby garrison. Out of the original 78 men of the 9th Infantry Regiment, 54 were killed or missing, 20 were severely wounded and only four managed to escape unhurt.

US RETALIATION

What became known as the 'Balangiga Massacre' was the subsequent brutal retaliation on the inhabitants of

Samar Island by the occupying US forces. The morning after the attack, two US batallions landed on Balangiga, along with two of the survivors of the attack. When they arrived they found Balangiga had been abandoned, so they buried their dead and razed the village to the ground.

The leader of the batallions, General Jacob H. Smith ordered Major Littleton Waller, commanding officer of the Marines, to tell his men to clean up the island of Samar, saying, 'I want no prisoners. I want you to kill and burn; the more you kill and burn the better it will please me.' He ordered that any Filipinos who did not surrender and were able to bear arms, should be shot, and this included anyone over the age of ten.

What ensued was a bloody massacre of the Filipino residents on Samar Island, leading to the death of thousands of Filipino. Smith's strategy was simple, cruel, but effective. By blocking all trade with Samar, he planned to starve the revolutionaries into submission. He said that all Filipinos were to be treated as enemies unless they could prove otherwise, for example, by giving the soldiers information as to where the guerillas were hiding or if they agreed to work as spies. Other than that anyone who appeared to be a threat should be shot on sight. Large columns of US soldiers marched their way across the island, destroying homes, shooting people and killing their animals.

The only thing that stopped a full-scale annihilation of Samar was that many of Smith's subordinates did not agree with his policy, which meant that many of the civilians escaped with their lives. When news of the abuses reached the USA at the end of March 1902, there was public outrage. Added to the atrocities committed by the US army, they stole three national treasures before they left Samar. One was a rare 1557 cannon and the other two were Balingiga church bells. Almost 100 years after the massacre, the current Philippine government is still trying to have these trophies of war returned to their shores.

COURT MARTIAL

The US Secretary of War ordered an investigation into the atrocities in the Philippines and brought court martial proceedings against General Smith and Major Waller. Waller was tried first, and the court martial began on 17 March, 1902. He was tried for the execution of 11 native guides, who had reportedly found edible roots during a long march, but had failed to share this knowledge with the starving US troops. Waller said that he was simply 'obeying orders' and was acquitted, a defence which the US army did not allow when trying enemies in Nuremberg decades later.

In May 1902, General Smith was tried, not for war crimes, but on the charge of 'conduct to prejudice of good order and military discipline' and that he had given orders to Waller to take no prisoners. The court martial found Smith guilty and sentenced him to be 'reprimanded by a reviewing authority'.

In an effort to try and appease the subsequent public outcry, President Roosevelt ordered Smith's retirement from the army. He received no further punishment for the atrocities that had taken place in the Philippines. It will always remain a matter of contention whether the killing of thousands of Filipinos was really justification for the murder of 54 US soldiers, and whether these killings amounted to war crimes or crimes against humanity.

The Sinking of the Lusitania

—————1915—————

*W*hen the German army marched into neutral Belgium on 4 August, 1914, they displayed a blatant disregard for international treaties and made it easier for Britain to become involved in World War I. Unlike World War II, World War I is not really associated with atrocities carried out by military forces against either civilians or enemy soldiers. However, this story proves that World War I was not fought with totally clean hands, as reports that came out of northern France and Belgium proved. During the months of August and September 1914, German troops are reported to have carried out wholesale murder of civilians without any obvious provocation. Stories of mass executions, rapes, mutilations and arson were widespread, and both the French and British governments set up special en-quiries into the alleged German 'atrocities' in Belgium. The report outlined horrific sexual and sadistic crimes, although there was a strong reaction to its content claiming that much of the information had been grossly exaggerated. Whatever the truth behind these atrocities, it does illustrate the ambivalent moral boundaries that are crossed during the time of war. What was regarded by one side as an 'atrocity' was simply seen by the other as a 'necessity' to win the war.

The incident of the sinking of the liner *Lusitania* on 7 May, 1915, had a major influence on the involvement of the United States in World War I, and it still stands out in history as a singular act of German brutality.

THE FATEFUL VOYAGE

The *Lusitania* was a British cargo and passenger ship that made its maiden voyage from Liverpool to New York in September 1907. She was a giant of a ship, built to speed through the water at an average of 25 knots. Powered by a 68,000 horse power engine, she had been dubbed the 'Greyhound of the Seas', and it wasn't long before she won the prestigious Blue Ribbon Award for the fastest crossing of the Atlantic.

The *Lusitania* had been built to Admiralty specifications, with the understanding that it would be turned over for government service at the onset of war. As the rumours of war started to spread in 1913, the *Lusitania* was secretly taken into the dry docks at Liverpool and was fitted out to be ready for service. This included the fitting of ammunition magazines and gun mounts, which were concealed under her polished teak deck, ready for when they were required.

The *Lusitania* had crossed the Atlantic many times over the years without any problems, but as World War I intensified and German submarines took a threatening role in the seas, her situation became far more precarious. Due to her speed, the *Lusitania* was considered to be unsinkable, believing that she would simply be able to flee if she came under attack. Because of this confidence in her construction and power, the *Lusitania* was allowed to set sail from New York on 1 May, 1915, with the sole purpose of delivering goods and passengers to England.

When she left for Liverpool, England, the *Lusitania* carried a large number of US passengers, despite the fact that the German authorities had published a warning in US newspapers on the morning of her departure. The notice read:

NOTICE!

Travellers intending to embark on the Atlantic voyage are reminded that a state of war exists between Germany and her allies and Great Britain and her allies; that the zone of war includes the waters adjacent to the British Isles; that, in accordance with formal notice given by the Imperial German Government, vessels flying the flag of Great Britain, or any of her allies, are liable to destruction in those waters and that travellers sailing in the war zone on ships of Great Britain or her allies do so at their own risk.

IMPERIAL GERMAN EMBASSY WASHINGTON, D.C., APRIL 22, 1915.

Many of the 1,257 passsengers believed that the luxury liner was unlikely to be a target to the Germans as it had no military value. However, unknown to her passengers, apart from her normal cargo of meat, medical supplies, copper, cheese, oil and machinery, the *Lusitania* also carrying a large quantity of munitions for the British to use during the war.

The *Lusitania* was captained by William Turner who, with his experience and a crew of 702, should certainly have been on alert for any Germany activity. As the giant liner left the shores of New York, a German U-boat was leaving, captained by Captain Walter Schwieger. He had been ordered to sail to the northern tip of Great Britain, join the Irish Channel and destroy any ships travelling from and to Liverpool, England. Schwieger was known to have frequently attacked ships without giving any warning, firing at any he suspected of being British.

Before the *Lusitania* set out on its voyage, it was decided to only light 19 of the 25 boilers on board to save on the enormous consumption of coal. This meant that the *Lusitania* was now limited to a speed of 21 knots, still much faster than a U-boat submarine, with a top speed of 13 knots.

The first few days of the luxury liner's voyage were uneventful, unlike those of the German submarine. As Schwieger rounded the south-west tip of Ireland, he attempted to destroy several ships, but was unsuccessful. The same day he spotted a small schooner, the

Earl of Lathom, and first surfacing to warn crew, opened fire and destroyed the boat. The following day Schwieger continued his journey to the Irish Sea, firing torpedoes at the steamer *Candidate,* and about two hours later he destroyed another ship, the *Centurion.* For some reason, even though the captain of the *Lusitania* received several warnings that a German U-boat had destroyed three British ships in the waters he was about to cross, he failed to take any action to avoid being attacked.

Schwieger was running low on fuel by this point and instead of travelling past Liverpool, he decided to turn back. This meant that the *Lusitania* and the U-boat were about to cross paths.

THE FATAL ENCOUNTER

On 7 May, the *Lusitania* entered the most dangerous part of her journey and, apparently concerned about poor weather conditions, Captain Turner actually slowed the boat down. On top of that, Turner was ignoring all the rules for avoiding attack, sailing too close to the shore, where the U-boats usually sat in waiting. However, Turner trusted his own instincts and experience and ordered extra lookouts and ordered that the lifeboats be swung out ready for evacuation.

Shortly before the U-boat and the *Lusitania* met, Schwieger had spotted an old war cruiser, the *Juno.* However, he was unable to hit his target because the captain was using the zigzagging tactic, which made it difficult to fire at due to its constantly changing course. Captain Turner, however, did not use this tactic because he felt that it wasted both time and fuel.

At 1.20 p.m. the U-boat spotted something large in its sight:

Starboard ahead four funnels and two masts of a steamer with a course at right angles to us . . .

Schwieger submerged and stealthily approached the enormous steamer. At 1.40 p.m. the *Lusitania* was about 700 m (765 yd) away and even turned towards the U-boat, making its target much easier. Schwieger ordered for a single torpedo to be fired.

On board the *Lusitania*, the passengers had just finished their lunch. As Captain Turner went down to his cabin, an 18-year-old lookout by the name of Leslie Morton spotted a burst of bubbles about 400 m (440 yd) from the liner. Then he saw another line of bubbles travelling at about 22 knots, heading towards the starboard (right) side of the ship. Aware that this meant trouble, Morton quickly grabbed the megaphone and shouted to the bridge:

Torpedoes coming on the starboard side.

Just a few seconds later, the lookout posted in the crow's nest, Thomas Quinn, sounded the alarm when he noticed the torpendo's wake. Captain Turner quickly ran to the ship's bridge, but as he reached it the torpedo exploded on impact.

There was a large explosion as the torpedo penetrated the hull just below the waterline. The initial explosion set off a violent secondary blast, which appeared to come from the bottom of the ship. The *Lusitania* tilted to the right at an angle of 25 degrees. The wireless room had to tap out its SOS message using battery power, as the main power had gone out with the explosion.

Because of the violent tilt of the ship, the lifeboats on the port (left) side were unable to be launched. The lifeboats on the starboard side were swung out so far, that it meant passengers had to make a huge leap from the deck to actually get into the boats. Many of the crew members panicked as the ship started to sink, launching lifeboats that only carried a few people. Some of the lifeboats capsized, and some were damaged when the torpedo hit, so, despite the fact that the *Lusitania* carried enough lifeboats for everyone on board, the simple fact was that the majority of them could not be launched for one reason or another.

Within 18 minutes of the torpedo hitting the ship, the *Lusitania* sank, taking with it 1,195 of the 1,959 on board. Captain Turner jumped as the water covered the bridge, and he swam around for about three hours before being rescued by a nearby lifeboat, which was already overloaded with people.

Captain Walter Schwieger had watched through his periscope from the moment the torpedo hit the *Lusitania*, and made notes in his log. It clearly stated that his U-boat only fired one single torpedo, but that it caused an unusually large explosion. The secondary explosion was due to the 4,200 cases of small arms ammunition that the *Lusitania* was carrying in its hold, making her a legitimate target for the German U-boat.

The distress signals sent out by the *Lusitania* reached Queenstown, Ireland, which was about 17 km (10 miles) away. Vice Admiral Sir Charles Coke organized as many rescue ships as he had available and told their captains to sail to where the *Lusitania* had sent its last signal. It took them about two hours to reach the six remaining lifeboats and any survivors still in the water. In total they picked up 761 people, a disaster that had only been rivalled by the sinking of the *Titanic* in 1912.

THE FULL IMPACT

News of the disaster was sent across the Atlantic to New York, and partly because of the large number of Americans on board, they were outraged at the sinking of the *Lusitania*. Out of the 197 who boarded the liner only 69 survived. Riots occurred in many countries at the injustice of the attack, and stores worldwide refused to serve any German customers. Anti-German protests and political cartoons started to appear with regularity, and President Woodrow Wilson sent the first of four notes regarding the *Lusitania* incident on 13 May.

The Germans tried to defend themselves by claiming that the *Lusitania* was not only armed, but that it was also carrying war munitions for the destruction of German soldiers. Although the first claim was not true, the second was proved many years later when some secret British documents were intercepted.

On the one hand the Americans believed that the Germans had violated the rights of humanity by attacking the *Lusitania* without giving any warning. On the other hand, the Germans retaliated by saying that they believed the British deliberately exposed the liner by going slowly in dangerous waters so that it could be easily destroyed. They said it was a plot on behalf of the British in an effort to get the Americans involved in the war.

The political fallout was immediate, and to placate the enraged Americans, the Germans gave an informal assurance to President Wilson that there would not be a repeat of the *Lusitania* disaster. The Germans abandoned their 'sink on sight' policy on 18 September, 1915, but this was to be a fairly short-lived solution, because it was resumed on 1 February, 1917.

Armenian Genocide

—————1915—————

*T*he most single horrific act committed during World War I was the suffering of the Armenian people, which became known as the Armenian Genocide. It was an atrocity of enormous magnitude, wiping out over one and a half million Armenians out of a total of two and a half million living in the Ottoman Empire.

The decision to carry out the genocide against the Armenian people was made by the political party that was in power at the time in the Ottoman Empire. The once-powerful Ottoman Empire was ruled by the Turks, who had already conquered lands extending across West Asia, North Africa and Southeast Europe. The main government of the Ottoman was centred in Constantinople (now Istanbul) and was ruled by a sultan who had supreme power. The Turks practised Islam, while the Armenians were Christians who had lived in the southern Caucasus region for over 3,000 years. They were the largest non-Muslim population in the Ottoman Empire, and they lived as second-class citizens, who were subjected to many legal restrictions.

Although the two classes had lived side by side for many years, by the 19th century the Ottoman Empire was in serious decline and this brought with it internal pressures that created ethnic tension.

The Turks started to see the Armenians as a threat, having never shared power in their country with any minority, and the government decided to take the matter into their own hands. During the reign of Sultan Abdul Hamid II (1876–1909), a series of massacres took place, with the intention of frightening the Armenians into take a back seat. In this first campaign of killing, around 200,000 Armenians lost their lives, but this was just a harbinger of the full-scale genocide that was to take place two decades later.

THE 'YOUNG TURKS'

In 1908, a group of modern-minded young officers – the 'Young Turks' – toppled the Ottoman sultan. At first the Armenians welcomed the new regime, believing that it was a progression from the old Ottoman dictatorship. Little did they realize how this new political party, the Committee of Union and Progress (CUP) was to change their lives forever.

The CUP was quickly taken over by a small group of fanatical nationalists, led by the triumvirate of Enver Pasha, Cemal Pasha and Talat Pasha. Wanting to eradicate any threat of political control by the Armenians, they started to plot the extermination of not just a few, but the entire population, who they saw as potentially traitorous.

When World War I broke out, the CUP steered Istanbul towards closer military and diplomatic relations with Germany and Austria–Hungary, and the Ottoman Empire became part of the Triple Alliance. The Alliance declared war against Russia and its allies Great Britain and France, and they used this guise to implement their abhorrent plan. Under the cover of war the CUP started to eradicate Armenians from Turkey and neighbouring countries, with the sole purpose of creating a new Turk empire.

One of the CUP's leading visionaries, Dr Nazim, spoke out at a meeting of the Central Committee in February 1915:

> . . . *if this purge is not general and final, it will inevitably lead to problems. Therefore it is absolutely necessary to eliminate the Armenian people in its entirety, so that there is no further Armenian on this earth and the very concept of Armenia is extinguished. We are now at war. We shall never have a more suitable opportunity than this.*
>
> (AS QUOTED IN G. S. GRABER'S *CARAVANS TO OBLIVION: THE ARMENIAN GENOCIDE*)

THE SLAUGHTER BEGINS

The genocide began on 24 April, 1915, and was

organized by a special organization (*Teshkilati Mahsusa*), set up by the CUP. They organized special 'butcher battalions', which were made up of violent criminals who were prematurely released from prison for the sole purpose of carrying out the genocide. The genocide was done in a systematic fashion and was well thought out beforehand. The first action they took was to round up any political and intellectual leaders who might possibly be effective in stopping the planned genocide. Around 600 people of distinction, all males, were taken from Istanbul and slaughtered.

The next tactic that the CUP employed was to disarm any Armenians serving in the army and turn them into nothing more than labourers. Instead of serving their country as soldiers, these men were stripped of their arms and uniforms and were treated like simple pack animals. They were made to carry heavy, army supplies on their backs and forced into the mountains of the Caucasus. They grew weak under the weight of their burdens, and as they stumbled and fell they were forced on by the whips and bayonets of the Turks. They had to sleep out in the open, laying on the bare ground in thick snow. With only meagre rations, the Armenians soon fell sick and those that were unable to carry on were simply left to die. Those that did make it to their destination were usually shot, sometimes being forced to dig their own graves before meeting their fate.

The CUP's main intention was to slaughter any

able-bodied Armenian male who would have been able to produce a new generation of Armenians. By removing these men from their cities, villages and places of work, it reduced the remaining community to near helplessness, leaving the way open for the next part of their plan. The authorities then turned their attention to the remaining male Armenian population. They were told that they were being deported to supposed 'safe havens', but this was merely a ploy to lead the men to their death.

As the caravans left the villages and cities, many of the young men were separated from their families, tied together in small groups, led to the outskirts and then shot. Public hangings without any form of trial were a regular occurrence. When the caravans eventually reached Angora, all the remaining Armenian men be-tween the ages of 15 and 70 were arrested, tied together in groups of four and were told to walk down the road towards Caesarea. After a few hours of walking they reached a secluded valley, where they decided to stop for a rest, little realizing that they were about to be ambushed by a mob of Turkish peasants. They fell upon them using clubs, hammers, axes, in fact anything they could lay their hands on, inflicting the most agonizing deaths. The horribly mutilated bodies were simply left on the ground to be preyed upon by wild animals. In this way, the CUP disposed of all the young Armenians who they considered might have been a threat to their future rule.

By the time the caravans moved again, they only

consisted of women, children and old men, little realizing what fate lay ahead for them.

GENDERCIDE AGAINST ARMENIAN WOMEN

The reports of what happened to those women, children and elderly people give rise to some of the most atrocious scenes of torture and carnage in the history of time. Although a few of the women were offered positions as slaves in the Turkish homes if they converted to Islam, it is generally thought that only about 1,000 actually accepted. The remainder were driven from their homes at the point of the Turkish bayonets, running the gauntlet between vicious soldiers and local tribespeople. Anyone who lagged behind was simply killed and left on the road, or pushed over a precipice to their death.

Every single caravan had a continuous battle not only against the soldiers, but the gendarmes, convicts who had been released from jail, and the local Turkish tribes. They had no strong, virile men to protect them, as the Turks had already made sure that they were out of the way, and so the weak were left to fend for themselves. Any of the Armenians who did manage to escape usually didn't get far before they were set upon, helpless without any form of weapon to defend themselves. Those that were not killed by the bayonet were ravaged by hunger and thirst, adding to their torment. The hot sun of the desert shrivelled the skin on their scantily clad bodies, and after several days of travelling, the once healthy Armenians were nothing more than pathetic skeletons.

The end result was an almost total extermination of the Armenian population, with only about 150 women and children reaching their final destination. They arrived naked, having had their clothes ripped from their bodies as they travelled. Already in an emaciated state, most didn't survive the squalid camps that had been set up in Syria and Mesopotamia (Iraq), as the spread of disease was rampant.

Although the majority of the massacres took place in 1915, the genocide continued until the end of World War I in 1918.

THE AFTERMATH

Turkey's final defeat at the end of World War I, and the subsequent collapse of the Ottoman Empire, gave the surviving Armenians a chance to try and rebuild their nation. In 1918 an independent Republic of Armenia was declared, giving them back some of the pride that had been stripped by the evil CUP. For several decades the rest of the world was unaware of the horrors inflicted on the Armenian people, and for a long time was overshadowed by the Nazi's genocide of the Jewish race in World War II. Turkish governments have maintained a constant silence on the subject, which has been sustained by lying, deliberately forged propaganda and bribes.

The day that it all began was 24 April, and Armenians living around the world commemorate the genocide at the site of memorials raised by the survivors, despite the fact that several governments do not officially recognize the genocide ever took place.

Amritsar Massacre
——————1919——————

The Amritsar Massacre, also known as the Jallianwala Bagh Massacre, took place in the city of Amritsar in Punjab, in the northern part of India. In the years following the end of World War I, India was still reeling from the effects of British rule. Indian soldiers who had returned as heroes from the front line found themselves once again being treated as natives. The actual issue that caused the sinister, if not extraordinary, event in the Jallianwala Bagh garden, was the government's passing of the Rowlatt Acts in March 1919. The Acts were introduced to try and curb the growing violence that was breaking out in various parts of India, in particular the Punjab. They allowed the government of India to arrest known agitators without a formal trial, giving judges the right to sentence without a jury. The Acts came just after the end of World War I, in a time of peace, when many Indians were hopeful of some form of self-government.

It soon became obvious that the British government had no such intention of relaxing its hold on India.

When the Acts were actually passed, the leader of the Indian National Congress, Bal Tilak, was away in London, leaving the way open for Mahatma Gandhi to emerge as the true leader of the Congress. Gandhi urged all Indians to take sacred vows to disobey the Rowlatt Acts and launched a nationwide movement for the repeal of such repressive measures. His appeal received the strongest response in the Punjab, where two nationalist leaders Kichloo and Satyapal addressed mass protest rallies. Gandhi was arrested when he was on his way to Punjab to attend one of their rallies, and was taken back to Bombay on the orders of Punjab's governor, Sir Michael O'Dwyer.

On 10 April, 1919, Kichloo and Satyapal were both arrested in Amritsar and deported from the district by Deputy Commissioner Miles Irving. Their followers were outraged and proceeded to march to Irving's residence, demanding the release of the two men. No sooner had they arrived than they were fired on by British soldiers. With several of their men either killed or wounded, the now incensed mob rioted through the old city of Amritsar. They set fire to houses and property associated with the British rule, and four European men were brutally murdered.

General Dyer was ordered to take Gurkhas and Balochi troops to try and restore order and, as a result, around 20 Indians were killed before the end of the day.

DEPLORABLE ACT

The protection of women and children by the white population in India had been a major priority since the Indian Rebellion of 1857. They were considered a defenceless and vulnerable part of society, open to the despoliation of the natives. So when an English woman, Miss Marcella Sherwood, a Church of England missionary, was molested on a street in the city of Amritsar, the repercussions were enormous.

Miss Sherwood had been a resident in Amritsar for over 15 years and, although she was not involved in the riots in any way, she was unable to escape the wrath of the crowd. As she was cycling down one of the narrow streets, she was set upon by an enraged crowd of Indians. They knocked her off her bicycle and hit her around the head with sticks while she lay on the ground. Miss Sherwood, despite her injuries, managed to get onto her feet and as she tried to run away from the crowd, she was once again brought down. On her second atempt, Miss Sherwood managed to run to a house to ask for help, but as she knocked on the door, the occupant simply slammed it in her face. Again the crowd set on her and left her criticially injured on the side of the road. After the crowd had dispersed, a rescuer came to her aid and prompt medical attention saved her life.

THE REVOLUTION TAKES HOLD

Although the city of Amritsar was quiet for the next few days, the rumbles of revolution could be heard in other parts of the Punjab. Government buildings were burnt, railway lines and communication cables were destroyed, and a further three European men were murdered in a period of three days. On the third day following the attack on Miss Sherwood, 13 April, the government decided to place Punjab under martial law. The troops at the disposal of General Dyer included 475 British and 710 Indian soldiers.

The 13 April also marked the Baisakhi festival, and a large number of people, mostly Sikhs, had poured into the city of Amritsar from the surrounding villages. In the morning, Dyer's soldiers had gone through the streets of the city to announce that any group meetings would be dispersed by force, using arms if it was necessary. At 4.30 p.m. a crowd of around 15,000 to 20,000 Indians had gathered for a meeting in the Jallianvala Bagh (or garden), a large unused piece of land in the heart of Amritsar that was surrounded by crude walls and just one, single exit.

As soon as Dyer heard of the defiance to his orders, he headed for Jallianvala Bagh with 50 riflemen (mostly Indian and Gurkhas) and two armoured cars. Dyer positioned his men by the narrow entrance into the bagh, ensuring that there was no possibility of anyone making a quick escape. The ground surrounding the entrance was slightly higher than the rest of the bagh, which gave the troops an excellent vantage point. It was here that they waited for the order from Dyer.

Dyer gave the command, without giving any warning to the crowd inside the bagh, for his troops to open fire where the mob was most concentrated. The firing continued indiscriminately for over 20 minutes, and they spent over 50 rounds of ammunition. People attempted to flee as best they could, but many were trampled in the ensuing stampede. Some mothers, still clutching their children, jumped into a well in an attempt to escape the constant rain of bullets.

Dyer and his men simply marched away down the same route they had arrived, leaving behind the carnage of dead, dying and wounded. Although there is no official record of the number of Indians killed on that day, it is estimated that 400 died and as many as 1,200 were severely wounded, although it is suspected that the numbers were far higher.

AFTER THE EVENT

Jallianwala Bagh was only the start of a prolonged phase of appalling violence and insurgence. When news of the massacre reached the surrounding districts, mass riots erupted in the Punjab, and the government placed a further five towns under martial law. Students and migrant labourers from Kashmir set fire to government buildings, destroyed the Kachi bridge, bungalows, local courts and also the railway station. Spontaneous riots broke out in Sheikhpura, Sangla and Chuharkhana. The local authorities appealed to the government for help, but as the bridges had been destroyed they had to deploy aeroplanes to quell the insurrections. On 14 and 15 April, aircraft from Lahore dropped three bombs on a the protesting crowds, followed by rounds of machine-gun fire.

Appalled by the escalating amount of violence and subsequent deaths, Gandhi called for *satyagraha*, which is the philosophy of nonviolent resistance. From then on colonial reprisals began, perhaps the most notable of which was the famous 'crawling order' introduced by General Dyer. This order meant that anyone passing down the street where Miss Sherwood was assaulted, had to pass on all fours with their noses close to the ground, just like an animal. Under marshal law there was even a mandate that said Indians must dismount in the presence of a European and raise their right hand as a sign of respect. Others who were suspected of being involved in any sort of trouble were beaten and made to work as *punkha-pullers* (or fan operators). A total of 1,229 people were convicted of involvement in the uprisings – 18 were sentenced to death, 23 were transported for life and 58 were flogged on the orders of the Martial Law Commission.

General Dyer was convinced that he had managed to crush the rebellion, but eventually a Disorder Inquiry Committee, known as the Hunter Committee, was set up to investigate what had taken place, and it was decided that he had committed a 'grave error'. Dyer was relieved of his commission and forced to take early retirement from the army. However, on arrival in England he was treated as a hero and presented with a purse containing thousands of pounds and a jewelled sword inscribed with the words 'Saviour of the Punjab'.

Back in India, the Amritsar Massacre had provoked feelings of deep hatred and it led to the freedom movement in the Punjab against British rule. It also paved the way for Mahatma Gandhi's Non-Cooperation Movement against the British in 1920.

The actual site of the massacre at Jallianvala Bagh became a place of national pilgrimage. A memorial was built on the site and was unveiled at a ceremony by the then-president of India, Dr Rajendra Prasad on 13 April 1961. To this day, the bullet holes can be seen in the walls and adjoining buildings. The well, into which several people jumped and drowned, has also been turned into a protected monument inside the garden. A semicircular verandah surrounding a children's swimming pool marks the spot where General Dyer's soldiers stood waiting to fire.

One man got his own revenge for the massacre, which he had witnessed first hand. An Indian revolutionary nationalist by the name of Udham Singh, shot dead Sir Michael O'Dwyer, the man believed to have planned the actual massacre, at Caxton Hall in London on 23 March, 1940. He would probably have liked to have killed General Dyer as well, but he had died many years earlier in 1927. Singh was a freedom fighter and *The Times* referrred to his action as 'an expression of the pent-up fury of the downtrodden Indian people'.

PART FOUR

WAR CRIMES AND ATROCITIES OF WORLD WAR II

Belgium in World War II

——————1940–45——————

*D*uring World War II, Belgium was invaded by the Germans. There was heavy fighting as the Belgium army fought to defend the country, and each side lost many men. Finally, on 27 May, 1940, the Belgians surrendered. King Leopold III of Belgium was made a prisoner of war but his ministers were able to flee to London, where they set up a government in exile, under the protection of the Allied forces.

The ensuing occupation of Belgium soon proved to be beyond everyone's worst nightmares as the Germans rounded up the population for extermination or forced labour in the notorious concentration camps. Over the next few years, more than 25,000 Belgian Jews met their deaths in Auschwitz-Birkenau, either through being gassed or through malnutrition, disease and neglect. In many cases, Belgian people collaborated with the Germans in sending their compatriots to their deaths; however, there were also hundreds of brave

Belgian citizens who risked their lives to help the victims of Nazi persecution, including two underground resistance groups called The White Brigade and The Secret Army.

In 1944, with the help of the Allies, the resistance proved victorious, and the Germans were defeated. However, the war crimes and atrocities that had occurred during the occupation were never forgotten, and they left an indelible scar on the nation's history. Thousands of innocent victims had lost their lives, and today they are remembered in the many war memorials across the country, whether in great cities, bustling towns, or tiny villages.

THE MASSACRE AT BANDE

By 1944, the Germans were near to defeat, and their troops' ferocity intensified as they realized that Hitler's plan was failing and Germany could now lose the war. Accordingly, the Nazis launched the Ardennes Offensive, colloquially known to the Allies as 'the Battle of the Bulge', referring to the dent that the Germans initially made in their lines as they advanced. The Ardennes Offensive, which aimed to split the British and American lines and encircle the Allies' armies, was planned in total secrecy and caught the Allies by surprise. However, the Allies eventually fought back and the Offensive was repelled, but not without great losses to each side.

During the Offensive, a unit of German soldiers arrived in the small village of Bande in the south of the country. It was Christmas Eve, and snowing heavily. They captured the village, and then set about tracking down local resistance fighters who had attacked and killed three German soldiers there several months before. Their method of doing so was to arrest all the men in the village and then question them about the events of 5 September, when the attack had occurred. Then, one by one, each of the men was shot in cold blood.

The way the Germans executed the men was to lead them to an open door and push them in. Inside the door, a gunman was hidden, and as each man entered, the gunman shot him in the neck at point-blank range. As the victim fell, the gunman kicked his body into the cellar of the building. In this way, 34 men were murdered, one after the other. Only one man, 21-one-year-old Leon Praile, escaped. In a hail of bullets, he ran to the forests surrounding the village and hid there, managing to avoid capture.

On 10 January, 1945, British troops arrived in Bande. The war was now over and the Nazis had, thankfully, been defeated. However, the memory of what had happened on Christmas Eve the year before still haunted the villagers, and many of them gave harrowing accounts of what had happened. Accordingly, a war crimes court was set up in Belgium, the massacre was investigated, and one of the culprits brought to justice.

The man involved was Ernst Haldiman, a Swiss national who had joined the SS in France in 1942. He spoke fluent German and had been sent to Bande during the Ardennes Offensive. After the war, he was identified as one of the soldiers who had taken part in the executions at Bande, and was arrested in Switzerland. He was tried in an army court there and convicted of the atrocity, receiving a sentence of 20 years' imprisonment. In 1960, after serving 12 years of his sentence, he was released on parole.

THE MALMEDY MASSACRE

Another appalling atrocity that took place in Belgium during World War II was the massacre of American prisoners of war near the town of Malmédy. Here, German troops from the Waffen SS, led by Major Joachim Peiper, shot over 80 American prisoners of war dead in a field. After the war, Peiper and others were found and brought to trial for their crimes, amid a great deal of controversy.

On the fateful day of 17 December, 1944, Major Peiper and his SS Unit encountered a batallion of American soldiers travelling to a new base. The Americans were not heavily armed and had no anti-tank weapons, so Peiper and his men immediately fired on the convoy, causing the Americans to surrender. A total of about 150 American soldiers were taken prisoner, disarmed and taken to a field near the small village of Baugnez, between the towns of Malmedy and Ligneuville.

Next, an SS soldier drove up in an army truck, pulled out a pistol and shot the medical officer of the battalion, who was standing in the front row. He then shot another officer in cold blood. After that, other SS soldiers appeared, armed with machine guns, and began to shoot at random into the group of American soldiers. Not surprisingly, some of the prisoners took to their heels and tried to escape into the nearby woods. Several were shot as they ran away, but many actually managed to reach the woods and hide there.

After the massacre, the bodies of the murdered prisoners of war were left in the field to rot while the SS battalion moved on. They were later discovered by American troops on 13 January, 1945.

THE STAVELOT ATROCITY

On the day after the Malmedy massacre, Peiper's unit passed through the village of Stavelot and set about decimating the civilian population there. The villagers were charged with sheltering American soldiers, and dozens were rounded up and summarily executed. Estimates vary as to the actual numbers of those who died, but some allege that there were more than 100 people were killed, some of whom were children.

CHENOGNE REPRISAL

On New Year's Day 1945, the Americans took their revenge for Peiper's work. In the village of Chenogne, American GIs marched 60 German prisoners of war out to a hillside and machine-gunned them to death. However, in this instance, the perpetrators of the massacre were never brought to justice, since the Allies won the war and did not see fit to try their own soldiers for their conduct during the fighting.

As at Malmedy and Stavelot, accounts as to what really happened at Chenogne differ. According to some sources, a US army unit had responded to the massacre at Malmedy by commanding their troops to take no prisoners and to shoot German soldiers on sight. Because of this, it was argued that the GIs were only following orders, and thus no punishment was meted out to them. Others argue that the GIs acted completely illegally and brutally, out of revenge for the murders of their fellow soldiers at Malmedy.

JUSTICE IS DONE

After the war, General Sepp Dietrich, Major Peiper and other members of the SS were caught and put on trial for the massacre at Malmedy. Their trial took place at Dachau, home of the notorious concentration camp, in May 1946. The proceedings were controversial, as there were several different stories as to what had happened. Some witnesses swore that they had heard German officers giving the order to 'kill all the prisoners', while others contested that the prisoners had only been shot because they had been trying to run away. Another account held that the Germans were only shooting all those who had been critically wounded during the fighting, as was their regular policy during the war.

Whatever the true story, the fact that so many prisoners died at the same time, and that their bodies were left unburied and unmarked in a field while the division moved on, gave the distinct impression that a brutal massacre had been carried out. Peiper and other members of the unit were sentenced to death, but this was never carried out, as a series of reviews questioned the findings of the court. Instead, the culprits received long prison sentences.

Peiper served his sentence until 1956, when he was released. In 1972, he went to live in Traves, northern France, and four years later he was murdered there by a group of French communists. His house was also burnt to the ground. Thus, the story of violence and reprisal that had started at Malmedy finally came to an end.

THE BELGIAN WAR CRIMES LAW

In 1993, Belgium passed a War Crimes Law allowing any individual to bring war crimes charges to Belgian courts, whether or not the crimes had been committed in Belgium. The law, which upheld the concept of 'universal jurisdiction', came to public attention over claims regarding the genocide in Rwanda, but became difficult to administer as more and more individuals began to file what were perceived as politically motivated cases. In 2006, the law was modified, much to the outrage of human rights organizations, who felt that it had been a great step forward in bringing perpetrators of war crimes and atrocities to justice.

France: Prisoners of War

————1940-44————

$\mathcal{T}$he French experience during World War II was a painful one, not only because of the heavy losses its military forces sustained in fighting the Germans, but because of its capitulation to the enemy in 1940. After this, France was divided into an occupied and an un-occupied zone, with a right-wing government at Vichy, under Marshall Pétain, which collaborated with the Nazis. This left many Frenchmen and women with a stark choice: either assisting the Germans with their policies of genocide and repression, or risking their own lives and those of their families to help the victims of persecution. Inevitably, many citizens were forced to collaborate, and after the liberation of France by the Allies in 1944, the nation as a whole suffered a terrible sense of shame for allowing dreadful war crimes to occur within its territory. However, France could also point to many instances of courage and selflessness on the part of the members of the French Resistance, who had covertly waged a campaign of sabotage against the Germans during the occupation, as well as steadfast determination on the part of the Free French, who had masterminded the resistance campaign outside the country. Even so, the war crimes that were committed in France in the name of the Third Reich remain a stain on the nation's conscience today, and there is no doubt that the war years are among the darkest in the nation's recent history.

PRISONERS OF WAR

One of the most shocking aspects of Nazi brutality was their treatment of prisoners of war, which not only contravened all hitherto accepted regulations as to how to deal with captured enemy soldiers, but went against the most basic standards of decency, humanity and morality. In many cases, Allied soldiers were gunned down in cold blood after they had been captured and rounded up, for no apparent reason other than to satisfy the bloodlust of the German troops. Towards the final days of the war, this aggressive behaviour became more marked, as the Nazis struggled to come to terms with the fact that they were losing the war, and lashed out at the enemy in response. After the war, the Nazis' actions were universally condemned, and it was clear that they had acted from the basest of motives, for the pleasure of killing, and to seek revenge for the indignities of their defeat.

LE PARADIS MASSACRE

On 26 May, 1940, soldiers from the British Royal Norfolk Regiment were stationed at Le Paradis in Pas-de-Calais. They were not fighting, but were part of manoeuvres by the British Expeditionary Force. However, they were captured by troops of the SS Totenkopf Division, or 'Death's Head' Division. The commander of the division, SS Obersturmführer Fritz Knoechlein, ordered that 99 prisoners were to be marched to some farm buildings in the countryside and lined up against a wall. They were then machine-gunned to death by his men. Only two survived: Private William O'Callaghan and Private Albert Pooley, who had managed to hide in a pig sty. Later, the pair were captured by the Germans and sent to a prisoner-of-war camp, but at least they had been lucky enough to escape with their lives. After the shootings, the German troops buried the bodies in shallow graves near where they had fallen. Two years later, local French people dug them up and gave them a proper burial in the local churchyard, which is now a war cemetery.

It was not until after the war that the crime was investigated, and the leader of the division, Knoechlein, brought to trial in Hamburg. He was found guilty of the atrocity and received the death penalty. On 28 January, 1949, he was hanged. Today, a memorial plaque on the barn wall where the men had been lined up and shot commemorates the terrible massacre that took place there during the dark days of France's occupation.

WORMHOUDT ATROCITY

Only one day after the massacre at Le Paradis, around 80 prisoners British and French soldiers were shot by the Liebstandarte SS Adolf Hitler, a German infantry regiment under the command of Sepp Dietrich. These unfortunate soldiers were taken to a barn outside the town of Wormhoudt, Pas-de-Calais, and pushed roughly inside. This included soldiers who were already wounded, who did not have room to lie down inside the building.

It was then that the nightmare began. The SS soldiers stood outside and threw stick grenades into the barn, causing many of the imprisoned soldiers to die or suffer terrible wounds as shrapnel tore into their bodies. Those who managed to survive were taken out of the barn five at a time, and each one shot dead by a hail of bullets as they emerged. In the wake of the massacre, the Nazis buried the victims in a mass grave near the barn, but the bodies were later dug up and buried in cemeteries nearby, in an attempt to cover up the crime.

Only 15 wounded soldiers survived the attack, and they were later found by other German troops. Luckily for them, these regular troops treated them better, dressing their wounds before sending them to a prisoner-of-war camp, where they remained for the rest of the conflict. After the war, the man held to be immediately responsible for the deaths of the soldiers,

Hauptsturmführer Wilhelm Mohnke, was tracked down. A campaign was mounted by a British MP, Jeff Rooker, to bring him to trial, but it was eventually found that there was insufficient evidence to charge him. Thus, sadly, no one was held accountable for one of the worst massacres of prisoners to take place in France during World War II.

ARDENNES CAMPAIGN

Another example of Nazi brutality was the treatment of Canadian soldiers in the Ardennes campaign, many of whom were shot after being captured. On one occasion, on 8 June, 1944, 37 Canadian prisoners, some of them wounded, were taken to a field near the village of Le Mesnil-Patty and ordered to sit down. They then waited until a group of German soldiers arrived on a truck, armed with machine guns. As they got out of the truck and walked towards the prisoners, they opened fire on them, killing all but two of them dead. The surviving pair escaped with their lives, but were later captured and sent to a prisoner-of-war camp for the duration of the conflict.

On a further occasion, around 40 Canadians from the North Nova Scotia Highlanders were captured and shot, one by one, as they were marched to the German headquarters. In some cases, the dead bodies were put into the centre of the road for passing trucks and tanks to run over. When French civilians tried to pull the bodies out of the way, they were ordered to leave them there. Back at headquarters, in the Abbaye Ardenne, 20 Canadian soldiers were locked up in a stable, then taken out and shot in the back of the head. In another instance, 26 Canadian prisoners of war were shot by an SS Hitler Jugend Division, at the Château d'Audrieu. So brutal were the Hitler Jugend Division as a whole that they were branded 'the Murder Division' by the Allied forces.

THE UNKNOWN SOLDIERS

In the aftermath of the war, the toll of war crimes against Canadian troops was assessed, establishing that a total of 134 Canadian soldiers had been victims of these atrocities. SS Brigadeführer Kurt Meyer, who had been responsible for the atrocity at the Abbeye Ardenne, was finally brought to trial at Aurich, Germany, and convicted by a Canadian military court. He received the death sentence, but this was later commuted and he was eventually released on parole in 1954, after spending many years in German and Canadian prisons. In 1961, Meyer died of a heart attack, aged 51.

Sadly, however, by the end of the war there were many Allied soldiers whose bodies were never recovered. In many cases, the Nazis had tried to cover up the massacres and atrocities, hiding the bodies or disposing of them in unmarked graves, so that the soldiers did not receive a proper burial. Neither did the Germans record the names of those who died. Also, it was the Nazis' practise to divest the soldiers of all their belongings before they were shot, removing their pay books, documents and identity tags, so that the bodies could not be identified later on. Naturally, the fact that the bodies had gone missing was a great source of anguish for their relatives and communities, who did not have the chance to visit their loved ones' graves and to mourn them properly. For this reason, many towns and villages commemorated their dead by erecting war memorials. In this way, they were able to ensure that even those whose bodies had been buried in unmarked plots and mass graves on the field of war would never be forgotten.

France: World War II
1940–44

During World War II, the Nazis wreaked vengeance on those civilians they suspected of opposing them, whether by harbouring or helping Jews, or by committing acts of sabotage, or by other acts of resistance. This was particularly so in France, which after the surrender of the French forces in 1940, pursued a policy of collaboration with the Nazis through the government at Vichy, in return for peace. This was widely opposed by many Frenchmen and women, and a resistance movement soon arose, both within and outside the country, which was secretly supported by many ordinary French citizens, particularly those living in the rural areas of France.

REPRISALS

Knowing how much they were loathed by the ordinary country people of France, the Nazis constantly suspected individuals – and sometimes whole communities – of helping the guerrilla resistance movement, or 'maquis', as it was known. The regime did not tolerate any form of opposition and took savage revenge on the suspects. In this way, the Nazis maintained a rule of terror in the country; however, there were many who were brave enough to risk their lives, and the lives of their families, to stand up against the tyranny of the regime.

One such example was at Oradour-sur-Glane in the Limousin region of France. This small town was in the occupied region of France (the country had been divided into occupied zones, with a zone ruled by the French government at Vichy). In 1944, towards the end of the conflict, as the Nazis were becoming more and more desperate to maintain their power, it became the locus of a terrible atrocity in which hundreds of residents were brutally slaughtered.

CAPTIVE GERMAN OFFICER

On the morning of 10 June, the Second Panzer Division of the SS, known as 'Das Reich', was travelling across the country to join the fighting between the Allies and the Nazis in Normandy. At this point, it was becoming clear that the Allies had a good chance of invading France and overwhelming the German presence. During the Division's journey, the soldiers met with constant sabotage and disruption to their progress from the French resistance, who had stepped up their activities as the defeat of the Nazis began to look like a distinct possibility.

That day, Stürmbannführer Otto Diekmann of the Waffen SS First Battalion had been tipped off that an important German official, Stürmbannführer Helmut Kampfe, was being held captive by members of the 'maquis' in the town of Oradour sur Glane. Diekmann, who was a friend of Kampfe, reported the news to Stürmbannführer Weidinger, who also knew Kampfe well. The tip-off had come from the hated French secret police, the Milice, who had also reported that the townspeople were planning to execute Kampfe and burn him at the stake as a way of celebrating the Germans' imminent defeat.

DREADFUL ATROCITY

Incensed at this news, Diekmann and his forces surrounded the town and ordered the soldiers to herd everyone into a public fairground. The soldiers told the townspeople that the authorities needed to examine their papers. When they were assembled, the soldiers singled out the women and children and took them to the church. The men of the town were taken to six barns nearby. Meanwhile, the troops set about looting the town.

What happened next has gone down in history as one of the worst atrocities of World War II. The Nazi troops, using machine guns, shot all the men in the legs, so that they would die slowly. They then set the barns alight, using kindling and torches, so that the men would burn to death. Out of 195 men, only five escaped: the rest met an agonizing end in the barns, having been shot and burnt to death.

SCENE OF CARNAGE

Having committed this dreadful atrocity, the soldiers then moved on to deal with the women and children in the church. They planted an incendiary bomb in the middle of the church, lit it and ran outside, leaving the women and children to die. Naturally, the occupants of the church tried to escape, but as they ran out of the doors or climbed through the windows of the church, the troops opened fire, machine-gunning the victims until they fell dead. In all, there were 247 women and 205 children who died that day.

Not content with this, the Nazis proceeded to burn the town to the ground. The soldiers then stole everything they could carry from the houses and continued on their journey to fight the Allies. When they left, the scene of carnage was discovered. A few dozen villagers had escaped as soon as the troops had arrived, and they returned to bury the dead. Over 640 victims had died, wiping out almost the entire community.

BURNT TO DEATH

When the news came out, the sheer brutality of what

had gone on shocked the nation. There were stories of soldiers roaming the streets, hunting down victims who were hiding from them. In one instance, an old invalid was burnt in his bed; in another, a baby was put in a bakery oven and baked to death; and in another, victims were shot and bodies were thrown down a well so that they could not be buried. However, there were also tales of those who survived: one townswoman, Madame Rouffanche, managed to throw herself out of a high church window, and then dug herself into the earth between some rows of peas. In this way, she managed to hide until the next day, when the troops departed.

There are various theories as to why the atrocity happened. Some believe it was done as part of a deliberate policy by the Nazis to quell any kind of resistance. It came at a time when the French Resistance, especially its guerrilla arm, the Maquis, had been extremely active, sabotaging the movement of German troops through France in any way they could. However, there are those who think this is not a persuasive explanation. Oradour was not, in fact, a place that had a strong history of resistance activity. Moreover, the German troops at the time gave no reason for their actions.

CONTROVERSIAL TRIAL

Many support the theory that Diekmann went to

Oradour purely to kill everyone in sight, acting on his own, out of sheer brutality, rather than because he had been given orders to do so. Some accounts report that his superiors, such as his commanding officer, Sylvester Stadler, were shocked at what he had done, especially with regard to his treatment of the women and children. It is believed that Stadler threatened to court martial Diekmann over the affair; however, he did not relieve Diekmann of his command. In the event, Diekmann was killed in action, on 29 June, so he was never tried.

In 1953, the perpetrators of the Oradour massacre were brought to justice. In February of that year, 21 former members of the Der Führer regiment of the Das Reich Division came before the courts at Bordeaux. There was much controversy about the trial, since none of the men tried were high-ranking former Nazis. Also, some of the defendants came from Alsace, which in previous times had been a French province. This meant that many French people viewed them as French nationals, and felt that they should have refused to commit the massacre. In their clients' defence, their lawyers argued that they were merely conscripted soldiers, who would have been shot had they disobeyed orders.

When the verdicts were finally reached, there was uproar in France. Two defendants were sentenced to death, the others to prison sentences of between eight and 12 years. Some felt these sentences to be too lenient, and demanded that all the defendants receive the death penalty, while others argued that there should be no penalties for acts committed by conscripted soldiers under pain of death in a war situation. Eventually, all the defendants were freed, which made a mockery of the whole trial.

MISTAKEN IDENTITY?

Some commentators have pointed out that what happened at Oradour may have been a case of mistaken identity. The town of Oradour sur Glane is not far from another town with a similar name, Oradour sur Vayres, where in 1944, a high-ranking German officer, Karl Gerlach was being held. According to this account, Diekmann's informants, the Milice, had got their facts wrong and named the wrong town. Not only this, but Diekmann had assumed, without checking, that it was his friend Kampfe, not Gerlach, who was being held there. Thus the massacre was the result of a mistake. Be that as it may, massacres and atrocities of this nature were not unusual among Nazi troops, and we know that little attempt was made to discipline Diekmann for his appalling crime.

Today, the town of Oradour still stands in its ruined state as a memorial to those who died, so that visitors can witness the true horror of what happened. Many people travel there to see the ghost town, which stands as a testament to the death and destruction wreaked by the Third Reich in its final days and as a reminder that such a regime of intolerance and hatred must never be allowed to exist in the future.

France: The Jews
———— 1940–44 ————

*O*ne of the most shameful aspects of the French capitulation to the Germans in 1940 was the country's collaboration in sending thousands of French Jews and others to the gas chamber. Because the French government decided to surrender to the Germans early on in the war, so as to gain favourable peace terms, many ordinary Frenchmen and women became involved in the process of persecuting the Jews and other groups that the Nazis thought undesirable, such as those with disabilities, homosexuals and others. Because the mass genocide of the Jews required a large administrative and bureaucratic structure, many French citizens became involved in the daily tasks of identifying individuals, arranging for their transportation to the death camps, and so on.

In this way, the French people became polarized into two factions: those who collaborated with the Nazis, and those who helped the Resistance forces. With the threat of death and torture hanging over anyone who resisted the regime, there were also many who changed sides, or who played a game of double dealing throughout the war. The whole atmosphere of the country was rife with paranoia, as spies and tale-tellers vied with resistance sympathizers, causing an immense burden of guilt and shame, together with bitter feuding on both sides, which lasted well beyond the war years. Even today, there is much controversy as to how much the French were forced to collaborate in sending the Jews to the concentration camps, and how much their actions were due to entrenched anti-Semitism within the country.

THE PARIS DEPORTATIONS

When the Germans first occupied the country, it did not immediately become clear that mass genocide of the Jews was one of their main objectives. The sheer scale of what was intended went well beyond most people's worst nightmares, and there were many – including Jewish people themselves – who simply did not believe what was going on, in terms of mass extermination in the concentration camps, until it was too late to escape. One such group were the Jewish people of Paris.

After the invasion of the Germans, many Jewish Parisians moved to the French countryside or abroad to avoid the restrictions that were placed on them. As the result of the Nazis' regulations, many lived in fear of the authorities and were unable to earn a living. Given the fact that many had been forced to flee communist Russia and were attempting to rebuild their lives in a foreign country, this new form of persecution was particularly harsh. However, most had no inkling that they would be rounded up, sent to concentration camps and gassed to death, and therefore remained where they were, rather than abandon everything they had built up and move abroad. Some went to the countryside with the intention of returning as soon as the war was over, or as soon as conditions became more favourable to their leading a normal life in the city once more.

They could not have known how swift, and how deadly, their end would be. On two days in July 1942, the 16th and 17th, the Nazis rounded up 12,884 non-French Jews to be deported to their concentration camps in Poland. Before they left, almost 7,000 of them were held in a single stadium, the Vélodrome d'Hiver, on the Boulevard de Grenelle. The majority of the victims were children. Incredibly, there were only four toilets available for them to use. After a whole week, during which they were not given adequate supplies of food or water, the victims were transferred to 'collection' camps at Pithiviers and Drancy, outside Paris, where the children were separated from their parents. The parents were then taken to Auchwitz, where they were herded into gas chambers and gassed to death. The children followed soon after. All 4,051 of them died. At the end of the war, only 30 of the adults who had been sent to Auchwitz in the Paris Deportations were still alive.

CHILDREN EXTERMINATED

In total, around 60,000 Jews died in France during the war, under the German occupation. Not only adults, but many children and teenagers were also sent to the concentration camps, often alone without their families. For example, on 11 June, 1941, 300 Jewish boys aged between 14 and 19, were deported to Mauthausen concentration camp in Austria. All of them died.

In another instance, Jewish orphans aged between fiveand 17, living at an orphanage in Izieu, central France, became victims of the Gestapo. On 6 April, 1944, Gestapo Officer Klaus Barbie, known as the 'Butcher of Lyon' because of his brutality, arrived with a convoy of trucks outside the building. His soldiers gained entry and forcibly removed 44 children and seven adults, throwing them onto the waiting trucks as they cried out in terror. The defenceless children were then taken to the camp at Drancy, where they were put on trains going to the concentration camps. Most of them were gassed to death in Auchwitz, while others met their end in Tallin, Estonia, shot by a firing squad.

After the war, Klaus Barbie was arrested for this and other war crimes, and was sentenced to life imprisonment. He died in prison of cancer in 1991. He was thought to have been responsible for the deportation of over 7,000 people to the death camps, and to have ordered the murder of over 4,000 more. In addition, he oversaw the torture of around 14,000 members of the Resistance movement.

THE FINAL SOLUTION

It was not until after the war that the full extent of the Holocaust became apparent. In the early days of Jewish persecution under the Nazis, death squads were used to round up and shoot Jews in conquered territory. However, this method proved too slow for Hitler and his henchmen, so from 1941, a policy of mass genocide was pursued, known as the Final Solution. Under this new scheme, extermination camps were set up with the specific aim to kill as many Jews as possible, as quickly as possible. Industrial methods were developed to exterminate victims in gas chambers and burn their bodies in large furnaces on a scale never known before. Jews who had been living in overcrowded, disease-ridden ghettos all over Europe were arrested and transported to the camps on trains and in cattle trucks, still in many cases unaware of the fate that was to befall them. Once there, they were either gassed, shot or left to survive as best they could, in conditions of unimaginable filth and neglect. Many did not survive the war, starving to death or dying of disease.

FRENCH ANTI-SEMITISIM

It became shamefully apparent after the war that the

French collaboration with this barbaric scheme had been extensive. Philippe Petain, leader of the Vichy government and a hero of World War I, supported the Nazi regime, arguing that the French people would suffer less under it if his government cooperated. However, it seems that his government did more than cooperate with the Germans: it actively participated in the persecution of the Jews, setting up a secret police, the Milice, to inform on individuals and have them arrested and deported. The Milice, along with right-wing activists, such as members of Jacques Doriot's Parti Populaire Français (PPF), are thought to have been responsible for arresting at least 75,000 Jews for deportation to the death camps. It has also been argued that it was the Milice, and not the Nazis, who were responsible for the Paris Deportations, in which over 12,000 Jews were rounded up in a stadium for deportation. According to this account, the Nazis did not demand the arrest of the 4,051 children who were included in the round-up.

Many commentators also claim that there were many far-right factions in French society who were all too eager to help the government in their task of sending Jews to the concentration camps, and that anti-Semitism had been deeply entrenched in France for centuries. Thus, when the Nazis took over power, this provided an ideal opportunity for the far right, both within and outside the government, to put their racist beliefs into practise on a hitherto unimaginable scale.

MAURICE PAPON

One individual who was singled out as a collaborator was Maurice Papon, a high-ranking government official and the supervisor of its so-called 'Service for Jewish Questions'. Papon switched allegiances during the war and moved up the political ladder swiftly, until his war crimes were uncovered. He was known to have had regular contact with Nazi Germany SS corps who were responsible for the mass cleansing of the Jewish population. As a high-ranking official, he is thought to have been responsible for the deportation of 1,560 Jews to Auchwitz from 1942 to 1944, but he skilfully managed to cover his tracks. Among his victims were children and the elderly.

After the war, Papon moved to Paris and went on to become a successful civil servant with many top appointments, including Chief of the Paris Police and Budget Minister for President Valéry Giscard D'Estaing. He was even decorated by General Charles de Gaulle and kept a position in the cabinet for 30 years before his past caught up with him.

However, Papon's history was eventually brought to light by the radical newspaper *Le Canard Enchaîné*, and on 2 April 1998, Papon faced the longest trial in all of French history. He was charged and convicted of 'crimes against humanity'. He was given a ten-year prison sentence, but he was released four years later because of health problems.

The decision to release Papon was met with angry outbursts by the relatives of those who had died. Human rights activitists, who had fought to bring him to justice, said that victims of Nazism felt 'insulted' by this decision.

Czechoslovakia

—————— 1938–45 ——————

Czechoslovakia (now The Czech Republic and Slovakia) was the site of some of the worst war crimes and atrocities of World War II. As in other European countries, such as Belgium, France, The Netherlands and Poland, once the Nazis had assumed control, the Jewish communities living there were mercilessly persecuted, along with other minority groups. The population figures for Czechoslovakia, as elsewhere, tell their own tragic story: at the beginning of the war, there were 350,000 Jews living in the country; by the end, only 20,000 remained.

The savage treatment of these peaceful, industrious communities who had contributed so much to the life of the nation met with little resistance from the majority of Czech people, where a strong current of anti-Semitism was apparent. However, there were also brave Czechs who fought to protect their compatriots, and who showed great courage in doing so, for the Nazis wreaked a hideous revenge on anyone found helping the Jews, or defying the regime in any way.

One of the most notorious instances of Nazi brutality towards the civilian population of Czechoslovakia was at Lidice, a small town whose inhabitants were exterminated, at the specific request of the Führer himself, in order to set an example to those who even considered resisting the Nazi reign of terror.

DEMOLITION OF A STATE

In 1938, Hitler signed the Munich Agreement with Britain, France and Italy. Under the terms of the agreement, an area of western Czechoslovakia known as the Sudetenland was to be taken over by the Germans. Although there was a substantial German-speaking population in this region, who were mostly anti-Semitic and complained that they were oppressed by the Czech majority, there was no legal basis whatsoever for this seizure of power. The other European nations simply allowed Hitler to walk in to Czechoslovakia, hoping that signing the agreement might appease him and gratify his need for territorial expansion. They could not have been more wrong.

When the Nazis arrived in Czechoslovakia, they met with little resistance. Within months, the entire autonomous structure of the country, including its armed forces and its democratic political apparatus, had been destroyed. First, the Czech army was demolished, and its arsenal of weapons taken over for use by German forces. Next, Hitler encouraged Slovakian fascists to declare independence for Slovakia, creating a state that was entirely under the power of the Third Reich. Subsequently, the Germans invaded the Czech provinces of Bohemia and Moravia, declaring them to be a German protectorate, and appointing one of their leading figures, Konstantin von Neurath, as the 'Reichsprotektor' of the new territory.

THE HANGMAN

Von Neurath immediately set to work, abolishing political parties and trade unions, and arresting students who protested against the situation. However, despite his brutal suppression of all forms of political opposition to the fascist regime, Hitler did not consider him fanatical enough, and in 1941 replaced him with one of the most feared figures of the Third Reich, Reinhard Heydrich. Von Neurath remained a nominal figurehead until 1943, but from that time, the real power lay with Heydrich.

Known as 'The Blond Beast' and 'The Hangman', Heydrich was soon to receive another nickname, as 'The Butcher of Prague'. As the head of the Reich Security Services, which included the Gestapo, he was also one of the chief architects of the Holocaust. It was Heydrich who had organized and chaired the infamous Wannsee Conference of 1942, laying out his plans for the extermination of the entire Jewish population of Europe: the 'Final Solution', as it became known. He was a close friend and confidant of the Führer, who much admired his skill and prowess as a sportsman, and considered him to be the prototype Aryan (even though it was rumoured that, in fact, Heydrich had a Jewish grandparent). According to some sources, Hitler considered Heydrich to be a possible candidate for leader of the Third Reich in the future.

THE FINAL SOLUTION

In his new position as head of government in Czechoslovakia, Heydrich lost no time in putting his nightmare plan into action. Already, von Neurath had announced a long list of anti-Jewish laws, designed to make the Jewish communities as powerless as possible, both in terms of business and social life. There had also been deportations of Czech Jews to concentration camps in Poland. However, under Heydrich the campaign was now stepped up, and thousands more Jews were arrested and sent to concentration camps. Most of them met their end in Auschwitz, either being gassed to death, or perishing from malnutrition and disease. By the end of the war in 1945, around 75 per cent of the Jewish population had been murdered in the death camps.

As in other European countries, the Nazi regime mined a deep seam of anti-Semitism running through Czech culture, and there were many who enthusiastically collaborated with the Final Solution programme instigated by Heydrich. However, there were also brave souls who were prepared to risk their lives to oppose the Nazis, and who eventually succeeded in ridding Czechoslovakia of its tyrannical ruler – but with devastating consequences.

OPERATION ANTHROPOID

Operation Anthropoid was a daring plan to assassinate Heydrich, masterminded by the British spy unit, the Special Operations Executive. Under the plan, several soldiers from Czechoslovakia's erstwhile army, including Jozef Gabcik and Jan Kubis, were to covertly enter the country to assassinate the Nazi leader. On the night 28 December, 1941, the soldiers were parachuted in by RAF planes. Once on the ground, they made their way to Prague, where they contacted anti-Nazi resistance groups and prepared to make their attack.

Heydrich was known for his habit of riding around Prague in an open-topped car. He was supremely arrogant and appeared to believe that he was invincible, especially since his henchmen had brutally suppressed all forms of opposition to his regime. However, on 27 May, 1942, his confidence in his total control of the country was proved wrong.

That day Heydrich set out to commute from his home to Prague Castle, the Nazi headquarters. Ever careless of security, he did not wait for a police escort that day, but ordered his driver to take him in to work in his Mercedes-Benz. As the car travelled along its accustomed route, Kubis and Gabcik stood at a bus stop outside a hospital. When the car passed, Gabcik stepped out and opened fire with a Sten gun, but it jammed. Heydrich promptly told his driver to stop, and stood up in the car to shoot Gabcik. At this point, Kubis intervened, throwing an anti-tank grenade at the car. The grenade damaged the right fender of the car, but did not penetrate into it. Nevertheless, Heydrich was badly injured as pieces of shrapnel and upholstery fibres lodged in his body. Undeterred, Heydrich continued to shoot at his assailant, but eventually collapsed, where-upon his driver, a man named Klein, ran out in pursuit of Gabcik. Klein was shot dead during the chase.

CONSPIRACY THEORIES

Heydrich was taken to hospital, but Czech doctors were forbidden to attend to him. Instead, he was operated on by the personal physicians of Heinrich Himmler, his direct superior. However, Heydrich died of his wounds, apparently in agony. Himmler maintained afterwards that Heydrich had died of blood poisoning, as the result of an infection set up by the horsehair in the car's upholstery. This odd diagnosis prompted speculation that Himmler was responsible for Heydrich's death, as it was known that Himmler was both afraid of Heydrich and jealous of his close relationship with the Führer. Other conspiracy theories suggest that the hand grenade lobbed into the car by Kubis contained botulin, and was the result of an experiment in biological warfare by British scientists.

Whatever the truth of the matter, the outcome of the situation was that Hitler's favourite had been assassinated. The Führer's revenge, whatever form it would take, was sure to be savage indeed.

WADING IN BLOOD

Hitler immediately gave orders that his men should 'wade in blood' until they found the assassins. However, the Gestapo were unable to find them until its officers bribed a resistance fighter named Karel Curda with the promise of a million Reichsmarks, a new wife and a new name. Curda accepted the bribe and led them to the Moravec family, who had been sheltering the soldiers. The family were arrested, held captive and tortured. Mrs Moravec managed to commit suicide, taking a cyanide capsule. With typical sadism, the Nazis later put her head in a fish tank and showed it to her son, Ata. Not surprisingly, the young boy told the Gestapo where the assassins were hiding. Over 700 Nazi troops laid siege to a church in the city, but were unable to take the assassins alive; Kubis was killed in the gun battle, while Gabcik and others committed suicide to avoid being captured alive.

Not content with this outcome, Hitler planned to unleash untold violence on the entire Czech people, but was persuaded out of this by his advisers who told him that military productivity would be adversely affected in the region if he did so. Instead, the Nazis went on to arrest more than 13,000 people, and also committed one of the worst atrocities of the war: the destruction of the village of Lidice.

MASSACRE AT LIDICE

The massacre that took place at the small village of Lidice, just northwest of Prague, on the night of 9 June, 1942, was one of the greatest atrocities to hit Czechoslovakia during World War II. The whole village was completely eradicated along with the majority of its inhabitants. The violence started following the assassination of Reinhard Heydrich, the chief of the Security Police and deputy chief of the Gestapo. Two Czech men, Jan Kubis and Josef Gabeik bombed Heydrich's car while he was on his way to the castle in Prague. Heydrich was badly wounded and died from his extensive injuries on 4 June.

The assassination incited the German people into taking revenge, and the village of Lidice took the brunt of their anger. Just five days after Heydrich's death, ten trucks full of Security Police stormed the village and forcefully removed all the inhabitants from their homes. No one was allowed to leave the village and anyone trying to escape was shot. All the men and boys over the age of 16, 172 in total, were separated from their families and locked in a barn. The next day they were all lined up in groups of ten, and mercilessly shot. The massacre lasted from dawn until 4.00 p.m.

The women, as a whole, fared better than their menfolk but they were still subjected to excessive cruelty. Seven of the women were taken to Prague where they were shot. The remainder, 195 in total, were sent to Ravensbrüeck concentration camp in Germany. They were kept in squalid conditions with very little nourishment and 49 of the women died. Seven were gassed while the rest died from the appalling conditions and treatment they received at the hands of the Germans. The children, who the Germans considered to be the fittest, were chosen and sent to live with German people with a new identity.

The village itself was completed razed to the ground, and any building that was not destroyed by fire was dynamited and bulldozed so that nothing was left standing. Today there is no sign of the village of Lidice except for the open fields where the children once played. It is a stark reminder of the grim atrocities that took place in the long and harrowing war.

Yugoslavia
—————1941–45—————

In April 1941, German Nazi troops, together with troops from Hungary, Bulgaria and Italy, invaded what was then known as Yugoslavia in the Balkans. Their combined military force quickly overcame all opposition, and the region was soon occupied. The victors then proceeded to share out their gains, with Germany and Italy establishing a puppet fascist state in Croatia. Germany also occupied Serbia and annexed parts of Slovenia, while Italy occupied the coastal regions of Yugoslavia. Bulgaria annexed Macedonia, and Hungary took control in Backa, an area in the north of the country. This complex division of power meant that there were many conflicts in the country, not only between the occupied peoples and their rulers, but between the rulers themselves. However, the invasion proved disastrous in all regions for the 78,000 Jews who, since the 1930s, had come to Yugoslavia to escape persecution. Not only the Jews, but thousands of Roma people (commonly known as gypsies) also lost their lives, as the fascists began on their programme of genocide, exterminating entire communities whose ethnic backgrounds or religious beliefs they considered undesirable.

Croatia was perhaps the country worst affected, mainly because the Croatian fascist movement, the Ustasa (which still exists to this day), set about murdering as many Serbs, Jews and Roma as they could lay their hands on. Immediately after the invasion of the Axis powers, they murdered, tortured and raped thousands of Serbs, burning down Serbian villages all over the country. Within a year, almost two-thirds of the entire Jewish population of Croatia had been sent to concentration camps, including Jadovno, Loborgrad, Djakovo, Tenje, Osijek, Kruscica and the notorious Jasenovac. In Jasenovac alone, more than 20,000 Jews met their deaths. Not only this but Croatia also deported thousands of Jews to concentration camps in Germany and Poland, especially to Auschwitz.

JASENOVAC CONCENTRATION CAMP

After the invasion of Yugoslavia by the Axis powers, the fascist Ustasa established a so-called Independent State of Croatia, and they set up Jasenovac between August 1941 and February 1942. The Ustasa were a far-right political group who had a long history of animosity towards the Serbian people of the former Yugoslavia, with whom they shared citizenship. With the Nazis now in control, the Ustasa took the opportunity to persecute hundreds of thousands of Serbs, as well as Jews and Roma people. Thus it was that over 250,000 Serbs died in the Croatian concentration camps, along with 20,000 or more Jews. And this was only in a single year: 1941 to 1942.

Situated only a few miles outside the Croatian capital of Zagreb, Jasenovac was a complex of several camps: Krapje, Brocica, Ciglana, Kozara and Stara Gradiska. Krapje and Brocica closed down after four months, but the others were not dismantled until the liberation of the country at the end of the war. Stara Gradiska was initially a camp for political prisoners, but then became a camp for women in 1942.

Conditions in the camps were absolutely horrifying. Prisoners were forced to live in cold, insanitary conditions without enough food to eat. The Ustasa guards, who were paramilitaries, showed extreme sadism in their treatment of the prisoners, torturing and murdering their victims on a whim. Often, prisoners would be taken out and shot at killing sites nearby, for example at Gradina and Granik. Others were rounded up and sent to concentration camps in Germany and Poland: a total of 7,000 Jews were sent to Auchwitz. Yet others, who had skills useful to the Croats, such as carpenters, electricians and tailors, were used as forced labour in workshops.

A SCENE OF CARNAGE

There was little opportunity for the inmates of these

camps to mount any opposition to their brutally violent masters, but towards the end of the war, news came that the Nazis were about to be defeated. In 1945, Communist leader Josip Tito, who later became a national hero and ruled Yugoslavia for many years, advanced on the camps with his partisan troops, and as the soldiers approached, the inmates rose up in rebellion against the Ustasa guards. However, in the fighting, many prisoners died. The rest met their deaths when the Ustasa guards, knowing the game was up, murdered as many prisoners as they could before surrendering. In May 1945, Tito's troops invaded the camps and found a horrific scene of carnage and devastation there that was far beyond anyone's worst nightmare.

In German-occupied Serbia, the nightmare continued, with a military government that set up concentration camps in 1941. Virtually the entire Jewish population of these areas were imprisoned in the five camps at Nisch, Schabatz, Sajmiste and Topovske Supe. They were dealt with in the most horrific way. In the summer of 1941, the majority of Jewish men in the camps were shot. The following year, at Sajmiste, the Nazis brought a specially designed 'gas truck' to the camp and proceeded to dispense with almost all the Jewish women and children there. The women and children were herded into a hermetically sealed gas compartment in the truck and gassed to death. In all, 8,000 women and children were put to death in this way, over a period of less than a year.

In the areas of Yugoslavia occupied by Hungary and Bulgaria, who had joined the Nazis, more horrifying events took place. As well as deporting Jews and Serbs from these territories, the Hungarian army police units took to murdering them in the streets. In January 1942, in the city of Novi Sad, thousands of Jews and Serbs were killed in this way. After the German occupation of Hungary in March 1944, Jews from the Hungarian-occupied territory of Yugoslavia were also deported to the death camps, along with thousands of others across Europe. In the Bulgarian-occupied areas of the country, non-Bulgarian Jews were handed over to the Germans for extermination at the Treblinka death camp in Poland: in total, about 11,000.

By the end of the war, around 60,000 Yugoslav Jews, out of a population of 78,000, were dead. Those who survived managed to do so by hiding with friends and relatives for the duration of the war, or by joining the partisan forces.

REPRISAL ATROCITIES

As well as the systematic genocide of innocent victims, including thousands of Serbs, in the concentration camps, the war years in Yugoslavia were characterized by appalling atrocities that took place in the cities, towns, villages and countryside. This was partly as a result of the activity of the National Liberation Army, the force commanded by Communist leader Tito, which was the largest resistance force in Europe. The Germans vowed that each time the liberation army killed a soldier, they would kill 100 civilians in reprisal; for a wounded soldier, the price would be 50 civilians. As a result, civilian losses in Yugoslavia were high, estimated at more than one million. However, on the more positive side, the NVA's campaign of guerrilla warfare resulted in the eventual defeat of the Axis powers, with the help of the Red Army and Allied forces.

In response to guerrilla warfare against his troops, Hungarian General Ferenc Feketahalmy-Czeyder launched a vicious reprisal campaign at the town of Novi Sad. There, his Arrow Cross militia rounded up a group of over 800 Jews and Serbs and forced them, at gunpoint, to walk over the frozen Danube river. The ice was too thin to hold them, and most of them drowned. Those who did not drown in this way were shot at point blank range. In the six days that followed, there was more carnage as the troops rampaged around the town, killing over 3,000 more victims.

THE SERBIAN MASSACRES

One of the worst aspects of the war in Yugoslavia was the wholesale massacre of a large percentage of the Serbian population by the Croatian fascist army, the Ustasa, who were given carte blanche by the Germans to pursue this objective without interference. As a result of this policy, thousands of Serb men, women and children all across the country were murdered at random, often being brutalized and tortured in the most sadistic way before they were killed. Stories abound of children's heads being cut off and thrown at their mothers, of women's breasts being severed, and childrens' bodies mutilated. The true facts of the mass genocide of Serbs during the German occupation of Yugoslavia were suppressed for many years after World War II, and in many cases, accurate records of what took place did not exist (or were destroyed). However, today there remains little doubt that the treatment of the Serbs by the Croatian fascist militia was at least as vicious as that of the Jews by the German Nazis, if not more so. For this reason, among many others, animosity between the Serbs and the Croats continued to run high for decades after the war, resulting a renewed period of conflict in 1980, after the death of President Tito, who had managed to hold these warring factions together during his premiership.

The Netherlands

—————— 1941–45 ——————

The Netherlands has a long history of tolerance within its society, and for this reason, many Jewish people over the centuries made the country their home. Amsterdam, in particular, became one of the largest Jewish population centres in Europe, a place where many Jews from around the world were able to settle: to do business, conduct their religious observances, and to build their communities, in an atmosphere of tolerance and respect on the part of the Dutch authorities and population.

During World War I, The Netherlands managed to stay out of the conflict, despite being at the heart of the European mainland. The Dutch aimed to take the same stance during World War II; however, when Germany invaded the Netherlands, they were forced to fight. After a brief conflict, during which Rotterdam was heavily bombed, the Dutch surrendered. The Netherlands was occupied by the Germans, and from then on, the Dutch became complicit in the Nazi war plan.

GENOCIDE PROGRAMME

This was a disaster for the many Jewish people who lived in the country, and over the period of occupation, more than 100,000 Dutch Jews were killed. There were also many Dutch Roma people (or gypsies) who were murdered as part of the Nazis' programme of genocide. As had happened in France, the Germans were able to draw on a deep strain of anti-Semitism running through Dutch society, and many ordinary Dutch citizens collaborated with the Nazis, sending thousands of innocent Jews and others to their deaths in the concentration camps. Towards the end of the war, the Dutch as a whole also suffered considerable hardship as the Allied forces invaded Europe, disrupting transport and food supplies. Indeed, when the Netherlands was finally liberated on 5 May, 1945, the entire population had undergone a harsh winter, with many dying of starvation and malnutrition.

THE DUTCH HOLOCAUST

During the occupation, the notorious SS ruled the country, under the aegis of Reich Commissar Arthur Seyss-Inquart. Seyss-Inquart was a favourite of Hitler's and was fanatical in his Nazi beliefs. He personally oversaw each and every aspect of the administration of the Netherlands. He banned all political parties except the Dutch National Socialist party and ensured that all

activities took place under the watchful eye of his paramilitary police force. He also imprisoned many former
officials, creating a reign of terror in which the most
innocent of activities, such as playing chess, were
subject to constant surveillance.

An open anti-Semite, Seyss-Inquart saw to it that
after the Dutch surrender all those of Jewish origin
were immediately removed from the government,
media, civil service and other positions of power in the
country. Many successful Jewish business people were
forced into poverty as a result of taxation and other
laws. Jews were required to register as such, including
many Jews who had fled to Holland to avoid the Nazis
in Germany. In total, 159,806 people registered, including many who were only partially Jewish.

THE YELLOW STAR

Initially, there was some opposition to this openly anti-
Semitic regime. In February 1941, a strike was
mounted by Dutch workers to protest against the
arrest and deportation of several hundred young
Jewish people who had been sent to forced 'labour
camps' as the concentration camps were euphemis-
tically called. However, this protest only provoked
further harsh measures on the part of the Nazis. With
amazing speed, the Jews' power and influence was
eroded, until many were living in ghettoes in reduced
circumstances, unable to work and to move around the

country. However, it had not yet become clear just how far-reaching the new regime's persecution of the Jews was going to be.

In a chilling development, a new law was passed on 29 April, 1942, requiring all Jews to wear a large yellow star on the left breast of their clothing. Anyone who did not comply with this could be fined on the spot or deported to a forced labour camp. From this time on, the SS police conducted raids on the ghettoes of Amsterdam, arresting Jews and sending them off to the concentration camps. Summons were also issued to Jews who had registered, telling them that they must report and leave immediately for Nazi 'forced labour' camps. Confused Jewish citizens turned to the Jewish Council, who represented their interests. The Council advised them to go, thinking that it might be able to oversee the process if it cooperated with the Nazis.

MASS DEPORTATIONS

Faced with this dilemma, many Jews chose to obey. There were unpleasant rumours about the 'forced labour' camps, but these were thought to be untrue (such rumours had persisted in World War I and had been found to be groundless afterwards). There were other Jewish families, such as that of Anne Frank, whose diary is an extremely moving account of the period, who decided to go into hiding. In all, about 25,000 to 30,000 Jews went into hiding, helped by the

Dutch resistance movement. Two-thirds of those who did survive, though sadly not Anne and her family.

In the summer of 1942, the mass deportations of Dutch Jews began. Thousands upon thousands of innocent victims boarded trains to the Nazi concentration camps of Buchenwald, Mauthausen, Auschwitz, Sobibor and elsewhere, never to return. There, men, women and children, were gassed to death, starved, beaten and abused, in the largest genocide in modern history. By the end of the war, over 75 per cent of the Jewish population of the Netherlands was dead.

In hindsight, it seems extraordinary that so many Jewish families went meekly and obediently to their deaths in the concentration camps. There have been many explanations advanced for this, but it seems that, in many cases, people genuinely did not believe that the Nazis could be conducting a mass genocide programme on such a scale. Whatever the truth, the murder of so many thousands of Dutch Jews stands as one of the greatest crimes in the whole of human history.

REPRISALS

The Nazis did not restrict their brutality and sadism only to the Jewish population. In many cases, they wreaked their vengeance on the population at large, especially towards the end of the war when they realized that they were about to face defeat as the Allies invaded Europe. During this period, anyone suspected of harbouring or helping underground resistance fighters met with the harshest of punishments.

PUTTEN ATROCITY

At the village of Putten, on the night of 30 September, 1944, members of the Dutch underground resistance movement ambushed several German soldiers. Three escaped and one remained prisoner. This soldier, Lieutenant Eggert, was eventually released after the Nazis threatened reprisals against the villagers. However, even when he was set free, General Helmuth von Wuhlisch of the SS went ahead with the reprisals anyway, rounding up 598 men from the village and ordering them to be sent to concentration camps in Germany. Of these, only 49 survived the war and returned.

DE WOESTE HOEVE

Another atrocity occurred on the night of 6 March, 1945, when a German general, Hans Albin Rauter, was ambushed by Dutch underground resistance fighters. Ironically, the fighters had intended to ambush a German lorry, but struck the general's BMW instead. Both the driver of the vehicle and another soldier were killed. Rauter sustained serious injuries and was taken to hospital near Apeldoorn, where he was given a number of blood transfusions.

Rauter recovered, but the Nazis were so incensed by this attack that they ordered immediate reprisals. Under the command of SS Brigadeführer Dr Eberhard Schongarth, 116 local men were arrested and taken to the scene of the crime, where they were all shot dead. Their bodies were buried nearby, in a mass grave at Heidehof cemetery, Ugchelen. Not only this, but all over the country, prisoners of the Gestapo were taken out and shot: in total, 147 more men lost their lives. Evidently, as the Allies invaded Europe, the Nazis were in a mood of desperation at losing the war, and reacted with appalling brutality.

After the Allied victory, General Rauter was arrested by British military police while in hospital at Eutin. He was then tried by a Dutch court in The Hague, and was sentenced to death. After a period of imprisonment, he was finally executed by a firing squad near Scheveningen Prison on 25 March, 1949. His colleague Schöngarth was also tried, this time by the British, and was later hanged.

TEXEL MASSACRE

The island of Texel lies off the coast of Holland. It was here that a mutiny of Soviet soldiers against their German masters took place in April 1945. Eight hundred Red Army soldiers, all from Georgia, had been taken prisoner and had volunteered to join the German army. As it turned out, however, this was just a ploy, and unbeknown to the German officers, the Soviet soldiers were plotting their revenge. One night in April, they struck: led by Lieutenant Shalva Loladze, they crept into the Germans' sleeping quarters and murdered over 200 of the Nazi soldiers in their beds. When news of the massacre reached the mainland, the Germans responded by sending in soldiers to hunt the rebels down. Those who were caught were tied together in groups of four or five and blown up with hand grenades. In this way, over 400 Soviet soldiers perished; a further 100 or more local people also died in the fighting. Today, their remains are buried at the Georgian war cemetery on the island.

Germany

1938–45

The Nazi regime in Germany under Adolf Hitler is thought to have been responsible for the deaths around 11 million people, including 6 million Jews. The Holocaust, as it has become known, in which the Nazis carried out their plan of genocide with ruthless efficiency, was the greatest war crime of the 20th century, and possibly of all time. What differentiated it from other instances of persecution and attempted genocide was the sheer scale of the programme. The Nazis used newly developed technology to commit mass murder on a much larger scale than had hitherto been possible. During World War II, Germany underwent an industrial revolution – no longer manufacturing goods, but effecting the mass production of death and destruction.

THE 'FINAL SOLUTION'

Perhaps the most disturbing aspect of the Holocaust, besides the sheer numbers of people killed, is the way in which the murders took place. They were organized efficiently and systematically, with the tacit or active consent of ordinary German people, who were persuaded that the Nazis' aim to 'cleanse' the nation of racial impurity was a civilized goal, rather than a descent into barbarity. Not only were Jews considered undesirable: Poles, Serbs, Hungarians and other nationalities were persecuted, as were Roma, or gypsy, people, homosexuals, people from minority religious sects such as Jehovah's witnesses, people with physical and mental disabilities, and others. Although the Nazi reign of terror meant that ordinary members of the public were often afraid to disobey orders, and acted out of fear, there is no doubt that many also used the opportunity to inflict violence on their fellow human beings.

The systematic persecution of the Jews and others deemed racially undesirable began with a series of laws requiring Jews to register their names, and passing laws that limited their business interests and social lives. Segregation then continued by herding the Jews into ghettoes in Europe's large cities, where many died of disease and starvation, or were weakened to the point that they became permanently sick. Next, the victims were sent to so-called labour camps, which were in reality death camps. Herded into freight trains without sanitation or food, many bound for the camps died on the way, particularly children and the elderly. Once at the camps, the 'Final Solution of the Jewish Question' became a nightmare reality as the victims, many of whom had no idea what was in store for them, were herded into gas chambers. Those who were left in the camps often died from torture, neglect and starvation. The Nazi guards and their civilian supporters behaved, on the whole, with no mercy: even young children were subjected to the most horrifying ordeals.

CRIMES AGAINST HUMANITY

Despite the fact that the treatment of the Jews in Germany and across Europe was more barbaric than anyone could possibly have imagined, the Third Reich operated an efficient bureaucracy that gave an air of supposed legitimacy to the murders. This was perhaps the most sinister aspect of the regime: that ordinary people were easily persuaded to take part in the most appalling crimes against humanity, simply because they were ordered to do so by the government.

After the war, chilling evidence came to light of the methodical way in which the Nazis had catalogued their horrific crimes. For example, the victims' belongings were carefully listed, and the victims given receipts, possibly to stop them realizing what was going to happen to them. It was this semblance of officialdom that caused many Jews and minority groups to trust their captors, not understanding that they were bound for wholesale slaughter until it was too late.

BODY DISPOSAL

Exterminating human beings on the scale that the Nazis envisaged required new technologies, and accordingly, German scientists, industrialists and others worked hard to find efficient killing machines for their victims. Often, the Nazis used mental patients from asylums as guinea pigs, trying out various methods, such as mass shootings, explosives and machine gunning. They found that the most successful method to use was poisoned gas, such as carbon monoxide or Zyklon B, which took less than ten minutes to kill large numbers of people and was an easy way to dispose of hundreds of prisoners at a time.

The next problem was how to dispose of the hundreds of bodies after the gas had done its work. At this point, German industrialists stepped in, eager to lend a hand. Furnaces were developed that operated at high temperatures, and burned using human body fat, making the disposal of thousands of bodies relatively easy.

HUMAN EXPERIMENTS

With these technical solutions in place, the Germans and the 35 other European nations that collaborated with them set about the mass extermination of the Jews and other 'undesirables'. However, for some unfortunate victims, the prospects were even worse than death in the gas chambers: the Nazis also carried out experiments on prisoners, including children and babies, under the pretext of advancing medical science, but in reality to feed their taste for sadism. For example, the notorious Dr Josef Mengele, under the guise of research into genetics, carried out horrific experiments on twins, dwarves and gypsies. Unbelievably, in one case he tried to sew two twins together to see what would happen. Another of his specialities was to inject dye into victims' eyes to see how they would change colour; he also performed amputations and subjected his victims to drug tests and various methods of dying, including freezing. Few of his experiments were of any medical interest, and afterwards, the hapless victims were almost always put to death.

As well as these experiments, there were cruel investigations with the supposed aim of protecting German soldiers. For example, many Russian prisoners were used in experiments, such as being frozen to death in iced water, or subjected to intense air pressure, ostensibly to see how soldiers would fare in a war situation. In other cases, prisoners faced the naked brutality of the Nazi guards for no reason other than to satisfy their captors' lust for violence; some were hung up on poles, others beaten to death.

CHILD LABOUR

The thousands of children taken to the concentration camps came in for the most terrible treatment, often being separated from their parents and taken straight to the gas chambers on arrival. Those who did not perish immediately were forced to work as slave labourers in factories and quarries, often ending the day by standing for hours waiting for their names to be read out in a roll call. Badly fed, with no proper medical care or sanitation, many children who lived and worked in the appalling conditions of the camps died before the end of the war.

DEATH MARCHES

Towards the end of the war, as the Allies were advancing through Europe, the Nazis began to move prisoners out of the death camps in an effort to destroy the evidence of what they had done. Inmates were marched miles through the snow to train stations, transported and then marched to their new camps. Many of the prisoners, who had suffered years of malnutrition and ill treatment, died during the 'death marches', as they became called – in total, around a 100,000. And this was not the end of the story. As Soviet and Allied forces began to discover the horrific truth of what had happened at the Nazis' concentration camps, thousands of inmates were liberated. However, many of the prisoners were so weak by that time that they died within a few weeks of being set free.

The genocide at the hands of the Nazis and their collaborators was so extensive during World War II that, after the conflict was over, new legislation had to be enacted to encompass the crimes. The charge of 'a crime against humanity', which had been brought in after World War I, was now extended to cover all crimes against humanity and civilization by the Axis powers committed during the war (significantly, any crimes committed by the Allied powers were exempt from this). These crimes included murder, extermination, enslavement, deportation and other inhuman acts committed against civilian populations 'whether or not in violation of the domestic law of the country where perpetrated'. What this meant in effect was that German ministers, officials, military officers and civilians could be charged in an international court of law for crimes committed during World War II, even if they were abiding by the rules of the Third Reich and its collaborators. This was because the crimes – whether committed by high-ranking officials, lowly guards or simply members of the public – went beyond the terms of the Geneva Convention, and constituted crimes, on a grand scale, against the whole of humanity.

Had the Allies failed to defeat the Axis powers, there is no doubt that the Nazis would have continued to carry out their programme of genocide in Britain and elsewhere. As it was, their avowed aim to exterminate all Jews in Europe in the 'final solution to the Jewish question' failed: but not before millions had been put to death in the most horrifying war crime of the 20th century, if not in the whole of human history.

Action T4 'Euthanasia Programme'

————————1939–41————————

One of the most horrifying aspects of the Nazi regime in Germany was the killing of up to 100,000 individuals with mental or physical disabilities. Under a programme known as 'Action T4', named after the address of the house where the headquarters of the operation was located (Tiergart enstrasse 4 in Berlin), Hitler ordered the killing of those identified as mentally or physically 'diseased', so as to cleanse the German people of 'racial impurities'. Along with Jews, communists, homosexuals and other minority groups, those with any genetic defects, impairments or peculiarities were seen as undesirable elements to be got rid of, that is, put to death.

BARBARIC PLAN

The programme was administered by qualified doctors, nurses and other trained medical staff, including Hitler's own personal physician, Dr Karl Brandt. The director of the operation was Philipp Bouhler, the head of Hitler's private chancellery. The T4 programme was often referred to as a programme of 'euthanasia', implying that the victims wished to be put to death to end their suffering, but that was not the case. In the majority of cases, the victims wanted to live, and most were not in extreme pain. Moreover, in most cases, their families desperately wanted to keep their relatives alive and had cared for them for many years. Despite this, Hitler was determined to carry through the programme, partly because of his crazed belief that only perfect human beings, as he saw it, should be allowed to inhabit the planet, and partly to save money: at the time the programme was launched, Germany was undergoing extensive rearmament in preparation for World War II.

In retrospect, it seems hardly believable that such a barbaric plan, including the murder of all mentally and physically disabled people, should have been conceived by a political leader and put into action by trained medical personnel. However, that is what happened between 1939 and 1941 in Nazi Germany, under the 'T4 Action' programme set in motion by the so-called 'General Foundation for Welfare and Institutional Care'.

Eventually, after meeting a great deal of resistance to the programme, not just from the victims' families but from political, religious and other figures, Hitler realized that he was not going to be able to mobilize public opinion against the disabled in the same way that he had done against the Jews, so the policy was abandoned in 1941; but by this time, between 75,000 and 100,000 individuals had been cold-bloodedly murdered in one of the most shameful war crimes in history.

'RACIAL HYGIENE'

The T4 Action programme appears to have been directly ordered by Hitler himself, as part of his policy of enforcing 'racial hygiene'. Hitler had a horror of mental illness, perhaps because he was afraid of his own tendency towards it, and there are accounts that he often ranted about how disgusting mentally ill people were. He seemed particularly fixated on those who were incontinent, or 'put their own excrement in their mouths' as he expressed it. In addition, he was horrified by physical deformity and believed that anyone with any kind of abnormality should not have children and should be sterilized to prevent such an occurrence.

The Führer, and other members of the Nazi regime, had been influenced by the writings of the late 19th-century scientist Adolf Jost, who had argued that euthanasia – that is the right to end a person's life to relieve suffering – should be the decision of the state not the individual. From this, it was a short step for Hitler to maintain that the state could choose who was to live and who to die. But in truth, the Nazi T4 programme had nothing to do with euthanasia at all, at least as most people understand it. Firstly, those chosen were not in a great deal of physical pain; and secondly, they were not put to death in a merciful way but subjected to a great deal of abuse and neglect. They were rounded up, separated from their loved ones, held as frightened prisoners in horrifying conditions and then put to death.

ENFORCED STERILIZATION

The T4 programme was also connected to the eugenics movement, which had become popular in Europe and the USA at the turn of the 20th century. According to this theory, selected breeding could improve the quality of the human race. Some countries, such as Sweden, had already passed laws to encourage sterilization of all those in the population with hereditary defects. In Sweden, thousands of people had been sterilized as a result. In 1933, Germany followed suit, passing a more draconian law 'for the prevention of hereditarily diseased offspring', which enforced sterilization for individuals with a range of mental conditions, from epilepsy and schizophrenia to alcoholism.

Under Interior Minister Wilhelm Frick, officials from what were known as Hereditary Health Courts visited psychiatric hospitals, special schools, retirement homes and prisons, assessing individuals and selecting them for the programme. In this way, over 360,000 individuals were sterilized. The enforced sterilization of people with any kind of physical disability was also considered, until it was pointed out that one of the most powerful figures of the Nazi administration, Joseph Goebbels, himself had a club foot. There were also moves to sterilize people whose disabilities were not congenital, despite the fact that this was totally illogical.

Besides holding the opinion that anyone with a disability was not 'worthy of life' and should be done away with, Hitler also favoured killing the incurably ill. However, his medical advisors, such as Brandt, tactfully put it to him that he would not be able to persuade the German public to go along with such an idea. Hitler then argued that, should war break out, the task of disposing of the mentally and physically disabled would be considerably eased, because people would be pressured by poverty and would see that resources needed to go towards the war effort rather than towards caring for these individuals. Unfortunately, he was to be proved right.

CHILD MURDERS

In May 1939, as Hitler prepared to invade Poland, a couple near Liepzig wrote to him to gain permission to have their severely deformed child put to death. Encouraged by this, Hitler authorized the setting up of the Reich Committee for the Scientific Registering of Serious Hereditary and Congenital Illnesses, whose directors were Dr Brandt, Philipp Bouler and an SS Officer, Viktor Brack. The task of this committee was initially to approve voluntary applications from parents and carers of disabled children for their charges to be put to death. However, the brief eventually came to be enlarged, in the most sinister way. Under the new programme, all severely disabled children under three were required to be killed, whether their parents wished this or not.

The disabilities listed by register included Down's syndrome, malformations, various spastic conditions and so on. In a parody of scientific rigour, three doctors had to give their consent to killing the child, and various other bureaucratic procedures had to be undergone. The selected children were then taken away from their parents to 'Special Sections' for assessment, where they were kept for a few weeks before being killed by lethal injection. Their deaths were recorded as pneumonia, and their brains and other body parts were removed for 'scientific research'. Strange as it may seem, this so-called 'research' helped many of the medical staff involved in the programme feel more comfortable about what they were doing.

HORRIFIC TRUTH

With the outbreak of war, the remit of the programme became wider. Older children and adolescents were now included, and a wider variety of abnormalities and malfunctions were 'assessed', until the programme expanded to include any kind of problem or difficulty, such as delinquent behaviour. By 1940, the mere fact of a child being Jewish, or an 'Aryan–Jewish half-breed' could qualify him or her for the Special Sections.

By now, parents were beginning to realize the horrific truth about what was happening to their children, but there was little they could do to resist. In many cases, they were terrorized into surrendering their children to the authorities: for instance, they were often threatened that they would lose custody of all their children if they refused to comply with the programme. Accordingly, many parents felt they had no option but to do as they were asked, and by 1941, 5,000 children had been killed under the programme.

MASS MURDER

Worse was to come as Brandt and Bouhler prepared to launch their so called 'euthanasia' programme on disabled adults. With the help of the minister for health, Dr Leonardo Conti, and the head of the SS medical department, Professor Werner Heyde, Nazi officials compiled a register of all institutionalized people in the country. Once this was done, they set about visiting the mental asylums and hospitals to claim their victims.

They began by taking inmates from an area of Poland recently invaded by Germany and shooting 7,000 of them, and went on to do the same in other Polish territories. Next, at Posen, they herded hundreds of inmates into an improvised gas chamber and gassed them to death, using carbon monoxide. This was an idea pioneered by Dr Albert Widman, the chief chemist of the German Criminal Police, and later taken up by SS Chief Heinrich Himmler to commit mass murder against Jews and other minority groups.

It is hard to imagine how the general public could have condoned such a programme of slaughter of the innocent, but as the privations of war began to make people's lives difficult, there was less and less resistance to it. The government argued that besides ridding the state of the expense of paying for the care of mental patients, gassing inmates also had the advantage of freeing up the hospitals for wounded soldiers. Thus, the Nazi troops were also keen to carry on the work of murdering the nation's most vulnerable people, especially in areas where war was being waged, such as in and around Poland. All in all, over 8,000 German patients were killed in this way, with the approval of Himmler and other high-ranking Nazi officials.

'MERCY DEATH'

It was not long before Hitler began to set his sights on the incurably ill. Brandt had advised him before the war that the German people would never agree to a programme of killing all those with incurable illnesses, but now in the context of war the situation had changed. Accordingly, Hitler ordered Bouhler and Brack to allow physicians to effect a 'mercy death' on all those they deemed incurable.

This programme never had the force of law, but it

was launched by a directive from the Führer and implemented by a team of doctors and psychiatrists, some of whom had worked on the previous programme and some of whom were new recruits. The team began by registering all inmates who had been in hospitals, retirement homes and so on for more than five years, and who were diagnosed as 'criminally insane'. Those of 'non-Aryan race' were also selected for 'assessment'. Next, a list of serious conditions, such as senile dementia, schizophrenia, syphilis and encephalitis, was issued to the institutions. Unfortunately, in many cases the staff from these homes assumed that selections were being made for labour camps and often overstated their patients' disabilities to protect them from being called up, with devastating consequences. In other cases, staff refused to co-operate with the authorities, especially in homes that were run by Catholic or other religious organizations – only to find that the selection was made for them, and inmates were removed without their permission.

At first there was a system with a semblance of order, whereby three 'experts' were required to deliver the death verdict on a patient, but after a while doctors began to make decisions on their own initiative. In the early days of the scheme, victims were killed by lethal injection, but this proved a slow and expensive way to kill large numbers of people, so Hitler told Brandt to gas the patients with carbon monoxide instead. (Incredibly, Brandt later described this development as a 'major advance' for medical history.) Accordingly, gas chambers were set up at Brandenburg in 1940, then at other towns across Germany.

Teams of SS soldiers, dressed in white coats to make them look like medical staff, were drafted in to escort the mental patients to the 'special treatment centres' by bus. In many cases, patients were sent to 'transit centres' in hospitals to be 'assessed' on the way: this was really so that their families would lose touch with them and give up trying to visit them. Once at the centre, the patient would be gassed immediately and then burnt, with a pile of other bodies in a furnace. Then, in an extraordinary display of macabre bureaucracy, the families would be sent an urn of the ashes from the furnace together with a falsified death certificate.

In 1940, the death toll at Brandenburg reached about 10,000 people; at other centres, such as Hartheim and Grafeneck, the figures were similar. In total, there were around 35,000 people killed under the Action T4 programme before it was closed down due to public opposition in August 1941. When this happened, the centres continued to operate, but their victims were now prisoners from concentration camps.

BACKLASH OF PUBLIC OPINION

Hitler had been careful to avoid passing laws sanctioning the use of the T4 programme, fearing that public opinion would be against it. In particular, there was intense opposition from the Catholic community, who now formed nearly 50 per cent of the German population. High-ranking members of the legal profession, including judges, also protested. The Nazis responded by trying to keep the programme as secret as possible, but this was difficult since there were thousands of doctors, nurses and administrative staff involved in it; also, there were thousands of families who lost loved ones in the purges. As well as the fact that staff talked to their friends and relatives about what was going on at the centres, despite strict instructions not to, many families had begun to realize that the hastily issued death certificates they received to notify them of the patients' deaths were false; for example, in one case, a patient was alleged to have died of appendicitis, when in fact he had already had his appendix taken out. In addition, those citizens who lived near the centres noticed that more and more busloads of patients were going in but none ever came out, and that there was a steady stream of smoke issuing from the furnaces. Gruesome incidents, such as clouds of ash and human hair falling on townspeople living near the centre at Hadamar, were clear indications of the carnage that was taking place; and it was reported that, in many places, children could be heard shouting about the gassings in the streets.

Not surprisingly, families began to take their loved ones away from mental asylums, hospitals and residential homes. There were also instances in which doctors worked to protect the patients from their fate. In other cases, staff took bribes to save the patients from the gas chambers. However, on the whole, the entire German medical profession cooperated with the T4 programme, either because they held the same beliefs as the Nazis about eugenics and 'racial purity', or because they were too afraid to protest.

HITLER JEERED

Despite the support for the programme from the medical profession, it's not surprising that the T4 programme could not last. Rumours began to be circulated that even wounded German soldiers would be subject to the T4 criteria and gassed, giving rise to public protests and increased opposition from outspoken members of the Catholic clergy. Protestant church leaders, who had hitherto supported the Nazis, also joined in the chorus of disapproval. In one instance, a Catholic bishop, Clemens von Galen, preached a rousing sermon against the killing of 'poor, unproductive people', and followed it up with a diatribe against religious persecution.

Naturally, the Nazis would have liked to arrest von Galen, but he, and others like him, had immense support from the general public. Thus the authorities were nervous of causing open revolt among the population against the regime. Matters reached a crisis point when Hitler himself was jeered at a public event in the town of Hof – the first time this had ever happened to him. He was reportedly furious, but he knew that his hands were tied: the Reich was busy fighting a foreign war and could not afford a major confrontation with the Church at that time. Faced with the choice of arresting and imprisoning hundreds of high-ranking Church and other leaders, which would have provoked public opinion against the party, or ended the T4 programme, the Führer chose the latter option. On 24 August, 1941, he personally ordered the closing down of the programme.

Unfortunately, this was a short-lived victory for humanitarian standards and common decency in Nazi Germany. Within only a few months, the T4 team of doctors, nurses and administrators had been given a new task. They were to perform the same role in another killing programme, that of exterminating the Jewish population under the terms of the 'final solution'. And, although the systematic murdering of the mentally and physically impaired ceased after 1941, the killings continued at a local level. Patients were no longer sent to the gas chambers, but were given lethal injections or starved to death.

THE AFTERMATH

After the war, the full scale of the horror regarding T4 programme emerged. In December 1946, 23 doctors and adminstrative staff, including Hitler's personal doctor Dr Karl Brandt, and the chief organizer of the programme Viktor Brack, were tried for their part in war crimes and crimes against humanity. The crimes included the systematic murder of physically and mentally ill people, and those with disabilities. Brandt and Brack, along with several others, were convicted and sentenced to death. They were executed in 1948. Philipp Bouler and Leonardo Conti, both leading Nazi medical officers, were also sent to trial, but they killed themselves while in prison.

In October 2006, skeletons of children and adults believed to have been part of the T4 'euthanasia programme' were unearthed in what appeared to be a mass grave in a cemetery at the village of Menden-Barge. The cemetery was near to the site of a former hospital run by Brandt, where mental patients had been gassed to death.

The Bombing of Dresden

February 1945

The bombing of Dresden in February 1945, during World War II, is considered by many to be a war crime, committed by the Allies against the German nation. This is because a heavily populated civilian area was specifically targeted and bombed on an enormous scale, using incendiary bombs to create a firestorm on the ground to maximize the death toll. So many bombs were dropped over the city by British and American aeroplanes that the area became a sheet of fire, drawing in cold air towards it like a tornado, and sucking in human bodies to be consumed in the flames. Eye-witness accounts of the bombing tell of extraordinary sights, such as seeing people reduced to cinders in front of their eyes, and whole streets blackened and burnt so badly that they were no longer recognizable.

The total weight of bombs dropped on Dresden was far greater than any bombing hitherto during the British air campaign and the bombing seems to have lacked any particular rationale, beyond creating sheer panic and terror in the population and thus destroying civilian morale. For these reasons, many doubt that it was necessary to wreak quite such appalling devastation on one of Germany's most crowded cities, especially considering the chaos and confusion that its inhabitants were already experiencing as a result of refugees fleeing to it from other areas of Germany.

However, there are those who maintain that the bombing was necessary to hasten the end of the war, and that to that degree it may have saved lives, at least on the Allied side. After the war, Air Marshal Arthur Harris of RAF Bomber Command – the man who helped to introduce the policy of 'area bombing' (or 'terror bombing' as it was known in Germany) – came under intense criticism for his part in the attack. However, he argued that the city was an important military target, being a communications centre for German defence, and that it was fully justified in the context of the war.

The policy of 'area bombing' (that is, directly bombing German cities and towns) had been advocated since by Charles Portal of the British Air Staff, and there had been attacks on Berlin and other German cities. These had not been successful, but they had encouraged the Germans to switch their air attacks from British military targets to urban areas. Many argued that this had helped the British win the Battle of Britain but had also invited the Blitz, which ravaged London during the war. In 1941, in conjunction with Arthur Harris, the Head of RAF Bomber Command, Portal introduced the policy of blanket bombing of urban areas at night to cause maximum civilian casualties. The campaign targeted Cologne, Hamburg, Nuremberg and Dresden, and is thought to have killed 600,000 civilians; the deaths of pilots were high, too, and more than 50,000 airforce personnel were killed in the raids. Eventually, the death toll from the campaign became too high, and the British prime minister, Winston Churchill, ordered that it should be abandoned. This was partly because Churchill did not want the whole country to be destroyed by the time the British won the war, which seemed likely by 1945.

MASSIVE FIRESTORM

The bombing attack on Dresden began on the evening of 13 February, 1945. First, British planes began to drop incendiary bombs, packed with magnesium, phosphorus, napalm and other combustible materials, onto the city, creating a massive fire that raged through the streets. Harris specifically intended this firestorm to be created, which shocked some of the pilots dropping the bombs. One wireless operator who took part in the raid, Roy Akehurst, recalled:

We seemed to fly for hours over a sheet of fire – a terrific red glow with a thin haze over it. I found myself making comments to the crew: 'Oh God, those poor people.' It was completely uncalled for. You couldn't justify it.

On the ground, the scene was worse than the worst nightmare. High buildings caught fire, creating a mass of hot air rushing upwards like a tornado, sucking up people and throwing them into the flames. Citizens fled through the burning streets to cellars, many of them fainting from the fumes and being burnt to cinders in front of onlookers. All the electricity in the city was out, so people were stumbling about in the darkness, clutching their children, many of whom were swept up in the flames. Down in the cellars, the dead and dying lay next to those who were still alive, and many were trampled to death as more and more people tried to cram in to get out of the firestorm.

The situation for those on the ground became worse when the weather cleared and the bombers were able to see their target better. American bombers were now called in, and a second wave of bombing began during daylight hours, in which the city was almost totally destroyed. Thousands were killed in the process in a most agonizing and painful way, being burnt to death. It is difficult to put an exact figure on the number of people who died, because so many bodies were completely incinerated in the firestorm, becoming cinders and ashes, but it has been estimated that the total death toll was around 35,000. However, some researches put the figure much higher, at around 100,000.

Whatever the truth of the matter, there is no doubt that the bombing of Dresden was one of the most destructive events of World War II. Almost the entire population was killed or injured, and few buildings were left standing. Sadly, Dresden had been a beautiful city, dating from medieval times, with many fascinating buildings and monuments that were a testament to the glories of German culture. Thus, its destruction was regarded not only as catastrophe on humanitarian grounds, but as a blow to European architecture, art and civilization.

CONTROVERSY

In the wake of the tragedy, there was great controversy about what had happened. After the war, the military personnel involved gave their side of the story, arguing that the bombing had been an effective way of bringing the war to a hasty close, thus saving the lives of hundreds of their men. In the view of Robert Saunby, Deputy Air Marshal at Bomber Command:

> *What is immoral is war itself. Once full-scale war has broken out, it can never be humanized or civilized, and if one side attempted to do so it would be most likely to be defeated. That to me is the lesson of Dresden.*

Others, however, had a different perspective. It was argued that Dresden had not been a city that had any particular military importance, and that nothing was achieved by bombing it, beyond destroying thousands of innocent people and desecrating one of the great cultural centres of the world. The burning to death of over 35,000 people, they claimed, was a war crime comparable to what went on in the concentration camps of Nazi Germany. Moreover, they pointed out, when the bombing of Dresden took place, victory for the Allies appeared to be a certainty and was only weeks away. It was unnecessary and seemed to spring from a mood of anger and revenge on the part of the Allies rather than being a careful military strategy to inflict damage on the German war machine.

Critics also point out that Britain has never apologized to Germany for the bombing of Dresden. While German politicians have spoken in public of the nation's guilt at the bombing of Coventry and other events during the war, there has been no public apology from Britain for similar attacks. Indeed, when the British queen visited Dresden, she did not lay a wreath for the dead at the cathedral there, or make a public apology about the bombing. She did, however, host a concert in Berlin to raise money for the rebuilding of the Dresden Frauenkirche, a building that was once regarded as an architectural masterpiece but was reduced to rubble in the bombing campaign.

At the end of World War II, Germany, Japan and other nations from the Axis powers became the focus of many investigations for war crimes and crimes against humanity. However, the Allies were not investigated for the simple reason that they had won the war and therefore became the legislators of the settlement made after the conflict. To many commentators, this seems a patently unfair situation, allowing Britain, the USA and the other Allied nations to get away with war crimes, atrocities and revenge killings of all kinds, while prosecuting the Germans and Japanese for their part in the war. Of course, it can be argued that Germany was the aggressor in World War II, and that the Third Reich was the most evil regime to come to power in modern history; but even so, it seems that the Allies were far from blameless in their conduct and that it is hypocritical to ignore this. Thus, in recent years, there have been several journalists, historians and researchers who have debated this state of affairs, claiming that the time has now come to redress the wrongs suffered by the losers in World War II, and that the bombing of Dresden must be regarded as one of the great war crimes that, to date, has gone unpunished.

Kristallnacht

10 November, 1938

Kristallnacht was a horrific attack on thousands of Jewish people living in German and Austrian cities. It took place on the night of 10 November, 1938, when, in a frenzy of anti-Semitism, Nazi stormtroopers and ordinary civilians rampaged through the streets, smashing the windows of Jewish homes, shops and businesses. Afterwards, the streets were covered in broken glass, and it was this that gave rise to the name, Kristallnacht, meaning 'Night of Broken Glass'.

Kristallnacht, or 'Pogromnacht', as it is now known in Germany, marked the beginning of the end for the Jewish population of Germany. It set in motion the events that led up to the Holocaust, in which over six million Jews were murdered. During the pogrom, many Jews were beaten to death and hundreds of synagogues burnt to the ground. Around 30,000 Jewish men were taken prisoner and sent to the concentration camps.

FORCED MARCHES

The pogrom took place against a background of rising

anti-Semitism in Germany that had been building up since the Nazis were elected in 1933. Up to that point, German Jews had been well assimilated in the population and had become successful in various fields, especially business, science and the arts. However, once the Nazis came to power, a series of harsh, anti-Semitic laws were passed that excluded them from the rest of the community and undermined their livelihoods. As a result, many Jewish families left the country, but it was not always easy for them to do so, because of anti-immigration laws elsewhere. Thus, many were forced to stay behind to face the full horror of German fascism.

According to some sources, the Nazi government planned the pogrom well in advance, hoping to whip up public sentiment against the Jews and thus gain the help of the general populace in persecuting this minority group. On 28 October, 17,000 Polish Jews were forced to leave the country and return to their homeland. This was despite the fact that many of these people had been living in Germany for over a decade. When the deported Jews got to the Polish border, the guards sent them back, and thus the refugees were forced to tramp back and forth between the two countries for days, in bad weather, until the Polish government finally interned them in a concentration camp. The camp was such a horrific place that many of the Jews tried to escape back to Germany, only to be shot on sight by German soldiers.

ASSASSINATION

It was this event that prompted a young Jewish man living in Paris, Herschel Grynszpan, to write to the head of the German embassy in Paris, Ernst vom Rath. Grynszpan's parents had been deported, and his mother had written to him describing the terrible treatment they had received at both the hands of the Germans and the Poles. Vom Rath was unable to help, however. In retaliation, Grynszpan – an intelligent, sensitive young man whose whole life had been characterized by anti-Semitic persecution, forcing him to move abroad from place to place – decided to take matters into his own hands. On Monday, 7 November, Grynszpan went to the embassy with a revolver and shot Vom Rath in the stomach. Two days later, his victim died.

The assassination provided the excuse Hitler needed to launch a pogrom against the Jews. He signalled to his ministers that, should anti-Jewish protests erupt among the public, they should be allowed to continue. Hoping to curry favour with the Führer, Hitler's propaganda minister, Joseph Goebbels, who had recently brought ridicule on himself as a result of an affair with an actress, immediately commanded the party leaders to organize the pogrom. Some of the party leaders privately disagreed with the action, realizing that it would prompt outrage from the rest of the European nations, and that Germany would soon be isolated because of its persecution of the Jews.

SMASHED WITH SLEDGEHAMMERS

Nevertheless, on 10 November, 1938, Gestapo Chief Reinhard Heydrich ordered the attacks to begin. Beginning from around 10. 30 p. m. , members of the Gauleiters, the SA and the SS, mostly wearing civilian clothing, stormed the streets of Germany's major cities, destroying Jewish property with sledgehammers and axes. The soldiers had received instructions not to harm German civilians or to endanger German property. Where a Jewish building stood next to a German one, it was smashed rather than burnt to the ground. In addition, the troops were ordered to arrest all Jews, especially healthy young men, and wealthy families. The authorities did not actually order the troops to beat or assault Jews, but this happened on many occasions, and the authorities turned a blind eye.

In the morning, there was glass everywhere on the streets of Germany's cities. Vienna, the capital of Austria was also awash with glass. Almost the entire total of German and Austrian synagogues had been destroyed in a single night: that is, around 1,600. Over 7,000 Jewish shops were destroyed, some of them large department stores. Scores of Jews had been killed, and several Gentiles who had been mistaken for Jews. Many Jews had committed suicide, realizing that the game was now up, and that anti-Semitic persecution had now reached epic proportions. In addition, over 30,000 Jewish men had been arrested and taken to concentration camps at

Dachau, Buchenwald and Sachsenhausen. Here, they met with brutal treatment. However, they were released three months later on condition that they leave the country immediately. Overall, the death toll was estimated to be around 2,500.

GRAVEYARD GHOULS

One of the most disturbing aspects of the pogrom, besides the loss of life and the destruction of property, was the sick way that the Nazis and their civilian sympathizers desecrated the synagogues and cemeteries belonging to the Jews. Graves were raided, tombstones smashed and bonfires lit in the graveyards, onto which were thrown prayer books, scrolls, statues, paintings and other religious artefacts. Even the smallest synagogues in little rural villages were razed to the ground, both in Germany and Austria. Not only this, but the Jews themselves were often forced to clear up the damage, being taunted by erstwhile friends and neighbours as they did so.

Not surprisingly, the events of Kristellnacht prompted outcry from abroad. In London newspapers, there were reports of the anti-Semitic violence on the streets, as well as an account of what had happened to interned Jews at Sachsenhausen, where 62 Jewish men had been beaten so badly by police that 12 of them died.

HOUNDED INTO EXTINCTION

However, despite public opinion abroad and the diplomatic repercussions for the German government, the Nazi leaders were determined to continue with their policy of persecuting the Jews. In fact, Kristallnacht seemed to mark a turning point: the Nazis' violent anti-Semitism was now out in the open, and, moreover, had ignited a deep vein of anti-Jewish feeling within the German population. Hitler's right-hand man, Hermann Göring, called a meeting of top Nazi officials 'to coordinate and solve the Jewish question once and for all, one way or another'. With these sinister words, the Nazis ushered in new phase of persecution, in which Jews were to be further hounded into extinction.

First, a collective fine of one billion marks was to be levied against the Jews for the murder of vom Rath. The government also decided to avail itself of all the insurance money that should have gone to the Jewish owners of properties destroyed on Kristallnacht, as 'damages' due to the German nation.

MASS EMIGRATION

Realizing that life in Nazi Germany was going to be made impossible for them, many Jews left the country: in total, in the ten months after the events of Kristallnacht, over one million Jews emigrated. Many found homes in other European countries, such as France, only to find themselves victims of persecution there later on in the war. Others went to the USA and to Palestine, and even to China.

After Kristallnacht, many European nations condemned the Nazi government. However, what was significant to the leaders of the Third Reich was that no one country actually came forward to oppose what was going on in Germany. After the events of World War I, none of the European nations was keen to involve its civilians in another horrific world war. Thus, Hitler and his henchmen were allowed to continue with their campaign of terror. They became aware that they could get away with whatever they wanted to, safe in the knowledge that neither Europe, nor the USA, would intervene.

Thus, Kristallnacht had a dual significance: signalling to the citizens of Germany that they could indulge their racist sentiments without fear of punishment from the government, indeed with encouragement from the authorities; and signalling to the rest of Europe that the Nazis were now in total control, and that Germany could be left undisturbed to carry out its cruel, inhuman programme of persecution and slaughter of the Jewish people.

Some historians have argued that had Kristallnacht provoked stronger opposition in Europe, German anti-Semitisim might have been nipped in the bud and the Holocaust might never have happened. However, through a combination of fears about another world conflict, and possibly a measure of anti-Semitism as well, the European powers left Hitler to his task of committing the greatest crimes against humanity that the world has ever known.

The Serbian Massacres

1941–45

$\mathcal{T}$he mass genocide of European Jews by the Nazis in World War II is well known. However, today many people do not know that, in the Balkans, fascist elements in Croatia and elsewhere persecuted and killed over one million Serbs, either interning them in concentration camps, where most met their deaths, or torturing and murdering them in their own villages and towns in the most unspeakably brutal way. This persecution had its roots in a long enmity between the different ethnic and national groups, and after the war, the wholesale slaughter of the Serbs was to have many repercussions, resulting in renewed conflict in 1991 in Bosnia.

SADISTIC BRUTALITY

The main perpetrators of the atrocities in Yugoslavia were the Croatian Ustase army, which was a militia created by the pro-fascist government under Prime

Minister Ante Pavelic. One of the first massacres they committed was on 28 April, 1941, when Ustasa troops appeared at the villages of Brezovica and Gudovac. The soldiers rounded up the villagers, singled out those of Serbian nationality, and ordered them either to convert to Roman Catholicism or to go back to their native land. During the raid, they killed 234 Serbs. Next, 520 villagers, including women and children, were attacked at Blagaj. They were beaten about the head until they died in a frenzy of violence that shocked even the most hardened inhabitants.

The violence continued at various areas around Livno, where over 3,000 Serbs were killed. At the Koprivnica Forest and the Risoveda Greda Forest, soldiers went on a rampage, hacking the bodies of women and children to pieces and throwing the bodies into ravines. Tales were told of terrible sadism, such as children being decapitated and their heads thrown at their mothers. Another instance of dreadful brutality occurred on 10 July at the small town of Glina, where 700 Serbs had gathered at a church to renounce their faith and convert to Catholicism. Instead, the Ustase attacked them, beating them to death with mallets, clubs and rifle butts, or stabbing them with bayonets. After this frenzied attack, members of the congregation were left to die, and the church was torched to the ground.

MASS MURDER OF CHILDREN

All this went on as the Nazis took control of the country. As far as the Nazis were concerned, as long as the Croatian militia carried out their orders to round up and intern Jews from the region, the troops were at liberty to persecute whoever else they pleased. Thus, as well as rounding up Jewish and Roma people, the Ustase interned many Serbs. In one of the worst war crimes to take place in Yugoslavia, over 6,000 children were separated from their parents and taken to a camp at Sisak. There, they lived in squalid conditions without enough to eat or drink, until around 1,600 of them died. A similar scene took place at the concentration camp of Jastrebarko, where over 3,000 children met with the same type of neglect, and hundreds of them dying in the process.

At the end of the war, the horrifying statistics on the carnage were revealed. It is estimated that in total, 11,176 Serbian children die between 1941 and 1942. Of these, the majority were boys. Tragically, the average age of the children was six-and-a-half years old.

THE ARCHITECT OF GENOCIDE

The architect of the Serbian massacres was Ante Pavelic, the leader of the Croatian National Socialist Ustase movement, who became head of the so-called Independent State of Croatia when the Nazis invaded the Balkans during World War II. Far from being an independent state, as its name suggested, Croatia in fact became a puppet state of the Third Reich, and it set about supporting the Germans in their persecution and murder of the Jews and Roma people. In addition, the Croatian Ustase pursued their own agenda, which was to rid the country of the Serbian nationals living there, without opposition from the German government.

Pavelic himself was a fascist activist who had campaigned for a separate Croat state and had been tried for terrorist activities before the war. In 1929, after being sentenced to death, he had fled the country, and while abroad, had founded the Ustase, an underground terrorist organization. He had helped to create a militia for the organization, setting up terrorist training camps throughout Italy and Hungary. In 1934, the Ustase had succeeded in assassinating the king of Yugoslavia, Alexander I, together with one of Alexander's ministers. For this, Pavelic was arrested and imprisoned in Italy, but before long, he was released. He remained in Italy until the outbreak of World War II. When the Nazis invaded Yugoslavia, he returned to his homeland and set up a pro-Nazi government there.

BARBARIC RITUALS

According to many sources, even the Nazis themselves were horrified at the brutal sadism of the Ustase regime. Barbaric rituals, such as gouging out victims' eyes, or wrapping prisoners in barbed wire before throwing them down pits to starve to death, were routinely used by Pavelic's Ustase troops. The stated aim of the pro-German, pro-Catholic Pavelic regime was to exterminate one-third of all Serbs in the country, which they succeeded in doing. Their plans were for another third to convert to Catholicism, while the remaining Serbs would be forced to move abroad.

After the war, it became clear that the Vatican had never condemned Pavelic's activities, and that in fact he had been given a private audience by the pope. Many commentators later saw the collusion of the Catholic Church in condoning the brutal Serbian massacres of World War II as one of the most shaming episodes in its history.

DEATH OF A WAR CRIMINAL

As the defeat of the Germans at the end of the war at last became a reality, Pavelic fled Croatia, first to Austria and then to Rome, where his Catholic friends in the Church helped to hide him from the authorities. However, since he was not a communist, the Americans were not, by all accounts, interested in pursuing him. Six months later, Pavelic managed to secure a passage to Argentina, where he found protection and help from the country's leader, Juan Peron. Peron also helped thousands of other Croatian Nazis and others who fled their homeland as the communist government of Josip Tito took control.

In April 1957, Pavelic became the target of an assassination attempt. He was not killed but was seriously injured. Rumours were that the assassins were working for Tito's security forces, but these were not confirmed. However, Pavelic was then forced to flee Argentina, since Tito's government was trying to make arrangements to have him extradited. This time, Pavelic went to Spain, where he was able to seek protection from the fascist government under Franco. On 29 December, 1959, he died in Madrid from complications caused by the injuries he had received in the assassination attempt.

COMMUNIST ATROCITIES

Sadly, towards the end of the war, Tito's incoming communist partisan troops, who had vowed to liberate the country, also behaved with extreme brutality. For example, at Siroki Brijeg on 7 February, 1945, 25 monks from a local monastery were attacked by the partisans, who tore down the crucifix in their church and demanded that they abandon their faith. The monks, not surprisingly, refused to do so, and knelt down to kiss the cross. In response, the friars – some of whom were ill in bed with typhoid – were dragged outside, doused in petrol and set alight. It was not until many years after the war that their bodies were finally given a proper burial.

In other instances, German and Hungarian civilians were set upon by Tito's communist troops at Vojvodina in southern Hungary. Helped by the local Serb population, who had suffered so much under the Nazi regime, the partisans murdered thousands of Germans and Hungarians. The victims were tied together in groups around stacks of corn and then set alight. Often, the perpetrators of these crimes were women, who wreaked their vengeance on the victims by torturing them to death. They devised horrible tortures, such as killing Catholic priests by tearing off their testicles with pincers, or chopping their victims up in sawmills. They also impaled their victims on sticks, putting them up on display for spectators to see. In one appalling case, they strapped a grenade to a small boy and allowed him to run away across a field before firing at the grenade so that it blew up, exploding his small body into pieces.

In all, Tito's partisans are thought to have murdered 34,000 victims at the end of the war, most of whom were Hungarian. Thus it was that, in the final years of the conflict, the most terrible brutality was unleashed, and the hideous carnage that ensued created resentments that lasted until the end of the 20th century and beyond.

Italy: Abyssinian War Atrocities

1922–41

*T*he fascist dictatorship of Benito Mussolini began in 1922 and provided a model for other dictators in Europe, such as Adolf Hitler in Germany, General Franco in Spain and Antonio Salazar in Portugal. Under Mussolini, all democratic liberties were taken away and state control was imposed on all aspects of citizens' lives. Only one party, the National Fascist Party, was permitted, and a secret police conducted constant surveillance on the population to maintain adherence to the regime. There was little opposition to Mussolini's regime within the country as the Italian economy had been decimated since World War I and many feared the rise of communism or the outbreak of civil war. Abroad, the European nations tended to turn a blind eye towards the rise of fascism in Italy because they had only just emerged from a full-scale war and were afraid of provoking another one.

Thus, Mussolini was largely left to indulge his grandiose schemes of Italian world domination without interference from the Allied nations. In October 1935, shortly before World War II took place, Italian forces invaded Ethiopia, then known as Abyssinia. Mussolini had dreams of a modern Italian empire, like the Roman Empire of antiquity, that would rule the countries around the Mediterranean. He was jealous of the large empires held by France and Britain, and believed it was Italy's right to colonize other countries in the same way.

Mussolini chose Abyssinia because it was one of the few African nations that had not been colonized by the Europeans, and it was also rich in natural resources. In addition, he already held colonies near Abyssinia, including Eritrea and Italian Somaliland. Mussolini believed Abyssinia was under-defended, though throughout their history the Abyssinians had fought bravely to maintain their country's independence, including defeating an attack by the Italians in 1896 (the first Italo–Abyssinian War). The rugged terrain of the country made it difficult for invaders to capture the population, who often retreated to the hills in times of conflict.

MUSTARD GAS ATTACKS

Nevertheless, Mussolini began to make plans to invade Abyssinia, and Emperor Haile Selassie gathered together a military force, armed with spears, bows and arrows, and weapons dating from the nineteenth century. When the Italians attacked, the League of

Nations was slow to act and the Abyssinians were left to defend themselves as best they could. Under General Pietro Badoglio, the Italians began to use chemical weapons, such as mustard gas, both in aerial bombs and on the ground. Not only did they target enemy soldiers, they also subjected civilians to mustard gas attacks, and even launched attacks on Red Cross camps and ambulance trucks. In total, around 300 to 500 tonnes of mustard gas was used by the Italians, in contravention of the 1925 Geneva Protocol that outlawed such attacks.

The Italian air force used bombs and grenades to drop the gas on their targets, also spraying entire villages with it. Flame-throwers were also used to ignite whole rural areas. Mussolini himself ordered the attacks as a solution to the problem of reaching enemy hideouts in the hills. The Italian government tried to keep these operations secret, but the International Red Cross and foreign journalists denounced their use of chemical warfare, in particular, the bombing of hospitals and Red Cross headquarters in the country. Mussolini's reaction to this criticism was that the Red Cross zones had been bombed by mistake, but since the bombings had occurred up to 20 times, this seemed unlikely.

MUTILATED BODIES

Not only was Italy's use of chemical weapons condemned, but there was also intense criticism of the way prisoners of war were treated. Mussolini had given orders that all rebels taken alive were to be shot, whether soldiers or civilians, so as to prevent counter-attack. There were stories of Italian soldiers killing and mutilating enemy corpses in the most horrible ways, including throwing individuals out of aircraft as they were flying along. The victors often had their photographs taken next to piles of corpses, or beside public gallows where hanged men and women were strung up. In addition, the Italians set up forced labour camps around the country, not only terrorizing the population but exploiting them as well.

In 1937, there was an assassination attempt on General Rodolfo Graziani, one of the leading generals in the campaign, at a public ceremony in Addis Ababa. In retaliation, the Italian military immediately had the 30 Abyssinians present impaled before launching an attack on the rest of the population, rampaging through the streets of the city killing men, women and children, and setting fire to buildings. The attack ended with the rounding up and mass execution of hundreds of ordinary citizens.

TRIBAL PERSECUTION

Eventually, the Italians won the war in Abyssinia, and annexed the country, proclaiming the Italian king, Victor Emmanuel III, the new emperor. They went on to merge the country with Eritrea and Somaliland, forming a single new colony, Italian East Africa. The new colony was short-lived, and was broken up at the end of World War II, but the colonization created rivalries and conflicts among the tribes there that were to last for the rest of the twentieth century.

After the defeat, the exiled emperor, Haile Selassie, gave an impressive speech on 30 June, 1936, to the League of Nations, chastising them for having done nothing to aid his country in its time of need and warning, 'It will be you tomorrow'. His speech turned out to be prophetic, as Adolf Hitler began to build National Socialism in Germany, ready to launch the evil of Nazi fascism on Europe.

Mussolini's fascist regime in Ethiopia, as Abyssinia later became known, was nowhere near as brutal as that of the German Nazis under Adolf Hitler, but nevertheless the population suffered under the Italians. In particular, the Amhara people living in the central highlands, who had remained loyal to Haile Selassie, were persecuted by the Italians. There were strict laws against miscegenation – that is, intermarrying between different races – and all activities were strictly con-trolled by the colonizers. However, the Italians did make some improvements, including building a network of roads through the mountainous terrain, which had never been done before.

During the years of occupation, there were numerous resistance attempts, including a revolt in 1938 at Gojjam, led by some of the educated elite of the nation. Exiled in Britain, Emperor Haile Sellasie tried to gain support among the Allied powers for an invasion of the country, but met with little enthusiasm. However, once Italy joined forces with Germany in June 1940, the position changed, and a campaign was launched to eject the Italians from the region, master-minded by Haile Selassie, who moved his operation to Khartoum to liaise between resistance forces in the country and British troops outside it. In 1941, after the East African Campaign in which hundreds of soldiers from Ghana, Nigeria, South Africa and India took part, Ethiopia was finally liberated from the Italians and Emperor Haile Selassie resumed control.

WAR CRIMINALS

After the war, the brutality of the Italian invasion of Ethiopia became known, and there were calls for those involved to stand trial as war criminals. Over 1,000 individuals were reported to the authorities for various crimes, including ordering and committing brutal atrocities. However, no leading Italian figures were ever tried for their crimes in Africa and elsewhere, and to this day, the crimes against humanity committed during World War II by the Italians have gone un-punished. This is despite the fact that, during the Italian invasion of Ethiopia, approximately 275,000 inhabitants of the country are thought to have been killed, over 15,000 of them by bombing. Ethiopian estimates put the death toll during the war at over 600,000. Yet, as one commentator put it, 'There was no Nuremberg for Italian war criminals.'

In a symbolic gesture, one of the national treasures of Ethiopia, the Obelisk of Axum, was recently returned to its rightful place. This 23.7 m (78 ft) granite monument, thought to be 1,700 years old, was looted by the Italians during the war and erected in Rome. Under pressure from the Ethiopian government and the world community, the Italy finally gave in to demands to return the obelisk, and in 2005 it was transported back to Ethiopia.

Italy: Massacres and Atrocities of the Axis Powers

1939–45

*D*uring World War II, many massacres and atrocities were committed against ordinary citizens by soldiers, both Allied and Axis troops, in the course of the conflict. There were also atrocities committed by communist partisan troops under the command of Marshall Tito. In the case of the Allied and Partisan troops, the crimes committed were never brought to trial, since these forces were on the winning side. In most of the countries of Europe, details of the massacres and atrocities were not widely known until after the war.

THE THUNDERBIRD MASSACRES

In Italy there were many cases where the full horror of events that had taken place was not revealed until many years later. In Sicily, for example, American

255

troops massacred many German prisoners of war in 1943. Units of the American 45th Division, known as 'Thunderbird', gunned down a group of German prisoners walking across the tarmac at Comise Airfield to board an aeroplane. On the same day, the division also gunned down 60 Italian prisoners of war. Instances of guards killing their charges were common. For example, at Buttera airfield, a US Captain machine-gunned his group of 43 prisoners to death, after lining them up against a wall. At a site near Gela, a Sergeant dispatched his 36 prisoners in the same way. The two soldiers, Captain Jerry Compton and Sergeant Barry West, were both arrested and convicted of the crimes, but they did not receive the death penalty. Instead, both were killed in action during the war. In their defence, the soldiers claimed that they were following the orders of General Paton, who had said: 'When we meet the enemy we will kill him. We will show him no mercy. He has killed thousands of your comrades and he must die.'

Soldiers of the 45th Division went on to augment their reputation for brutality when they liberated the concentration camp at Dachau, killing more Germans prisoners of war. Interestingly, during the conflict, the 45th Division was forced to abandon their insignia, which was a red square with a native American symbol for good luck picked out in yellow. This symbol became the swastika, adopted by the Nazis.

GANG RAPES AT MONTE CASSINO

The Allied invasion of Italy was intended to liberate the country's people from the yoke of fascist oppression, but instead many ordinary people met their deaths or were brutally raped and tortured in revenge atrocities that took place both in rural and urban areas. At Monte Cassino, the site of a sixth century Benedictine monastery, one such atrocity occurred when Allied troops, consisting mainly of North African soldiers, ran amok in the nearby villages, raping over 2,000 women there. No one was spared: girls as young as 11 and elderly women aged over 80 met with the same brutal treatment. In some cases, young girls were raped repeatedly by dozens of men. Villagers who tried to protect the women were attacked and many of them murdered: in total, about 800 men died. Not only this, but the villages were looted and razed to the ground.

In 1945, these same North African troops went on to commit similar crimes in Freudenstadt in the Black Forest region of Germany, where around 500 women were raped. In Stuttgart, they rounded up approximately 2,000 women and forced them into the underground, where they were repeatedly raped.

MASS MURDER

At Bretto, Partisan troops under the command of the

Yugoslav communists captured the power station, which was being guarded by a group of Italian soldiers. The partisans ransacked the barracks where the soldiers were sleeping, rounding them up and forcing them to eat food contaminated with caustic soda and black salt. Realizing they were poisoned, the Italian soldiers begged for mercy, but were frogmarched up to an alpine retreat in the nearby mountains, where they were stripped and beaten. Many of them were attacked with pick axes in a senseless frenzy of bloodlust, their eyes being gouged out and their genitals cut off and stuck into their mouths. The Partisan troops were never prosecuted for the incident.

Elsewhere, Tito's troops committed massacres of thousands of men, women and children, throwing their bodies into the 'foibe', deep valleys and crevasses in the mountains. The victims, all of whom were ordinary Italian civilians, were first forced to stand on the edge of the chasms, tied together with lengths of chains. The first few were machine-gunned to death, dragging the others with them as they fell into the chasms below.

The truth about these horrible crimes was suppressed for many years, mainly because some of the Partisans were Italian communists. However, in recent years there has been more honesty about what happened, and today, on Remembrance Day in Italy, the civilians massacred in the 'foibes' are honoured.

Poland

1939–45

*D*uring World War II, Poland was occupied by the Nazis and became the locus of some of the worst excesses of the regime. Initially, there was extreme persecution of the Jewish population, who were hounded into ghettoes, where many of them died from disease or starvation. Later, a huge number of Poles, both Jews and non-Jews, were sent to concentration camps, including Auschwitz, where they were tortured and murdered. (This was so widespread that virtually every family had a member who met their end in this way.) Yet others died from hard work, ill treatment and appalling living conditions. In total, around six million civilian Poles died during the war, about half of them Jews, while others struggled to survive in a nightmare situation. By the end of the war, the death count for the Poles was higher than any other nation in Europe.

Today, it is often said that, of all the nations of Europe – including Germany – it was Poland who really lost the war, in terms of having its land and its people completely decimated by the conflict. Despite contributing enormously to the defeat of the Nazis, Poland was eventually forced to give up 20 per cent of her territory under the Yalta agreement, causing many minority ethnic groups in these areas to become refugees. Not only that, but after the defeat of the Nazis at the end of the war, Poland was colonized by the Soviets, whose brutal communist regime continued until the 1990s, leaving the country ravaged by poverty and unemployment.

MASS EXECUTIONS

The German invasion began on 1 September, 1939, when over one million Nazi troops bombarded their way into the country, using 'Blitzkrieg' tactics of bombing defenceless civilians in cities, towns and villages. Although the Nazi arsenal was much more powerful than that of the Poles, the Polish army fought bravely to protect the country and inflicted a great deal of damage on the German troops. They also held off the enemy for much longer than any of the Allies had expected. However, on 17 September, when Soviet forces invaded from the East, the capital of Warsaw was forced to surrender, and shortly afterwards, the rest of the country followed suit. Many were forced to flee, and a government in exile was set up.

The victors, under the Nazi-Soviet pact, set about carving up the country between them. In the eastern Soviet zone, one-and-a-half million Poles, including women and children, were taken to labour camps in

Siberia and other parts of the Soviet Union. Former Polish officers were executed by firing squads in forests around the country. In the German zone, the Nazis announced their intention to destroy the Polish race, along with the Jews, and began by dismantling the cultural structure of the country. Universities were closed down and Polish intellectuals were sent to concentration camps around Poland. One of the worst of these was at Oswiencim, renamed Auschwitz.

THE FINAL SOLUTION

Next, Polish Jews were rounded up and forced to live in ghettoes in the major cities, where they were deprived of basic commodities, such as proper food, clean water and decent shelter, and were forced to live in filthy conditions on the streets. Many were taken to concentration camps, such as those at Auschwitz and Treblinka, where they were gassed to death, along with non-Jewish Poles, gypsies, disabled people and others. In total, about four million Poles were exterminated at Auschwitz alone.

As the war progressed, 2,000 concentration camps were set up in Poland, mainly to service the program of extermination of the Jewish and Polish people. For most of the Polish population, the war years became a struggle for survival, whether inside or outside the camps. As well as being sent to the camps, Poles were transported to Germany to be used as slave labour. In addition, there were frequent revenge killings of ordinary civilians in both urban and rural areas, where citizens were rounded up and shot in reprisal for anti-German resistance activity. In hundreds of cases, whole villages were destroyed, along with their inhabitants.

However, despite this intimidation, the majority of Poles flatly refused to collaborate, unlike other countries, such as France, and continued to resist their invaders with an active underground force of around 400,000 individuals, who sabotaged the German regime at ever opportunity. Yet there were instances in which non-Jewish Poles participated in massacres of the Jewish people, such as that at Jedwabne, where over 1,000 Jews were tortured and beaten to death by the people of the town. The extent of Polish participation in such massacres, which occurred at towns all over the country, remains a controversial subject to this day, but it is clear that, of all the countries in Europe, Poland suffered the worst devastation of all, both at the hands of the Nazis and the Communists.

Warsaw Ghetto

1940–45

*T*he Warsaw Ghetto was established in 1940 as part of the Nazis' programme of persecution against the Jews. Walled off from the rest of the city, it became the largest Jewish ghetto in Europe: as well as citizens from Warsaw itself, Jews from towns and villages all over Poland were brought in to live there. Food for the inhabitants of the ghetto was strictly rationed and was well below the levels that other Polish people received during the war and many people starved to death. In addition, medical and other social services were entirely lacking in the ghetto, and thus disease was rife.

In 1942, the Nazis decided to exterminate all Jews in Europe under the notorious 'final solution' program, and thus began the wholesale transportation of the ghetto inhabitants to concentration camps around Poland and elsewhere. The following year, the Jewish population staged a major revolt against this, known as the Warsaw Ghetto Uprising. However, after a brave attempt to hold off the Nazi war machine, the resistance fighters were crushed.

By the end of the war, the Jewish population of the Warsaw ghetto had been reduced from a total of about 450,000 to a mere 37,000. The herding of Polish Jews into the Warsaw Ghetto, and their miserable conditions of existence there before being sent to extermination camps across Europe, is one of the greatest war crimes of the twentieth century and remains a reminder of the terrible consequences of intolerance in our modern age.

BRICK WALLS AND BARBED WIRE

In 1939, Reinhard Heydrich, known as 'the Butcher of Prague', ordered the SS to begin the rounding up of Jews in Poland, commanding that Jewish people be confined to special areas in the towns and cities. These areas were to be patrolled by armed guards and cut off from the rest of the towns by brick walls and barbed wire. Prior to sending them to these newly created ghettoes, Jews had their property confiscated and in many cases were barred from employment.

The Nazis then began to deport Jews living in other parts of Europe, particularly Czechoslovakia and Austria, to the Polish ghettoes. By now, large ghettoes had been set up at Lodz and Warsaw. Herded into locked passenger trains without basic facilities, such as food and water, many Jews died on the journey to Poland. Once they got there, they realized that no proper accommodation had been made available to them, and many were forced to live in shelters on the street.

In the Warsaw Ghetto, the Nazis allowed a Jewish council, or Judenrat, to preside over the organization of the area. The Judenrat did their best to provide a police force in the ghetto to keep order, and it joined forces with youth movements to provide basic amenities for the refugees. They organized soup kitchens, feeding almost two-thirds of the ghetto population, and allocated housing: on average, families were forced to live in homes with seven people per room. The Judenrat also provided education for children and young people, sometimes in secret, and ran orphanages and hospital services. In addition, they established a lively cultural scene, with a ghetto newspaper printed in three languages, and a program of cultural events, using the talents of many Jewish artists who had been herded into the ghetto along with everyone else.

THE EXTERMINATION CAMPS

However, the Judenrat was also forced to negotiate with the Nazis, and it was involved in providing labour 'battalions' for the oppressors. And, despite their brave attempts to feed, clothe and house their people, conditions in the ghetto were so bad that between 1940 and 1942 around a 100,000 inhabitants died of disease and starvation. The situation then deteriorated further as SS chief Heydrich began to put his plans for genocide into action. At the Wannsee Conference on 20 January, the Nazis decided on the 'Final Solution':

to exterminate all European Jews as quickly as possible by gassing them to death in extermination camps.

With horrifying speed and enthusiasm, the Nazis began to build new extermination camps that had the capacity to kill thousands in a day. These camps, which included Majdanek, Belzec, Treblinka and Sobibor, were intended to dispense with between 15,000 and 25,000 people per day. In a sickening display of obsequiousness, in January 1943, Gestapo leader Heinrich Himmler gave orders for the Warsaw ghetto to be 'Jew free' as a present to Hitler on his birthday at the end of April. Accordingly, over 300,000 Jews were deported from the ghetto to these new extermination camps, never to be seen again.

OPEN REVOLT

It was not long before the Jewish ghetto citizens realized what was going on and decided to stage a revolt. There was little hope of them winning the fight against Nazi military might, of course, but with the prospect of certain death at the extermination camps before them, there was no other alternative. Thus, the various resistance groups – including The Jewish Fighter Organization, the Jewish Military Union and the Polish Home Army – combined forces to make their stand against the Nazis.

The Waffen SS, the Nazi army, arrived in the Warsaw Ghetto on 19 April, 1943. As they entered, the

Jews opened fire with machine guns, petrol bombs, grenades, rifles, and pistols. The heavily armed Nazi soldiers were caught off their guard, and took many casualties, so much so that they were forced to retreat. However, their leader, Jurgen Stroop, ordered all the buildings in the ghetto to be set on fire. As the inhabitants ran from the flames, they were captured and sent in large numbers to the Treblinka camp. Storm troopers then closed in on those hiding in the ruined houses, using poison gas to kill them. By the end of the fighting, only about 100 ghetto inhabitants were left: these people had managed to escape from the gas by going into underground sewers.

After the uprising, the Final Solution programme intensified as the Nazis tried to complete their programme of genocide before the end of the war. By 1944, a new threat had emerged: from the Soviet Red Army, who were now threatening to colonize Poland rather than hand it over to the government in exile once the Nazis had been defeated. As the Red Army advanced, members of the Polish resistance movements captured parts of Warsaw, but the Nazi military responded with a massive attack on the city, forcing the resistance fighters to take to the sewers once more. Heinrich Himmler gave orders that that all inhabitants of the city should be killed as an example to the rest of occupied Europe and accordingly, after heavy aerial bombing, thousands of ordinary citizens were taken out and shot by firing squads. By the time the Red

Army arrived, 70 per cent of the city had been destroyed and hundreds of thousands of its citizens killed by the Germans, thus making it easy for the Soviets to take control.

AFTERMATH

In recent years, more information has come to light about the way of life in the Warsaw Ghetto during the nightmare years of World War II. Historian, politician, and social worker Emanuel Ringelblum, who lived in the Warsaw Ghetto during the war, organized a secret society there called Oyneg Shabbos, which translates from Yiddish as 'Sabbath Pleasure'. This was a group of writers, scientists and others who made a collection of diaries, documents, posters, reports and descriptions of what was going on at the time, both in the ghetto and in the extermination camps at Treblinka and Chelmno. In 1943, just before the destruction of the ghetto, Ringelblum hid the archive in some milk cans and metal boxes. He and his family were then smuggled out of the ghetto and hidden by a Polish family in the city. However, the following year, he and his family were discovered and executed, along with the Polish family who had looked after them. After the war, parts of the archive was discovered in the ruins of the city. This contained newspapers, information regarding deportations and public notices from the Judenrat, as well as souvenirs of everyday life, such as concert invitations, chocolate wrappers and milk coupons, giving a fascinating picture of how people survived and pulled together in the darkest days of anti-Semitic persecution at the hands of the Nazis.

As the war drew to a close, it became clear that Poland's ordeal was far from over. Stalin wanted to maintain Soviet control in Poland, but was opposed by Churchill and the British government, who insisted that Poland should be a free and sovereign state. As Churchill pointed out, Britain had entered the war over the issue of Poland's sovereignty, when Hitler had invaded the country. However, Stalin would not compromise, although he did promise to hold elections there. Thus, having endured the regime of Nazi Germany, the Poles were now under the thumb of a new oppressor: the Soviet Communists.

At the Nuremberg Trials, which began in 1945, a number of leading Nazi officials were tried and hanged for their part in the invasion of Poland, the genocide of the Jews and the killing of Polish citizens in Warsaw. These included Joachim von Ribbentrop, Wilhelm Keitel, and Hans Frank, known as the 'Jew Butcher of Cracow'.

Greece

———1940–44———

*G*reece was occupied by Germany during World War II, despite the brave resistance of its people to the Nazi invasion. On 28 October, 1940, Mussolini sent a message asking Greek dictator Ioannis Metaxas to allow his troops to enter the country, and to surrender arms to the Axis powers. Legend has it that the Greek government responded with a simple 'No' (*Ochi* in Greek), though some historians dispute this, saying that the Greek government, in fact, sent back a message saying – in French – that it would choose to go to war with the Axis powers rather than surrender. Whatever the case, 'Ochi Day' has been celebrated in Greece ever since, as the moment when the Greek nation said no to fascism and stood up for its independence as a sovereign state.

As a result of the Greeks' refusal to capitulate, Italian troops stationed in Albania attacked the mainland, and after a period of bitter fighting, the Germans invaded and occupied Greece. However, during the period of occupation, Greek resistance fighters constantly sabotaged the regime, particularly on the island of Crete, causing direct disruption to the Axis powers' military campaign in Russia, as well as other campaigns.

REVENGE MASSACRES

However, the Axis powers responded to these acts of resistance with terrible reprisals, in the form of massacres and atrocities perpetrated on the civilian people of Greece. One of the worst massacres of the entire war took place on the island of Cefalonia in September 1943. An Italian division of more than 12,000 men and officers, known as 'Acqui' and commanded by General Antonio Gandin, were stationed on the island. Earlier that month, the Italian troops had been told to end hostilities against the Allies, since the alliance between Germany and Italy was beginning to break down. On Cefalonia, the Italian troops were jubilant and they celebrated the news by singing, dancing and drinking, overjoyed to think that Italy's support of the Nazi regime was coming to an end and that defeat for the Nazis seemed to be in sight at last.

German troops stationed on the mainland of Greece were, however, bitterly disappointed at the news, as well they might be. Their resentment and anger reached a crescendo when they heard of the merriment on Cefalonia, and they decided to attack the Italian troops. German aircraft began to bomb the island, and a German battalion commanded by Major Harald von Hirschfeld travelled to the island to attack the Italians. The German troops immediately began fighting, and soon shot General Gandin, along with groups of other Italian prisoners. According to witness accounts, the Nazis took out Italian prisoners in groups of four to ten people, and shot them together. Unbelievably, they shot over 4,000 Italian soldiers in this way, leaving their dead bodies all over the island. Another 4,000 soldiers were taken by ship to the mainland and then transported to labour camps in Germany. Sadly, some of the ships travelling through the Ionian sea on their way there were hit by mines, and many of these soldiers died on the way.

In total, about 10,000 Italian soldiers died as a result of fighting between the Germans and Italians in Greece. Afterwards, the case came to the courts at the Nuremberg War Trials, but by this time von Hirschfeld was dead, killed by a bomb in Warsaw in 1945. However, another general involved, Hubert Lanz, who had commanded some of the troops, was charged with the massacres. He gained a sentence of 12 years' imprisonment, and was later released. The case was re-opened in 2002, and a further ten ex-Nazi officers (now in their eighties and nineties) were investigated to determine their part in the killings.

In order to honour those who had died in this tragic episode, the remains of more than 3,000 soldiers were dug up in the 1950s and taken back to Italy to receive a proper burial. Today, their graves remain in the war cemetery at Bari.

WEDDING PARTY MASSACRE

Another hideous massacre took place at the village of Kommeno in Northern Greece on 16 August, 1943, when a wedding party was taking place. Thedoros Mallios gave a wedding reception for his son Spyros, which lasted the whole night through. In the early morning, the revellers left the party, only to be gunned down by soldiers from the First Alpenjager Division, known as 'Edelweiss'. The bride, groom and all the guests were shot dead, and the house then razed to the ground. A total of 34 people died in this incident. The soldiers also rampaged around the village, killing over 300 people – almost half the inhabitants of the village, including 74 children aged from one year old to ten years old. Finally, they set fire to the houses and burnt the village to the ground.

On the island of Kos, a terrible massacre of prisoners of war took place on 4 October, 1943. By now, Italian troops were fighting on the British side in the war. However, despite the combined Allied forces, Germany gained the upper hand at Kos, and took over 4,000 soldiers prisoner. Hitler ordered all the Italian soldiers among them to be executed, including the officer commanding the Italian troops, Colonel Felice Leggio. The Italian prisoners were taken to a deserted area just outside the town, where they were shot in groups of ten. Afterwards, the victims were buried in a mass grave. In all, 102 men perished in this way. Once the war was over, the Greek authorities had the bodies unearthed and taken back to Italy, where they were buried at the war cemetery in Bari.

SADISTIC KILLINGS

Resistance activity was high in Greece throughout the war, resulting in terrible reprisal atrocities committed by the German troops. On the morning of 13 December, 1945, in the town of Kalavryta in the south of Greece, a German army unit called the 'Kampfgruppe Ebersberger' attacked civilians in revenge for resistance activity around the area. The soldiers rounded up inhabitants and took them prisoner in the local school, before taking the men out to a hillside where they were all shot dead. Over 600 men, forming the whole male population of the town, were murdered in this way. The German soldiers also set the town on fire, killing many more victims and leaving only a few houses standing. The massacre is remembered today with a memorial, listing the names of the men who died at Kalavryta and the surrounding villages on that fateful day.

Another horrifying massacre took place at Distomo in central Greece on 10 June, 1944. In this incident, an SS Police unit known as the Panzergrenadier Regiment Number Seven was attacked by resistance fighters as it drove through the area. Seven SS soldiers were killed in an ambush outside the village, whereupon the SS convoy doubled back and wreaked their revenge on the civilian population there. The soldiers ran amok in the village, raping women, looting the houses and setting fire to the buildings. Their attacks on the local people were savage: in one case, a woman and her baby were mutilated, her breast cut off while the nipple was still in the baby's mouth. All along the main street, bodies were strung up on the trees. All in all, 218 civilians were murdered, some of them in the most horrible ways.

Later, it was found out that the commander of the unit, SS Hauptstrumfuhrer Lautenbach, had falsified a report on the episode, but no action was taken as the massacre was judged a 'military necessity'.

AFTERMATH

After the war, the full extent of the suffering of the Greek people during the German occupation of Greece became clear. It was calculated that around 60,000 men, women and children lost their lives in massacres at the hands of the Nazi troops during the war years. Not only that, but the suffering continued when a bitter civil war erupted in Greece after the war, claiming thousands more victims. Hostilities only ended in 1949, when the communist-led Democratic army were defeated by the Hellenic army.

In 1960, the German government paid the Greek government a total of a 115 million marks as compensation for the war crimes committed during the occupation. In 1990, officials from the German embassy took part in a ceremony commemorating the victims of the massacre at Distomo, but to date no compensation has been made for them in particular.

Today, at the Mausoleum there, the skulls and bones of the victims are displayed for visitors, so that what happened on that fateful day in 1944 can never be forgotten. The history of the Nazi occupation of Greece is a shameful one, and it is important that the massacres and atrocities that took place there – both against the Italian soldiers and the Greek civilians – should be remembered, not only as an indictment of the Nazi regime, but of all forms of intolerance and hatred throughout history.

Russian Ethnic Cleansing and Other Atrocities

1939–49

During the years 1939–49 the Soviets, under the leadership of a powerful and dangerous dictator, Joseph Stalin, caused the suffering and death of millions of ordinary individuals. In fact, Stalin may be responsible for more intentional human slaughter than any other single human being in recorded history. His dream was to have a powerful industrial state which he tried to fulfil with a callous disregard for human life. His victims were either executed or imprisoned in labour camps that turned out to be little better than 'death' camps.

UNTOLD HORROR

By 1928, Stalin had established himself as a supreme leader and he wasted no time in setting in motion a number of campaigns. These campaigns were aimed at firstly the collectivization of agriculture, which cost million of lives, and the cleansing of 'enemies of the people', whereby he sent millions to the famous Gulag system of slave-labour camps.

The infamous Gulag was established in 1934, with its own brand of murderous security police called the Smersh. They were responsible for the execution of thousands of captives during the war of 1941–45, and their system of mass execution, although extremely primitive, was highly effective.

Having purged the country of many people who were not deemed suitable citizens, many of them members of the Red Army Corps, Stalin was ill-prepared for Hitler's massive attack in June 1941. After heavy losses and enforced months of retreat from the Germany army, Stalin and his henchmen began to panic and decided to destroy any records that had been kept from the notorious Lubianka Prison, for fear of the secret leaking out to the rest of the world. Torture tactics in Lubianka were prolonged and vicious. Eyeballs were left hanging from their sockets as the hapless victims were beaten again and again in an effort to obtain a confession. One of the most infamous of Stalin's security police at Lubianka was a man named Lavarenti Beria. He has been labelled as a sadist, rapist, murderer and someone who loved to inflict pain.

As the Germans infiltrated the Soviet Union, many of the Soviet citizens welcomed them, hoping it would put an end to the sadistic reign of Stalin. However, where the Red Army were still in control, people who they considered to be disloyal to the state were eliminated either by shooting or by being deported to the slave camps of Vorkuta and Karaganda, which were all part of the massive Gulag network. Right from the start the conditions in these camps were so bad that prisoners were not expected to survive more than a couple of years. A camp at Kholmogori became known as a 'death camp' because everyone who was sent there feared for their life. It is thought that as many as 30 per cent of new inmates died in their first year from exposure, disease, malnutrition, overwork or from overzealous interrogation methods.

If a prisoner managed to survive the interrogation, the second stage was even more perilous. In fact, transportation of prisoners became as dangerous as the camps themselves. In 1941, 12,000 prisoners being held in cells on board the Soviet steamer *Dzhurma* froze to death when the ship sailed too close to the ice at Wrangle Island. A trainload of Polish deportees, approximately 1,650 in total, perished in the winter of 1940–41, due to the cramped conditions and lack of heating in the cattle cars. Of the estimated two million Polish civilians who were deported to the Russian Arctic regions of Gulag in railway convoys, it is believed that as many as half were dead before the year was out.

People who Stalin considered to be nonessential intelligentsia – i.e. scientists, engineers, doctors and teachers – were rounded up and deported to camps.

In April 1940, as many as 15,000 from three large Soviet detention camps located in Ostashkov, Kozielsk and Starobielsk mysteriously disappeared in the Okchotzk Sea.

The camps continued to eat up millions of supposedly disloyal civilians and the situation became even worse during World War II. In 1943, the Germans uncovered what turned out to be the most notorious of all Stalin's wartime atrocities, in a forest in western Russia.

THE KATYN MASSACRE

In April 1940, approximately 22,000 Polish prisoners were rounded up and transported to Katyn Forest and surrounding areas, where they were executed. The prisoners included army officers, civil servants, landowners, policemen, ordinary soldiers and prison officers. After being made to dig their own graves, they were shot in the back of the neck and buried on the spot. Stalin personally ordered the executions in his effort to eradicate the intellectual elite in the Polish army. His order for the 'cleansing' campaign was sent by memo directly to the head of the NKVD (predecessor of the KGB), Lavarenti Beria.

When the graves were uncovered in 1943 by the occupying Nazi forces, Goebbel felt it was a gift in the making and advertised their discovery to the world. This was not only a major embarrassment to Stalin, but to his wartime allies, Roosevelt and Churchill, too.

At first Roosevelt dismissed the report as 'German propaganda', while Churchill, who was a little less explicit, said, 'The less said about that the better'. Consequently, the whole matter was covered up until 3 March, 1959, when the then head of the KGB, Aleksandr Shelepin, sent full details of the atrocity to Krushchev.

In his memo, he revealed the full extent of what had taken place – a total of 21,857 people had been needlessly and heartlessly executed:

- 4,421 in the Katyn Forest
- 3,820 in the Starobelsk camp
- 6,311 in the Ostashkovo camp
- 7,305 in other camps and prisons in western Ukraine and western Belorussia

All the bodies were dressed in Polish uniforms and wore insignia indicating their rank. It soon became obvious that the officers came from a camp at Kozielsk, which was situated on the grounds of a former monastery, near Orel.

It wasn't until nearly 50 years later, on 13 April, 1990, that the Soviet president, Mikhail Gorbachev admitted his country's involvement in the massacres. Two years later, the Polish president, Lech Walesa, received documentation stating that Stalin had directly ordered the killing of the Polish people. They were businessmen who had been called up for national service following the Nazi invasion of Poland, but instead of fighting for their country they found themselves prisoners of the Red Army. The only survivors of the Katyn massacre were 448 officers, who had been transferred for no apparent reason, to a camp at Pavlishchev Bor.

The Katyn massacre is a prime example of the hypocrisy and conspiracies of international politics in an effort to cover up the enormity of human rights violations carried out during World War II.

BRUTAL MURDER AT BRONIKI

On 1 July, 1941, approximately 180 German soldiers of the 2nd and 6th Infantry Regiments and the 5th Artillery Regiment were taken prisoner by the Red Army in the town of Broniki in the Ukraine. Most of the soldiers were wounded from fighting, but the majority did not die from their injuries but at the hands of the Soviet soldiers. The following day, advancing German troops found the bodies of 153 men in a clover field near Broniki. According to the 12 soldiers who survived the attack, they were taken to a field just off the main road and forced to remove their clothes. Any valuables such as rings, watches and money were stolen along with all their clothes. Standing naked, with their backs towards the soldiers, they were fired on with machine guns and automatic rifles. The survivors managed to escape by running into nearby woods. Similar reports from other regiments brought to light that the Soviets were not taking any prisoners of war due to the bonuses they were being offered. It was alleged that for every 20 German soldiers, a Russian soldier would be granted a three-day pass to return to his family and would also receive a decoration or promotion in rank.

MASSACRE AT GRISCHINO

Grischino was an important industrial region in the Ukraine, which was initially occupied by German forces and then recaptured by a Soviet armoured division in 1943. In an counteroffensive attack in February 1943, the German 7th Armoured Division uncovered evidence of a horrendous massacre. They found the bodies of 406 German soldiers, 58 of whom were members of the Todt Organization, 89 Italian soldiers, 9 Romanian soldiers, 4 Hungarian soldiers and some Ukrainian volunteer workers. All 596 were Axis personnel that had been captured by the Red Army and brutally murdered and horribly mutilated. The female personnel had been bestially mutilated and raped. Their breasts and genitals were cut off and one had died with her legs splayed apart with a broomstick rammed into her vagina. The men had received similar treatment, with their ears and noses cut off, and genital organs removed and stuffed into their mouths. In a cellar room at the main train station, 120 German soldiers had been herded into a large storage room and gunned down.

PRISON MASSACRES

Soon after the Germans attacked the Soviet Union, the Soviets made a hasty retreat, which resulted in tragic consequences for all the political prisoners held in their jails. During the week of 22 to 29 June, 1941, literally thousands of Ukrainian and Polish prisoners were murdered in their cells, as the Soviet officers had no time to take care of them. In their panic to get away, the Soviets set fire to some of the prisons and the helpless inmates were burnt to death. In Lutsk, for example, out of the 4,000 inmates, 2,800 lost their lives. Some of them had been killed by hand grenades thrown into their cells and many more had been executed by a shot in the neck. In the cellars of Brygidki Prison, 423 bodies were recovered, with hundreds more piled up in the courtyard outside. In a military prison in Samarstinov, 460 charred bodies were discovered, many of them showing evidence of torture. The bodies were literally piled up layer upon layer until they nearly reached the ceiling. The stench of decomposing corpses was so nauseating that the German commander who made the grim discovery ordered that the bodies be covered in lime and that all doors to the cellars were to be bricked up. On 26 and 27 June, 520 Ukrainians were shot at Sambor. Another 700, including the entire local intelligentsia, were arrested and shot at Zlochev on 16 July. When bodies were discovered at Kremenets, they had no skin covering their bones, having been thrown into boiling water. It is estimated that as many as 10,000 Ukrainian and Polish prisoners were killed in their prisons by members of the Red Army.

UNIVERSITY OF LVOV

An Einsatzkommando unit killed 45 professors at the University of Lvov when the city was taken by Germans on 30 June, 1941. With the help of the Ukrainian 'Nachtigall' battalion, they started to round up the professors, their families and relatives, while the Jewish inhabitants of the city were shot on sight. Some of the professors, 38 in total, were taken to a place of execution just outside the city and shot to death. Another seven, including the former prime minister of Poland, Professor Dr Bartel, were shot in the courtyard of Brygidki Prison. Ironically, this was exactly the same courtyard where just days before they had discovered the bodies of the murdered prisoners.

VIOLENCE IN VINNITSA

When the Germans took occupation of the town of Vinnitsa in July 1941, they uncovered a mass grave in the prison courtyard. The grave, which was 20 m (65 ft) long by 6 m (19 ft) wide, contained the bodies of 96 Ukrainian political prisoners. Behind the prison, in another courtyard, they discovered a second grave.

It is alleged that the prisoners were executed because the Soviets did not have time to evacuate them prior to the arrival of the German troops. Many other graves were uncovered in the area, but the true extent of the atrocity was never uncovered because the Red Army reoccupied the area a short while later. By the time the city was taken by the Red Army, a total of 9,439 bodies had already been discovered, all with bullet wounds to the neck. Ukrainian witnesses testified that trucks kept coming day and night carrying dead bodies to the burial grounds. It would appear that most of the victims were either farmers or field workers (*kulaks*), who Stalin classed as 'enemies of the people'.

PINSK MASSACRE

At the beginning of German occupation in July 1941, Pinsk was occupied by approximately 26,000 Jews. Before World War II the Jews lived peacefully side by side with the Soviet people, but under the so-called 'cleansing' programmes, it wasn't long before they became the persecuted race. Helped by their Polish accomplices, members of the SS murder squads started to round up between 7,000 and 8,000 male Jews in the area. All of them were executed. The remaining 18,287, including 6,400 women and children, were held in a newly established ghetto and forced to work for the occupying forces.

The ghetto covered an area of 23 streets, with 240

houses, with as many as ten people per room. The whole area was surrounded by a barbed-wire fence and it was here they lived in appalling conditions under the watchful eye of the military. On 27 October, 1942, all the occupants of the ghetto were ordered to gather near the Jewish cemetery at Karlin, which was about 4 km (2H miles) outside of the town. Each person was deprived of their money and valuables before being led to their site of execution. Left behind at the ghetto were around 1,200 people who were not well enough to make the journey. None of them survived – they were simply shot. In the three days of killing, as many as 11,000 Jews were murdered.

When Pinsk was liberated by the Red Army, they only found 17 half-starved Jews who had managed to hide for over 620 days and nights. Unfortunately, the majority of the Gentile population of Pinsk did little to help their Jewish neighbours. Instead, they waited for the opportunity to steal their possessions and move into their houses, and today, only about 500 Jews are left living in Pinsk.

UKRAINE

Ukraine had already suffered untold hardships before World War II, when Stalin engineered a famine in 1933 to destroy the *kulaks* and crush Ukraine's growing spirit of nationalism. All roads in and out of the Ukraine were blocked, which meant that the farmers were deprived of seed stocks, grain and animals, and it wasn't long before the farmers started dying of cold, hunger and disease. In an attempt to stay alive, they resorted to eating their pets, their boots, in fact anything they could get their hands on. It is estimated that as many as seven million, one-quarter of Ukraine's population, starved to death.

As if this wasn't bad enough, after the German invasion, the Ukraines were to suffer even more. Stalin put into action his 'scorched earth' policy, which called for the wholesale evacuation of industries, factories, machinery, skilled workers and livestock. From the capital city of Kiev, alone, some 197 major industrial plants were evacuated east to Russia in a period of two months. Anything that could not be physically moved was destroyed and burnt.

Two years later, when Hitler's army started its retreat from the Ukraine, orders were given to loot and take back to Germany any works of art, rare books, engravings, libraries, sculptures and museum collections, adding up to hundreds of thousands valuable items. The Ukraine was stripped of all its cultural wealth, and 151 museums, 62 theatres, 19,200 libraries and 600 cinemas were destroyed by the retreating Germans. In addition, approximately 28,000 villages and 714 towns were razed to the ground leaving over ten million people without any form of shelter. Whatever the Soviets failed to destroy in their retreat was destroyed by the Germans when they finally left the Ukraine.

ABOVE: *From 1895 to 1915 about 1.5 million Armenians were massacred by the Turks, but despite their bloodthirsty methods, the main perpetrators, Talat and Enver Pasha, failed in their efforts to eradicate the Armenian race. Turkey still denies to this day that the genocide took place, but it is hard to forget that the world closed its eyes while the lives of innocent people were being shattered.*

ABOVE: *The newspaper article that carried this picture was headed:* A Crime that has Staggered Humanity: The Torpedoing of the Lusitania. *Despite being dubbed the 'Greyhound of the Seas', the* Lusitania *could not outmanoeuvre the U-boat of Walter Schwieger, and in May 1915 she was struck by torpedoes. Unbeknown to her passengers, the* Lusitania *was carrying munitions for the war, and mounts, concealed under the teak deck, were ready for the addition of the guns when needed.*

BELOW: *This was how Hiroshima looked following the first dropping of the atomic bomb by the USA on 6 August, 1945. The dropping of two nuclear weapons on the city of Hiroshima, followed three days later by another over Nagasaki, Japan, has gone down in history as the greatest man-made disaster in the world.*

ABOVE: *Nazi political and military leader Hermann Goering, founder of the Gestapo, on trial at Nuremberg, Germany, in 1946. He is seated in the witness box, with a young officer standing to his side. Goering was condemned to death for his part in the atrocities committed by the Nazis during World War II, but he committed suicide before his scheduled execution.*

BELOW: *Almost immediately after his rise to powr, Adolf Hitler began the creation of his famous concentration camps. Conditions were horrendous, treatment of the prisoners was appalling, and death rates were high. This shows an inmate, in a pitiful condition, breaking into tears when he learns that he will not be leaving with the first group following the US liberation.*

ABOVE: *The Warsaw Ghetto in Poland was the largest of the Jewish ghettos established by Nazi Germany during the Holocaust in World War II. In the three years of its existence, starvation, disease and deportations to concentration camps and extermination camps dropped the population of the ghetto from an estimated 450,000 to 37,000 people. Here families are being forced out of their homes by German officers.*

The Guantanamo Bay Detention Centre became an international matter of controversy. Images released of blindfolded prisoners kneeling, shackled by wire cages, raised fears that the USA was mistreating suspected Taleban and al-Qaeda prisoners. This picture shows a detainee being held in one of the cages in Camp X-Ray in February 2002.

ABOVE: *A Congolese woman mourns the charred remains of a member of her family on the outskirts of the Gety camp for displaced people in July 2006. Both militia and members of the Congolese army have been accused of vast atrocities against civilians in eastern Congo.*

By the end of the war, the Ukraine lay in ruins. The population had been decreased by 25 per cent. It is believed that as many as 6.8 million died of hunger or disease, while the remainder either evacuated or were deported as political prisoners and ended up as slave workers in Hitler's Germany.

UNTOLD MASSACRES IN UKRAINE

The treatment of the Ukraine civilian population during World War II was ruthless, something that the rest of the world was never really aware of. On 23 September, 1942, SS execution squads aided by local pro-German Ukrainian police, burnt to the ground the village of Kortelisy, killing all of its 2,892 population of men, women and children. In fact, all over the Ukraine a total of 459 villages were completely destroyed, with all or a portion of their population executed by the German army. The Nazis set up around 160 concentration camps in the Ukraine to hold the tens of thousands of prisoners, while others were sent to Auschwitz and other so-called death camps in Poland.

ILJA ATROCITY

Ilja was a small town in western Russia, where a number of Jews were sent to work on a small farm. They managed to escape into the nearby forest and joined up with a group of partisans who had set up their headquarters there. The following day, two prominent Jews also fled into the forest to join the group of partisans, and the revenge was appalling. All the old or sick Jews living in Ilja were rounded up and shot in the streets or in their own homes. A further 900 were locked inside a building, which was then torched, causing all those inside to be burnt alive.

MASSACRE AT DUBNO

Another horrifying massacre of the Jewish people took place in the western Ukraine town of Dubno. The SS and Ukrainian troops had dug deep pits near the town's airstrip, each one measuring approximately 30 m (98 ft) long and 3 m (10 ft) deep. Over the next few days the troops rounded up all the Jewish men, women and children, took them to the execution site and shot them to death. It is estimated that as many as 1,500 people were killed each day, until over 5,000 helpless civilians had been massacred. The bodies in the pits were piled up, row upon row, and then only crudely covered with earth.

The massacres were witnessed by an officer in the elite 9th Infantry Regiment, Capt Axel von dem Bussche, who was so nauseated by what he had seen that he offered to assassinate Hitler personally. In February 1944, dem Bussche agreed to blow up Hitler and himself while he demonstrated a new army winter uniform to the Führer. However, fate intervened that day when a British air raid destroyed the uniforms, forcing the assassination attempt to be cancelled.

MASSACRES IN VOLHYNIA

Volhynia was an area in north-west Ukraine, where a number of local Ukrainian nationalists formed themselves into a resistance army, the Ukrainian Uprising Army (UPA). Their primary aim was to fight the Nazi occupiers, but unfortunately their anger was diverted towards the local Polish minority, some 346,000 people. In an effort to drive all the Poles out of the Ukraine, with the aim of creating an independent Ukrainian state after the war, the UPA started their own programme of ethnic cleansing. They went from village to village, killing anyone of Polish nationality and leaving behind them a trail of death and destruction. These massacres continued for more than a year in all the rural areas, until either all the Polish residents had been killed or were forced to leave their homes.

The German occupation forces simply turned a blind eye to the atrocities and, although the exact figure has never really been assessed, it is believed to be as high 60,000. Today there are more than 600 mass graves in the Volhynia area, containing the bodies of the murdered Polish civilians.

KOVNO MASSACRE

Lithuanian mercenaries, with the help of the German police, put to death 136,421 Jews in 1941. Of these, 55,556 were women and 34,464 were children, all shot to death in a deep pit just outside Kovno. The Jews were marched in groups of about 200 to their place of execution, stripped of all their clothes despite the freezing conditions and told to stand on the edge of the pits to await their fate. One by one, they were gunned to death. To cover up what they had done, the mercenaries forced 72 men and women from the ghettos to dig up the bodies and set fire to them. The prisoners were all chained together to prevent them from running away, and at the end of their ordeal they were killed and their ghetto completely destroyed.

Kovno was not an isolated incident, and there are records of Jews being eradicated throughout Lithuania. Prior to the Germans invading, around 240,000 Jews lived in Lithuania, but it is estimated that only 6,000 or 7,000 survived the holocaust.

ATROCITY AT FEODOSIA

The port of Feodosia stands on the shores of the Black Sea, and in December 1941 it was occupied by German forces. To prepare for the attack on Sevastopol, the majority of the soldiers had left Feodosia, leaving behind a small detachment of troops and wounded soldiers, who were convalescing in the city's hospitals. On 29 December, the city was bombarded by the Soviet Black Sea Fleet, which managed to land and take occupation of the port.

On 18 January, 1942, the Germans returned and retook Feodosia, only to find that the majority of the German personnel had been brutally murdered. Wounded German soldiers had literally been thrown out of hospital windows to make room for Russian casualties. Buckets of water had been thrown over the bodies and they were left to freeze to death. Many other badly mutilated bodies were found on the beach, having been thrown from a wall. Their bodies were floating in the surf covered by thin sheets of ice. There were only 12 survivors, who had hidden in cellars when the Russian troops arrived, and they managed to tell the tale of what had taken place.

CHILDREN DIE IN CHARTSYSK

Retreating Soviet soldiers passed a small ravine between the the Chartsysk and Snizhy stations about 60 km (37 miles) from the city of Stalino. Although they were used to the sight of death, what they saw that day made them sick to their stomachs. They found the the bodies of 370 slain children, aged between 14 and 16 years, in the ravine. They were all dressed in the black uniform of the FSU Trade and Craft School in Stalino. It was later discovered that the children were being evacuated from the school ahead of the advancing German troops. After walking the 60 km (37 miles), they had become exhausted and hungry and had begged for transport to take them the rest of the way. Their guardians told them to sit down and promised to send trucks. However, instead of the transport they expected, a detachment of Russian political police from the NKVD arrived, carrying machine guns. Far from helping the desperate children, they simply killed them in cold blood and threw their bodies into the ravine.

SLAUGHTER AT BABI YAR

Huge explosions rocked the city of Kiev following the German takeover in September 1941. A number of buildings that housed the German administration and army were destroyed, and in retaliation, the military governor, Major General Friedrich George Eberhardt, decided to condemn to death all Jews living in the city. On 29 September, every single Jew living in Kiev was marched to a picturesque ravine, Babi Yar, situated in the Syret suburb, and the systematic slaughter of 33,771 civilians began. The killings took two days and two nights, and the naked bodies being thrown into the ravine. Only a thin layer of sand was used to cover the corpses, before the next lot of hapless victims were brought in.

In the months that followed, the Einsatzgruppen

shot a further 160,000 Jews, 20,000 gypsies and Soviet prisoners of war at Babi Yar. It has been alleged that because the executioners were running out of time, they made two people stand side by side with their heads together so that one bullet would kill two people. Others were hit with shovels, and it is believed that many, including children, were buried alive.

By the middle of 1943, the Germans started to retreat and thought it best to try and destroy the evidence of their mass killings. Jews from the nearby Syretsk concentration camp were brought to Babi Yar to do their dirty work for them. They were made to dig up all the bodies, while the SS flirted with the local women, and then all the bodies were burnt in enormous funeral pyres on gravestones removed from the local cemetery. As more and more bodies were exhumed, evidence showed that many had died a slow and painful death, some desperately holding each other while others held their hands in prayer.

After the bodies had been dragged from the ravine, they were lined up between stacks of logs on top of the gravestones, in effect forming enormous ovens. They were placed with their heads facing outwards and then liberally doused with petrol. With their hair and bodies thoroughly soaked, as soon as a torch was lit they immediately burst into flame. It is estimated that as many as 5,000 bodies a day were burnt in this way. As the fire did not burn some of the larger pieces of bone, the Nazis arranged for them to be crushed into a fine powder, so that nothing was left to incriminate them. No one was ever brought to trial for this atrocity.

COUNTLESS ATROCITIES

The amount of atrocities that took place in the Soviet Union during World War II are too numerous to list, but it is fair to say that, second only to the 'cleansing' of the Jewish population, the massacre of Russian prisoners of war must rank as one of the greatest atrocities. During the first seven months of the war, it is estimated that over four million Soviet soldiers were captured, but by the end of February 1942, just over one million remained alive. Many died from the severe weather conditions they had to face when they were forced to march in the open day and night. They fell by the roadside in their thousands. When they did eventually reach the prisoner of war enclosures, sometimes as far away as 400 km (250 miles), they simply collapsed and died before they could even have their first meal. Held in inhumane cages, the prisoners often resorted to cannibalism after they had eaten everything else available to them, even down to the last blade of grass. For example, a dead dog, which was thrown over the wire fence, was quickly pounced upon by the prisoners and torn to pieces with their bare hands in their desperation to eat.

Thousands more died from torture or as slave labourers, who were forced to work in quarries and factories. Out of 9,000 prisoners sent to the Buchen-wald concentration camp, only 800 were alive when US troops set them free in 1945. In the famous Dachau camp, only 150 survived out of a total of 10,000 prisoners of war who arrived there in 1941. It is estimated that, by the year 1944, over three million Russian prisoners of war died in this way.

The camps continued to be used after the war, still full of German, Polish, Hungarian, Rumanian, Bulgarian prisoners of war and refugees. After Stalin's death in 1953, his successors slowly started to reform the camps. Many of the prisoners were released as the worst of the camps were shut down. Others were renovated to improve their conditions, and by the mid-1980s the population of these camps was down to about four million.

With the collapse of the Soviet Union and the fall of communism in 1991, many articles have been published about the atrocities and war crimes that took place during World War II. The estimated death toll of these atrocities is believed to be over 39.4 million, but if all the evidence came to light it is fair to say that this figure is probably grossly underestimated.

Japanese War Crimes and Atrocities

—————1937–45—————

Japanese military aggression in East Asia and the Pacific region between the years 1937 and 1945 was so bestial and savage that it is hard for most Westerners to comprehend. Among the list of atrocities carried out include slave labour, massacres, executions, medical experiments, germ and gas warfare, beheading, rape, torture, boiling victims alive, impaling on bayonets, burning alive, starvation, neglect – and so the list goes on. As many as 200,000 women were sold as sex slaves, and the years of nightmare did not end until late 1945, when the Allied forces entered the territories held by the Japanese.

Evidence of their brutality, racism and fanaticism can be seen in the mass slaughter of hundreds of thousands Chinese civilians and prisoners of war after the collapse of the Chinese capital Nanking (now called Nanjing) in 1937. It was also witnessed in the brutal death marches in which thousands of allied prisoners were murdered.

Women and children were brutally treated as were other non-combatants during the Pacific War of 1941–45. For example, Australian army nurses who served overseas during World War II had to put up with not only uncomfortable conditions in makeshift field hospitals, but also the risks and horrors of war. Out of 65 nurses who were evacuated from Singapore on board the small ship *Vyner Brooke* in 1942, only 24 survived to return to Australia. The bombing and sinking of the ship by Japanese planes led to the death of 12 nurses. Of the survivors, 21 were slaughtered by Japanese soldiers when they reached Bangka Island in lifeboats, and eight died as prisoners in the Japanese camps of hell. Clearly marked hospital ships and field stations were indiscriminately bombed by the Japanese, killing both patients and medical staff alike. On the Alaskan island of Attu, Japanese troops attacked a US base camp and slaughtered everyone in the field hospital.

On 14 May 1943, an Australian hospital ship, *Centaur*, was struck by a Japanese torpedo off the east coast of Australia. The ship was clearly marked with large red crosses prominently displayed on each side of its white funnel. As a hospital ship, it should have been protected under the Geneva convention, and the attack was classed as Japanese barbarity. The ship exploded and sank within three minutes, leaving those on board no time to send a distress signal. A total of 268 crew, doctors, nurses and other medical personnel died, leaving just 64 survivors. Another deliberate attack on a hospital ship took place while it was anchored in Darwin harbour. Again, the *Manunda* was clearly marked and the majority of the nurses, medical staff and crew were killed in this barbarous attack.

Japanese submarine crews regularly murdered any survivors of merchant ships that had been sunk by them. Lifeboats were either rammed or machine-gunned and survivors in the water were shot. Survivors from the US merchant ship *SS Jean Nicolet* were taken on board a Japanese submarine and brutally stabbed to death before being thrown into the shark-infested sea.

These instances are only a small cross-section of the extensive range of war crimes committed by the Japanese armies during the Pacific War and also Japan's brutal undeclared war against China.

GERM WARFARE

One of the most heinous acts of former officers of the Japanese army was the setting up of a top-secret germ warfare research centre, called Unit 731, in the desolate area on the Manchurian Peninsula. Using American, Chinese, Soviet, Korean, British and other prisoners of war as human guinea pigs, they deliberately infected them with the plague, anthrax, cholera and other pathogens. It is believed that as many as 200,000 people could have been affected by this form of experimentation before and during World War II.

The victims of these cruel experiments suffered

indescribable misery and suffering; some were vivisected without the use of an anaesthetic, while others were tied to stakes and pounded with shrapnel laced with gangrene. After the victims became sick, they were cut open while still alive so that the doctors could chart the course of the infection. Others were put into pressure chambers to see how much they could stand before their eyes literally popped out of their sockets, or they were exposed to subzero weather conditions to find out how quickly they developed frostbite after being periodically drenched in water. Medical researchers also confined healthy prisoners with diseased ones to see how quickly the the disease would spread. The corpses were disposed of quickly in three large incinerators to destroy any evidence of mistreatment, especially as the majority were missing internal organs.

Away from the research centre, the Japanese army carried out long-range germ warfare field tests, as far away as Burma, Thailand and Indonesia. Planes dropped plague-infested fleas over China, which caused outbreaks of the disease killing at least 30,000 people in the Harbin area between 1946 and 1948. In 1942, germ warfare specialists distributed dysentery, cholera and typhoid bacteria in Zhejiang Province in China, but the operation backfired when many of the Japanese soldiers became ill, killing 1,700 of their own men.

The mastermind behind all this atrocity was General Shiro Ishii, a physician with a flair for sadism. He built up a unit of approximately 300 men, using special 'cover-up' identities. The site at Pingfan near Harbin, covered an area of 6 sq km (2.3 sq miles) and housed more than 150 buildings – administrative, laboratories, dormitories and barracks. It is alleged that by 1945, Unit 731 had stockpiled as much as 400 kg (882 lb) of anthrax that they planned to use in a specially designed defragmentation bomb. Inside Unit 731 were numerous jars containing specimens, such as feet, heads or internal organs, all neatly labelled.

Many of the human experiments were intended to develop new vaccines or treatments for problems that inflicted the men of the Japanese army. However, their methods of obtaining information were so scandalous that the whole operation was kept a closely guarded secret. When the war ended in 1945 and the Japanese surrendered, the specialists from Unit 731 destroyed war crime evidence and fled to Japan. The Soviet army took over the facilities, but it was to be many more months before they learned the truth about what had taken place there.

As soon as the USA occupied Japan, it started negotiations with known war criminals, offering them immunity from prosecution in return for their data, information and scientific skills. Although this was somewhat of a dilemma for the USA, they were concerned that the Soviet Union were far more advanced in their development of biological warfare and, despite the fact that the Japanese used horrific methods, they felt their knowledge would be invaluable to US military leaders.

After three years of talks, the USA offered General Shiro Ishii immunity and no other member of the now notorious Unit 731 was ever prosecuted as a war criminal. General Ishii lived in peace until his death from throat cancer in 1959. Other specialists from the unit saw their careers flourish in the postwar period, achieving high-ranking positions, including Governor of Tokyo, president of the Japan Medical Association and head of the Japan Olympic Committee.

More than five decades later, the subject of Japanese germ warfare – like many other atrocities related to World War II – remains an extremely sensitive issue.

THE DEATH MARCHES

Bataan

Not many prisoners of war ever returned to tell the tale of the inhumane treatment received at the hands of the Japanese army in the Philippines. The degradation, the brutal treatment, the torture and barbarism started when the Japanese invaded the Philippines in December 1941. The Japanese soon overpowered the sparsely distributed US and Filipino soldiers, forcing them to retreat to the Bataan Peninsula. Due to lack of supplies, General MacArthur had placed his men on half rations, so by the time the Japanese launched a second attack on 3 April, 1942, the US soldiers on the peninsula were so weakened by starvation and sickness they were unable to offer any effective resistance.

Commander of the US troops, Major General Edward King, decided to surrender his troops, but if he had known what lay ahead he would never have made this decision. Thousands of prisoners were herded together on the Mariveles Airfield at dawn on 10 April. Although some were in possession of meagre rations, they were not permitted to eat. All of their personal belongings were seized, and any prisoners carrying Japanese money or tokens were immediately beheaded.

Next came the 'march of death' when, in groups of 500 to 1,000 they started their terrible six-day ordeal along the road from Bataan towards San Fernando in the Pampanga province. Already in a weakened state from lack of nutrition and disease, the soldiers were forced to march without even the luxury of water. One soldier who was lucky enough to still have a canteen, had it seized by one of the Japanese soldiers, who taunted him by feeding the water to one of his own horses. The sun beat down on their uncovered heads and the prisoners staggered on through clouds of dust. On the roadside were the bodies of men who had been recently killed, many flattened by the Japanese trucks. Patients who had been forced to leave a field hospital were forced to march with the column, regardless of the severity of their injuries.

At night the men were put into enclosures that were too small to enable any of them to lie down, and they were still denied drinking water, except for the occasional dirty wallowing hole. This went on day after day. Any men that fell out of the column had to be left as no one was permitted to stop and help. These men were left to the mercy of the Japanese soldiers, who usually killed them on the spot.

On the third day of marching a new type of torture was introduced to further test the prisoners' endurance. While the Japanese stopped for a rest and food, the prisoners were forced to sit in the boiling midday sun without any form of cover. Many of the men, who were already seriously dehydrated, just collapsed and died. The only luxury afforded to the prisoners was the odd handful of contaminated rice, which only added to their problems of diarrhoea and dysentery.

On the fourth day, crazy through the lack of water, six Filipino soldiers made a dash for one of the watering wells at the side of the road. They were immediately shot, gutted and hung over a barbed wire fence to act as a deterrent to any other prisoners who dared to break rank.

On the fifth day 115 prisoners were packed into a small narrow-gauge box car, with the doors closed and locked. It was impossible for anyone to move and by the morning the stench was unbearable. When the doors were opened the following morning, the occupants were subjected to another three hours sun treatment and then forced to march to Camp O'Donnell. Many of the prisoners made the 137 km (85 mile) journey without any food or water whatsoever, and prisoners taken at Corregidor fared little better. Although they were not made to march, around 7,000 US and 5,000 Filipino soldiers were packed for a week with no food on a small concrete area. There was only one water point for all the men and the average wait to fill a canteen was 12 hours.

When the men arrived at Camp O'Donnell the conditions were no better, as there were virtually no drinking facilities. The prisoners would stand for hours on end just waiting to get a drink, and they had to stay in the clothes they arrived in, with no facilities for washing. The basic food ration was rice, with the odd luxury of a piece of meat about 2.5 cm (1 in) square. Sometimes they were thrown pieces of rotting vegetables, but the prisoners formed guards to try and stop the more crazed men from eating the contaminated scraps. There was a black market for those who had any money, and it was possible to buy a small can of sardines for the pricely sum of $5.

There was a dilapidated old building at Camp D'Donnell, which doubled as a hospital, but the conditions were appalling and little could be done to help the suffering. There were no washing facilities which meant that the dying had to lie in their own excrement and hundreds had to lay on the bare floor without anything to cover them. The sick were forced to work until they dropped dead, and the daily death rate after just two weeks in the camp was approximately 50 Americans and 150 Filipinos.

In June, the US soldiers were moved to Cabanatuan,

which was little better than O'Donnell, although there was adequate drinking water and muddy water for bathing. However, the diet did not improve and the brutality continued, with the men beaten with shovels if they didn't work hard enough. Three officers who attempted to escape were quickly recaptured, stripped down to their underpants, their hands were tied behind them and they were hauled up by ropes. They were kept in this position, in the blazing sun, for two days, occasionally being beaten as a Japanese guard walked past. In the end, one was beheaded and the other two were shot. By October, 3,000 of the US prisoners had died.

Eventually the remaining prisoners were taken to another penal camp at Davao, Mindanao, and put to hard labout. The beatings, murder and humiliation continued and conditions were no better, but their salvation eventually came in the form of Red Cross parcels providing them with food and clothing.

Three soldiers managed to escape on 4 April, 1943, and it is through their account that we have so much evidence of the Bataan death march.

Sandakan

The story of the Sandakan death marches is one of the most tragic of World War II, but also one of the most heroic. Despite the appalling conditions, the prisoners never gave up hope, and it is their heroism and determination that are testimony to the strength of the human spirit. Of the 2,434 prisoners held at Sandakan, 1,787 were Australian and the remaining British. Out of these, only six Australians escaped to tell their story.

The Japanese army decided to build a military airfield at the port of Sandakan, on the north-eastern tip of Borneo, to protect the oilfields they had recently captured. To complete this task they shipped in Australian and British prisoners of war from Singapore and neighbouring islands. The conditions at Sandakan were appalling – water was drawn from a filthy creek, their food was a couple of handfuls of contaminated rice and sometimes a few vegetables. At first security at the camp was lax, and several prisoners managed to escape into Borneo's steamy jungles. However, the remaining prisoners were punished by denial of food, and Japanese guards routinely shot any prisoner who attempted to escape or who was recaptured. Indiscretions, such as stealing a coconut to supplement their diet, or forgetting to bow to the guards, were treated with beatings or being locked in cages in the hot sun for hours on end.

Any prisoner who was suspected of assembling or operating an improvized radio could find himself at the mercy of the feared Kempei Tai, the Japanese military secret police. Torture methods included burning flesh with cigarettes, hammering metal tacks under the nails and force-feeding the prisoners water until their stomachs became distended. The Kempei Tai would then jump on the prisoners' stomachs.

The arduous work on the airstrip and the appalling lack of nutrition soon started to take its toll on the prisoners, many of them becoming totally emaciated. As the sickness took hold and the work slowed down, the brutality of the Japanese heightened and the already meagre rations were further reduced. To force the men to work harder, the Japanese brought in a gang of tough guards, who became known as 'the bashers. They carried wooden pick handles or bamboo canes and seemed to take great pleasure in beating the prisoners for no real reason. The victims were often left unconscious, with broken arms or legs.

By the beginning of 1945, only 1,900 prisoners were left at Sandakan and, as the war in the Pacific entered its final stages, the Allied prisoners were chosen to act as porters to undertake an arduous journey through the marshlands and dense jungle. This was the first of the Sandakan death marches, and only 470 prisoners were found strong enough to actually carry the supplies. The journey of 192 km (120 miles) would have been a test of endurance for even the fittest soldier, but already sick, weak and exhausted from their treatment at Sandakan, only 190 men survived the trek. Ill-equipped and severely undernourished, many of the prisoners simply collapsed from exhaustion. Those that did survive were forced to build huts for the Japanese soldiers and a temporary camp for themselves on the outskirts of Ranau, a village high on a plateau. The men were forced to carry heavy loads from Ranau back to the camp, including barrels of water from a nearby stream. Their rations were cut even further, until they only received 100 g (4 oz) a rice per day.

The second death march started on 29 March, 1945, with 536 prisoners who had been chosen because they were still able to stand without assistance. They set off in groups of about 50, with Japanese guards at the front rear and sides of each section. They had been ordered to shoot anyone who collapsed from exhaustion or attempted an escape. This march took 26 days and at the end only 183 prisoners reached Ranau. When the second group arrived at the camp at Ranau, they discovered that only six prisoners out of the original 470 who had left Sandakan were still alive. The survivors of the second march, like the men in the first one, were immediately put to work and the death toll soared.

After the second death march, there were about 250 prisoners left at Sandakan. Most of these men were so ill that the Japanese had decided to just leave them there to perish. However, on 9 June, 1945, they changed their minds and set out on a third expedition to Ranau. Only one man made it further than 50 km (30 miles), and as each one collapsed, he was shot by a Japanese guard.

By 1 August, just 38 prisoners remained alive at Ranau. The rest had died as a result of the brutality and starvation. What they thought had been an idle threat by one of the Japanese guards when they set out on their marches, turned out to be a reality. He had said that the prisoners would be killed as soon as they reached their final destination – this order was eventually carried out. A Japanese sergeant addressed the prisoners, saying, 'There is no rice, so I'm killing the lot of you today. Is there anything you want to say?'

Out of the original 2,434 prisoners of war, only six managed to escape the Japanese guards. It happened one afternoon when a US reconnaissance plane flew low over the camp at Ranau. The Japanese guards ran for cover, which gave the men the chance to run off in the opposite direction. Despite being riddled with disease and skeletal, they found the strength to slide down a long, steep slope and hide in the brush until it became dark. For the next few days they hacked their way through the dense, humid jungle and marched towards, what they thought, was the sea. They soon discovered the secrets of surviving in the jungle by watching the animals around them. They survived on bugs, wild fruit and fish, and simply spat out anything that tasted too bitter. Unfortunately, five of the men was so weakened by malaria and beriberi they were no longer able to move and died before they could get help. One man did make it out, though, and he was rescued by fishermen who took him to a group of Australian commandos stationed close by. He was taken to a US navy ship, where he was nursed back to health.

When it became certain that Japan would have to surrender, they made every effort to cover up for their atrocities by destroying incriminating evidence. For many years the rough track through the jungle was overgrown but in recent years it has been uncovered.

MASSACRE ON BANKA ISLAND

In February 1942, the fall of Singapore to the Japanese army seemed imminent. The British ship SS *Vyner Brooke* was carrying some of the last citizens to escape Singapore, including 65 Australian army nurses who had been evacuated from the besieged city. Also on board were over 200 civilians and English military personnel, who were also evacuees. The *Vyner Brooke* was only licenced to carry 300 passengers, so conditions were cramped and there was not enough food on board for regular meals. There were no bunks on board, so the nurses had made makeshift beds on the deck. As the ship sailed through the treacherous trait between Sumatra and Bangka, it sighted Japanese bombers. The ship sounded its warning siren, and the passengers crowded below deck. The first missile missed its target, which gave the *Vyner Brooke* time to change its course and fire its one token cannon in resistance. However, the Japanese planes returned and this time made three direct hits. The overloaded ship sank quickly.

The trained nurses automatically ran to any part of the sinking wreckage to administer morphine and dressings to the wounded. When they could do no more to help, the nurses jumped overboard and swam to a partly submerged lifeboat. In total 12 nurses (three of them wounded), two civilian women, one man and a ship's officer either clung to the side or managed to climb into the lifeboat. Although they could see land in the distance, it took them eight hours to reach the shores of Banka Island. Seeing fire in the distance, the survivors walked along the shoreline and found other survivors from the *Vyner Brooke,* who had managed to make their way using pieces of the ship as rafts. Others joined them in the night, many of whom had literally been washed in on the drifting tide.

The following morning the groups divided into three and went in search of food, clothing or anyone who could assist them in any way. One of the parties found a village, but when they asked for help they were told that the Japanese troops had already taken control of the island, and that they feared retribution if they were to offer them any assistance. The other two groups came back and reported similar stories.

That night another group of survivors – 20 English soldiers – from another ship that had been sunk, joined the crowd from the *Vyner Brooke,* bringing the total up to 100. One of the officers explained to the new party that there was no food or shelter, and he advised that they gave themselves up to the Japanese.

A party of men went off to find the Japanese, while 22 nurses stayed behind to look after the injured. Another party of women were told to walk to Muntok to ask for help. They made sure that they were easily recognizable as non-combatants by erecting a red cross. By mid-morning, the ship's officer returned with about 20 Japanese soldiers. They proceeded to separate the men from the women. The Japanese then divided the men into two groups and marched off down the beach out of sight. The nurses heard gunfire coming from that direction and shortly afterwards the Japanese soldiers returned on their own. They proceeded to sit down in front of the women and cleaned their rifles, wiping blood off the bayonets.

The nurses were then told to form a line and walk into the sea. They all knew exactly what was going to happen, and putting on a brave face, their matron said, 'Chin up girls. I'm proud of you and I love you all.' As the water reached their waists the soldiers opened fire. One of the nurses, sister Bullwinkle, was hit in the back by a bullet, which knocked her off her feet into the surf. Realizing that she had only been wounded, she lay still pretending to be dead. The waves brought her back to the edge of the shore, where she lay for about ten minutes before daring to open her eyes and look around. Seeing that the Japanese soldiers had gone, she got up and went into the jungle, where she lay semi-unconscious for about two days.

By the third day she had recovered enough to be able to walk to a fresh water spring close to the beach. She bathed her wounds, which had been sterilized by the salt water, and was then startled by the sound of an English voice coming from the trees. A soldier, who had been left on the beach laying on a stretcher with the other wounded, had managed to also survive the Japanese attack. Although he had received a bayonet wound to his chest, it had missed his vital organs and he had been able to crawl into the jungle. The remainder of the wounded still lay on their stretchers on the sand where they had been slaughtered.

The nurse dressed the soldier's wounds as best she could and then helped him to hide in the edge of the jungle. Over a period of a few days, the nurse managed to beg food from the fearful Indonesian women in the nearby villages, and eventually the two survivors had enough strength to attempt the walk to Muntok. They didn't get far before they were picked up by a Japanese officer in a truck and driven to the army's headquarters. They were questioned for several hours and then made to line up with the already crowded coolie lines of prisoners and refugees. Unfortunately, the English soldier who had arrived with the nurse died a couple of days later from his wounds.

Aware that if she told the Japanese what she had witnessed she would be killed, sister Bullwinkle kept her story secret for the three years that she spent in the prisoner-of-war camp, unable to tell anyone of the atrocities that had taken place following her shipwreck.

EVIDENCE OF CANNIBALISM

Horrifying evidence came to light after the war that the

Japanese soldiers had committed acts of cannibalism on Australian prisoners of war. What is even more horrifying is that this was not as a direct result of shortage of normal food, but just a sick desire to eat human flesh.

Between 21 and 26 August, 1942, 13,500 Japanese troops landed at the villages of Gona and Buna on the northern coast of Australia's territory of Papua. Their mission was to cross the precipitous terrain of the Owen Stanley Range and capture the Australian stronghold of Port Moresby on the southern coast. The Japanese army were tough, jungle-trained veterans, but they were unprepared for the narrow dirt track called the Kokoda Track. The track crossed some of the most rugged and isolated terrain in the world and was only passable on foot. Hot humid days with intensely cold nights, torrential rainfall and endemic tropical diseases, such as malaria, made it a challenge for even the toughest soldier and the Japanese troops set off with just ten days of rations.

There were 500 Australian militia defending the Kokoda Track, and these poorly armed and supplied men were outnumbered by the Japanese by ten to one. Many of the Australian soldiers were only 18 and lacked adequate training or experience but they fought hard to defend their post. They forced the Japanese army to fight every step of the way and they succeeded in blocking their advance for over five weeks.

The exhausted and starving Australian militia were eventually relieved by another battalion on 26 August.

These new militia were more experienced and used to combat, but they were still outnumbered by the Japanese five to one. Bloody fighting broke out on the Owen Stanley Range and both sides suffered heavy casualties. The Japanese, who were now low on supplies and totally exhausted, came to a halt on the top of the ridge. Unable to get any backup, they were forced to retreat to the beaches on the northern coast, closely followed by the Australian reinforcements.

The Japanese were furious at having been forced to retreat by the Australians, and any prisoners of war taken by the Japanese were not allowed to survive. Already short of supplies, they were not prepared to give their precious rations to the prisoners, but what was even more horrifying was the evidence that the Japanese actually ate their victims even though they had not exhausted their own food supplies. When the Australians pursued the Japanese, they found that they had left gruesome evidence behind them. Many of the Australian soldiers were found with the meat stripped off their legs and half-cooked human meat in the Japanese pots. Next to these dead soldiers were supplies of rice and tins of food that hadn't been touched.

Two Japanese officers, Major Sueo Matoba and General Yoshio Tachibana, were both tried and executed for war crimes, including cannibalism, that took place in September 1944. They were accused of eating American flesh washed down with sake in a feast that was laid on for officers on the island of Chichi Jima.

The Rape of Nanking
————1937–38————

*T*he Rape of Nanking, also known as the Nanking Massacre, is one of the most well-known of the war crimes committed by the Japanese army. In December 1937, the Japanese Imperial Army marched into Nanking, China's capital city, and committed numerous atrocities, including rape, looting, arson and the mass execution of prisoners of war and civilians alike.

The six weeks of atrocities were preceeded by a tough battle at Shanghai against the Chinese in the summer of 1937. The Japanese had expected to defeat the Chinese easily, but when the fighting continued into late autumn the infuriated troops were ready to take their revenge. When they eventually defeated the Chinese in November, 50,000 Japanese troops stormed the capital city with instructions to 'kill all captives'.

Their first job was to eliminate all Chinese prisoners of war, which started as soon as they were transported by truck to remote areas outside of Nanking. The young Japanese soldiers, who were goaded on by their superiors, were encouraged to inflict as much pain as possible on their captives. Filmed footage that was taken at the massacre, shows Japanese soldiers using the prisoners for bayonet practise and shows prisoners being decapitated and their heads being held up as souvenirs. Other victims were drenched in petrol and burnt alive, while some were simply shot.

After the Japanese soldiers had taken their revenge on the prisoners of war, they turned their attention to the women of Nanking. Regardless of age, old women and young girls were dragged off and sexually abused. It is estimated that as many as 80,000 women were gang-raped by the Japanese and then either shot or stabbed to death so that they could not bear witness to the inhumane cruelty. Even pregnant women were not spared, with many having their bellies ripped open and the foetuses torn out of their bodies.

Many Chinese men were forced to rape their own daughters, while sons were forced to rape their mothers, brothers and sisters, as the rest of the family were made to watch. Shops were looted, shopkeepers were killed and the buildings were set on fire with people locked inside. It appeared that the Japanese soldiers took great pleasure in watching the suffering of their victims.

The untold carnage took place over a period of six weeks. Corpses littered the streets and Nanking was described as literally 'running with blood'. Those who were not killed on the spot were taken outside the village and relatives were forced to bury each other alive. Following this period of heinous bloodshed, things quietened down and the Japanese settled in for occupation. To try and pacify the remaining horror-struck inhabitants of Nanking, the army supplied them with highly addictive narcotics, which included opium and heroin, regardless of age. It is estimated that as many as 50,000 people became addicted to these drugs. Young Chinese women were forced to become sex slaves, being used entirely for the pleasure of the Japanese soldiers.

Even the hospital was not safe from the Japanese, and it became the site of some of the worst atrocities. Bandages were torn from the bodies of the wounded, plaster casts were smashed to pieces and nurses were repeatedly raped. The unabated violence continued from mid-December 1937 to February 1938 until as much as two-thirds of the city were destroyed.

HELP COMES TO NANKING

As the stories leaked out of China, the world looked on in horror, finding the stories that had been smuggled out of Nanking just too incredible to believe. However, back in Nanking not everything was hopeless and samaritans turned up in the form of 20 US and Europeans civilians who had survived the massacre. They consisted of missionaries, doctors and business-men who took it on their own heads to form an International Safety Zone within the capital. Bravely displaying Red Cross flags, they declared a 4 sq km

(2.5 sq mile) area in the middle of the city as off limits to any members of the Japanese army. On many occasions they risked their own lives to try and rescue Chinese men, women and children from ultimate death or abuse. They worked day and night to the point of exhaustion to give aid to the persecuted Chinese civilians and became the unsung heroes of Nanking. Around 300,000 Chinese took refuge in their safety zone, and those who did not make it into the safe area were ultimately killed.

The Japanese eventually evacuated China when the USA dropped the atomatic bombs on Hiroshima and Nagasaki, but Nanking bore the scars for a long time. Not only was the city in ruins, but bodies were still floating in the river a year after the atrocities had ended, leaving a nauseating stench for miles around.

The samaritans described Nanking as 'hell on earth' and one claimed, 'I did not imagine that such cruel people existed in the modern world'. The official estimate of the death toll is 300,000, and this is engraved on the stone wall at the entrance of the Memorial Hall in Nanking.

In Japan, the severity of the massacre remains widely divided and, while most do not deny that the massacre took place, some government officials have stated that they feel the extent of the crimes has been grossly exaggerated, claiming it is purely Chinese propaganda. This is despite the fact that there is both photographic and independent eyewitness evidence.

On 15 August, 1995, which was the 50th anniversary of the massacre, the Japanese prime minister, Tomiichi Murayama gave the first formal apology for the actions of the Japanese army during the war. Chinese people are now beginning to accept the formal apologies, and the majority feel it is a step in the right direction.

CRIMINAL TRIALS

Many years after the Nanking massacre, criminal trials were held at the Tokyo Trials and lasted from May 1946 until November 1948. The prosecuting team consisted of judges from 11 different countries, including China and the USA. A total of 28 men were charged with mass murder, pillage, torture and other atrocities, and of these 25 were found guilty, two died during the trial and one had a nervous breakdown. Seven of the accused were hanged, and the remainder received life sentences, although none served longer than eight years.

Hiroshima and Nagasaki
————1945————

Since the Japanese attack on Pearl Harbor in 1941, the USA and Japan had been at war. The Japanese were warned of the consequences of continued resistance in July by the terms of the Potsdam Declaration, which had been signed by the US president, Harry S. Truman and the UK prime minister, Clement Attlee, in agreement with the president of the National Government of China, Chiang Kai-shek. However, when Japan rejected the Declaration, Attlee authorized the use of two atomic bombs. The dropping of these two bombs on the cities of Hiroshima and Nagasaki bought the long World War II to an abrupt end, but the bombings caused untold suffering.

THE FIRST BOMB IS DROPPED

Wanting to have the ultimate possible effect on Japan, the USA prepared to release their nuclear weapons, knowing full well the unimaginable power of the atom bomb. The target, Hiroshima, was a city of appreciable industrial and military significance, with military camps located nearby. On 6 August, 1945, people turned their eyes towards the skies above Hiroshima as they heard the drone of a B-29 bomber flying across an almost cloudless sky. As there were only three planes visible that day, the Japanese did not consider them to be a significant threat and decided to conserve their fuel and munitions for use against more serious threats.

For anyone who didn't hear the planes overhead, the sudden flash of a bright light was the first sign of something out of the ordinary. The plane that was nicknamed 'Little Boy' dropped its deadly cargo at 9.15 a.m. Tokyo time on Hiroshima, Japan's seventh largest city. The bomb was the equivalent of 14,330 tonnes (13,000 tons) of TNT, which projected an intense amount of radiation in every direction. Shortly after the fierce light, the heatwave arrived, and witnesses said it was like standing directly inside an oven. Within minutes, half of the city had vanished.

The sky over Hiroshima was stained with red and the air became saturated with smoke and dust. Those who had survived the impact helped the injured to flee the area, not fully realizing the magnitude of the destruction. The pressure wave that had spread with such speed across the city had left literally tens of thousands of people dead or dying.

Hiroshima was now one big ball of fire, and radio stations within sight of the city started to broadcast reports of a terrible explosion. The sky turned dark as a mushroom cloud towered over the city, spraying a sticky black rain over everything. Makeshift hospitals were quickly set up to try and treat the thousands of injured people, many suffering from severe burns, others from shrapnel wounds with sharp shards of glass and pieces of wood puncturing their skin. Hundreds of other people swarmed into the ruins of the city to try and find their loved ones. They searched frantically among the rubble; more than 60,000 of the city's 90,000 buildings had been reduced to ruins.

The news reached the government in Tokyo a few hours later, but it wasn't until 16 hours had elapsed that they learned what had caused the disaster at Hiroshima, when the White House made a public announcement about the nuclear attack on Japan.

THE SECOND BOMB

Three days after Hiroshima, 9 April, a B-29 bomber, nicknamed 'Bocksar', dropped its lethal cargo over the city of Nagasaki. The original target was to have been Kokura, but because of smoke cover, the plane was forced to change course. Nagasaki was another industrialized city with a natural harbour in the western Kuushu district of Japan. At precisely 11.02 a.m. the bomb known as 'Fat Man' was dropped from about 550 m (1,800 ft) over the industrial part of the city to achieve maximum blast effect. Despite the fact that hilly terrain protected much of the city, the devastation and loss of life was enormous. Most of the inhabitants suffered from flash burns from the first set of heat waves that swept across the city. Others were burnt alive as their homes burst into flames, and thousands received wounds from flying debris. A strong wind followed the initial blast, which caused air to be drawn back to the centre of the burning area, turning it into one immense furnace. The bomb at Nagasaki killed 42,000 people and injured 40,000, and it destroyed 39 per cent of all the buildings.

EFFECTS OF RADIATION

In the first stages of the two explosions, temperatures as high as tens of millions of degrees were produced, and the light emitted was roughly ten times as bright as that of the sun. Added to this, various types of radiation, such as gamma rays and alpha and beta particles, were spread for miles around, and it is these radioactive particles that are the atomic bomb's deadliest weapon. The effect of this radiation may last for years, or even centuries, and thousands of cases of radiation sickness were recorded in Japan. Firstly, the blood was affected and then the blood-making organs, including the bone marrow, the spleen and the lymph nodes. In severe cases, the organs of the body became diseased, usually resulting in death after just a few days. Anyone within a radius of 1 km (0.6 mile) of the two cities, would have received severe radiation poisoning; between 1 (0.6 mile) and 2 km (1.2 mile) away, serious to moderate; within 2 to 4 km (1.2 to 2.4 mile) slight.

Radiation sickness took the lives of many people in the days following the two explosions, and over 200,000 people were exposed to heavy nonfatal doses during the fallout in the intervening weeks. The victims of Hiroshima and Nagasaki became known as *hibakusha*, which literally translated means 'people exposed to the bomb'. These men, women and children are entitled to a monthly allowance from the government as compensation, since many have ongoing health problems and are more susceptible to the ravages of cancer.

Realizing they had been the target of the worst possible attack, the Japanese government, who at one time seemed ready to fight to the death, surrendered unconditionally on 2 September.

Out of the ruins of Hiroshima and Nagasaki sprang two new, vibrant cities. The majority of the surviving *hibakusha* still live in Japan and are believed to be as many as 266,598 in number. As of 2005, the death toll from these weapons of war stood at around 400,000 – some from the blast itself, others from the radiation exposure in the following years. Because of the lack of knowledge of radiation sickness, many of the *hibakusha* have been ostracized for fear of the 'disease' spreading. Even today, employers still refuse to hire the *hibakusha* or their children out of fear of the unknown.

On a brighter side, nuclear energy has become an important part of the life of each city today, but in a completely different way. Half of Nagasaki's and one-quarter of Hiroshima's electricity is supplied by nuclear reactors, which are testimony to the positive benefits of atomic energy.

General Eisenhower and General MacArthur both thought that the bombs were totally unnecessary as they felt that Japan was on the brink of surrender even before the attacks. A number of other notable individuals and organizations have criticized the bombings, describing them as war crimes or crime against humanity. Two early critics of the bombings were Albert Einstein and Leo Szilard, who had together instigated the first bomb research in 1939.

There is still controversy over the use of the Hiroshima and Nagasaki bombs. Those that oppose the action believe that the naval blockades around Japan would have soon forced them into submission, while supporters argue that without the bombs, many people would have lost their lives with the expected invasion of the home islands. The Japanese nation has sought the abolition of nuclear weapons from the world ever since the attacks on Hiroshima and Nagasaki.

Wake Island

—————1941—————

*W*ake Island, also known as Wake Atoll, is a ring-shaped coral atoll in the North Pacific Ocean. The battle that took place on Wake Island is a compelling story, which started on the same day as the Japanese attack on Pearl Harbor. The garrison on Wake Island consisted of 449 US Marine officers and men and 68 naval personnel, all commanded by Major James Devereux. The base's weapons were minimal – twelve 76.2 mm (3 in) anti-aircraft guns, six 127 mm (5 in) cannons, which had been salvaged from an old cruiser, and 50 machine guns which were not all in working order.

In 1939, the US Congress allocated $2 million to the Secretary of the Navy to develop Wake Island into an efficient air station and, after its completion, it became a regular stopping point for servicing and refuelling of the famous Pan Am 'Clippers', four-engined flying boats. However, at the time of the Japanese attack in 1941, the development of the naval air base was still under way and far from being completed. Although a number of structures had been constructed, the defensive systems were incomplete, in that there was no radar and a number of the gun batteries lacked the height finders or the gun directors. Consequently, Wake Island was ill-prepared for the attack that was about to hit the small atoll.

WORD OF WAR

The news broke about the Japanese attack on Pearl Harbor on 8 December, 1941, just as one of the huge silver-winged Pan Am Clippers roared off the water bound for Guam, a flight that was destined to never reach its destination. Major Devereux immediately ordered a 'Call to Arms' and assembled his officers to inform them that the war with Japan had started and that Wake could 'expect the same thing in a very short time'. Little did he realize as he said this that it was to be a very short time indeed.

Meanwhile, the senior officer on Wake Island, Commander Winfred S. Cunningham, called Pan Am's airport manager, requesting him to recall his Clipper. The pilot on board the Clipper was told about the outbreak of war and he immediately turned his plane around and returned to the lagoon he had left just 20 minutes earlier. Cunningham requested that the pilot carry out a reconnaissance flight and the Clipper was unloaded and refuelled with a planned take-off time of about 1.00 p.m., to be accompanied by a two-plane escort.

By midday, Japanese bombers who had taken off from Marshall Islands shortly after dawn, started to attack the small naval base. Although the base was prepared for attack, the sound of the pounding surf drowned out the noise of the approaching planes and the alarms were not sounded until the planes were just a few hundred yards from the atoll's south shore.

The first attack concentrated on the airfield, destroying all but four of the F4F Wildcat fighter planes, the majority of the fuel tanks, aviation spare parts and oxygen, which severely diminished the effect of the US air cover. Pan Am's facilities were totally wrecked and an attack from the Japanese bombers had set fire to the hotel in which five Chamorro employees died. Out of the 66 Pan Am staff, nine lay dead and two of the Clipper crew were badly wounded.

Many of the US pilots were trapped as the Japanese bombs turned their planes into balls of fire. The explosions rattled the windows of Commander Cunningham's office and he quickly ordered his troops to open fire. However, their small guns were ineffective against the Japanese aircraft, and in about seven minutes they had rendered the air base inoperable.

FIRST ATTEMPT AT LANDING

Three days later, on 11 December, under the command of Rear Admiral Sadamichi Kajioka, the Japanese attempted to land on Wake Island. It was a small contingent of only 450 assault troops as Kajioka had thought the operation would be fairly simple.

The US troops played a waiting game and withheld their fire until the Japanese vessels were well within their range and then fired their cannons. In the ensuing battle, the US managed to sink the Japanese destroyer *Hayate* and seriously damaged most of the others in the fleet, including their flagship *Yubari*.

The US assault was sufficient to force the Japanese to abort their landing attempt. The retreating vessels were attacked by the four remaining US Wildcats, who succeeded in sinking another destroyer, the *Kisaragi*. This battle went down in history as the first time an amphibious assault was foiled by land-based guns.

The Japanese were determined to effect a landing on Wake Island and in the next few days they continued to bombard the atoll relentlessly in an effort to render their forces useless.

RELIEF OPERATION

Aware that another landing attempt was imminent and that the situation on Wake Island had become untenable, naval strategists at Pearl Harbor decided to send a relief force to resupply the island with aircraft, ammunition and men. The plans were complicated, however, because the forces that were left afloat after the attack on Pearl Harbor were now widely scattered. It was decided to send USS *Tangier* with an accompanying oil cargo ship to be escorted by Admiral Frank Fletcher's *Saratoga* Task Force 16, who were currently approaching from Hawaii. However, Task Force 16 was making slow progress and the *Tangier* was forced to leave Pearl Harbor with no escort, followed the next day by *Saratoga* and her escorts.

By 21 December, 11 days after the marines on Wake Island had managed to repel the Japanese landing, the relief force were still 965 km (600 miles) away. Wake Island was now bereft of any air defence, and the promised relief was nowhere in sight. Little did they know that Fletcher's force were refuelling and, due to heavy seas, had sailed away from Wake. Fearing that the relief force was sailing into a trap, they were ordered to go no closer than 320 km (200 miles) of Wake Island. *Tangier*, who was closer and ready to land reinforcements and supplies, was ordered to evacuate. It is still a matter of conjecture why the Task Force ships and planes returned when they were so close, as they could have provided much-needed support in the second confrontation with Japanese forces.

SUCCESSFUL SECOND ATTEMPT

The second landing attempt by the Japanese came at 2.30 p.m. on 23 December, and consisted mostly of the same ships from the first attempt with a few additions, including 1,500 Japanese marines. Once again the Japanese met with heavy resistance, but this time they were taking no chances. The Japanese succeeded in getting their landing crafts to the shore and a desperate battle was fought across the island, with groups of men fighting with rifles, bayonets, grenades and some simply using their fists. The fighting lasted through the night but the US troops were seriously outnumbered and were driven towards the centre of the island. Cunningham made the decision to surrender by mid-afternoon on the 24th. The Japanese took captive all the remaining men on the island, the majority of whom were civilian contractors employed by the Morrison-Knudsen Company.

The total number of casualties on Wake Island from the onset of the fighting was 81 marines, eight sailors and 82 civilian workers who had been either killed or wounded. The Japanese, however, paid a heavier price for their victory; it cost them two destroyers, one submarine, seven ships were damaged, 21 aircraft were shot down, and almost 1,000 of their men were killed.

WAR CRIMES

The Japanese were angry and they took it out on their prisoners of war, both military and civilian. Fearing a counter-attack on the island, the Japanese started to build defences on Wake. The US prisoners were forced to build a series of bunkers and other fortifications. During this initial period, one civilian was beheaded to set an example to the others and one civilian died. Two others had set out in a stolen boat, however, they perished at sea.

Early in the morning on 23 December, 1,603 captives, including 1,150 civilian contractors, were taken to the northern end of the island and ordered to strip naked. Most of them had their hands tied behind their backs with wire, with an additional wire looped tightly around their necks, so that if they lowered their arms they would strangle themselves. They were then blindfolded and jammed into two claustrophobic concrete ammunition bunkers. Later that day they were all herded out onto the airstrip and made to sit, naked, in the blistering heat of the midday sun. The prisoners watched the Japanese set up machine guns close by, expecting to be shot at any minute. However, their ordeal was not over as the heat of the sun was replaced by the bone-chilling winds of night. They remained sitting on the airstrip for two days without food, water or any medical supplies.

The original plan was to murder each one, but through the intervention of Rear Admiral Sadamichi Kajioka, their lives were spared. They were given food and water, despite the fact that it had been contaminated by the heat and the unclean gasoline drums. Their clothes were returned to them and Kajioka read out a proclamation that said, 'The Emperor has gracefully presented you with your lives.' They were marched back to their barracks and for the first time the Japanese treated their captives with due consideration.

This was not to be the case for 98 contract workers, because fearing an imminent invasion, Rear Admiral

Shigematsu Sakaibara ordered their execution. They were all blindfolded and gunned down before being buried in a mass grave. One of the captives managed to escape and carved an inscription on a large coral rock near the site of the grave. It said, '98 US PW 5-10-43'. This inscription is still visible today on Wake Island and has become a famous landmark. This unknown American was captured again within a few weeks and personally beheaded by Sakaibara.

The Japanese finally surrendered to US marines on 4 September, 1945, and all the officers were taken into custody. While some of them committed hara-kiri, others told of the massacre. Sakaibara and his immediate subordinate were convicted of war crimes, and Sakaibara was hanged on Guam while his subordinate had his sentence commuted to life. Until the end, Sakaibara maintained, 'I think my trial was entirely unfair and the proceeding unfair, and the sentence too harsh, but I obey with pleasure.'

Port Blair

---1942---

The Andaman Islands are located 960 km (596 miles) off the east coast of India, and they make up a group of more than 200 islands. The islands, which share history and traditions with each other, are inhabited by ancient tribes that today remain some of the most traditional in the world. Today Port Blair, the main town for the islands, is a prime tourist spot, offering luxurious hotels along with fascinating rainforests and unspoilt beaches.

During World War II, Port Blair was the main military objective on Andaman, consisting of 300 Sikh militia and 23 British officers, boosted in 1942 by a Gurkha detachment. After Rangoon fell to the Japanese on 8 March, the British became aware that Port Blair was becoming impossible to safeguard. When the Gurkhas withdrew to the Arakan peninsula on 10 March, the garrison at Port Blair were even more exposed. With only the one British company to maintain law and order, the islands did not have any elaborate defence structures and, with no hope of defending the island, the British evacuated, leaving a skeleton staff.

Wishing to secure their sea defences, the Japanese sent a sizeable force to seize the islands on 23 March. They met no resistance from the British or the local population, and within hours the Sikh militia were disarmed and placed under captivity without the firing of one single bullet. The British militia were sent to Singapore as prisoners of war, while the officers were held on the island in Port Blair's prison, the Cellular Jail. The prison is named after the shape of its construction, which was started in 1896 and completed in 1906. It was built with seven wings with a central tower and turret. Connected to this were seven wings, each three storeys high, with 698 isolated cells.

The Japanese soon started to assume their control of the islands, with the army commander taking the position of governor of the civilian population. At first, the Japanese were welcomed by the islanders, many finding new and higher positions that had been vacated by the British officers. In return, the Japanese treated them with respect and paid fair prices for goods purchased in their shops.

After one year in occupation, the Japanese established the 'Andaman Miniseibu', with the prime objective of:

To protect the local population and also to promote their welfare, maintenance of public peace and order, development of industries, repairing of roads and prevention of epidemics in the islands but its main

work to increase the production of food stuff, by
establishing a self-sufficient system, on the other hand
recognizing their religious freedom much attention
was given to education and also attempts were made
to make the local people happy by encouraging whole
sale amusement . . .

A Japanese school was opened as well as the
Government High School, which was originally run by
the British. Roads were constructed across the island,
and the previously unfinished airstrip was finished
within three months. However, underneath their
seemingly friendly facade, there is evidence that the
Japanese committed many atrocities during their term
of occupation.

NUMEROUS ATROCITIES

Although some of the evidence is a little vague, due to
the fact that the Japanese destroyed all their records
when they left the Andaman Islands, there are reliable
stories of people who witnessed the atrocities. The first
victim came after just four days of Japanese occupation.
A young man, by the name of Zulfiqar Ali, became
enraged when some Japanese soldiers chased some of
his chickens into his house. After Ali fired an airgun at
the soldiers, he was taken captive and marched in front
of the Browning Club, where his arms were twisted
until they broke and then he was shot.

Over the next few months the situation for the locals deteriorated as the Japanese soldiers started holding unthinkable orgies in the towns and villages, with young girls being forcibly raped and young boys sodomized. In Port Blair, eight high-ranking Indian officials were tortured and then buried up to their chests in pits, which they had been forced to dig themselves. Each time a Japanese soldier walked past the men, they prodded their heads and eyes with bayonets, and after a few hours the helpless victims were pumped full of bullets.

In an effort to try and protect the local civilians, a group of locals (mostly officials and doctors) were encouraged to become members of Rash Behari Bose's Indian Independence League. They formed a Peace Committee, headed by Dr Diwan Singh, which made every effort to try and alleviate the pain and suffering of the population at the hands of the Japanese. However, their efforts were to little avail, and Dr Singh was arrested along with approximately 2,000 of his Peace Committee associates. They were taken to the Cellular Jail, where they were subject to water torture, electric shocks and many other unimaginable forms of torture for a period of 82 days. Any survivors were taken off the island and shot and buried.

One of the British captives, Major A. G. Bird, who had imprisoned in Singapore, was used as an example by the Japanese. They used a fellow convict, Sarup Ram, to set Bird up in front of an improvised 'trial', where he was accused of spying. Wireless parts had been planted in the house where Bird had been held prisoner. Bird was found guilty, and his arms and legs were twisted and broken before he was decapitated by a sword in the hands of Colonel Bucho.

After the massacre of the majority of the Peace Committee, the Japanese resorted to inflicting terror on the women. They were abducted from their homes and taken to the officers club, where they would be raped by high-ranking officers. Shiploads of Korean girls were also brought in to appease the sexual appetite of the Japanese soldiers.

Towards the end of their three and a half years of occupation, the Japanese resorted to more desperate measures. It is believed that about 700 people from the south of Andaman were deported to an uninhabited island to grow food. According to one of the survivors, almost half of these people died as a result of drowning or being eaten by sharks, as they were pushed out into the darkness in inadequate boats. Others died of starvation or at the hands of Burmese pirates. A rescue mission went to the island after the Japanese left, and although they found only 12 survivors more than 100 skeletons were lying along the edges of the shore.

GOVERNMENT OF CHANDRA BOSE

In December 1943, political control of the islands came under the Azad Hind government of Subhas Chandra Bose. There is much controversy as to how much Bose was really aware of at the time, although the judgement of some was that he had 'failed his people'. On the only visit he ever made to the Andaman Islands, Bose went to Port Blair to raise the tricolour flag of the Indian National Army. The Japanese army made sure that he was sufficiently shielded from the local population so that information didn't leak out regarding their treatment of the locals. There were quite a few attempts made by the Andamans to let him know about their suffering, and also that local Indian Nationalists were being tortured at the Cellular Jail. Bose placed the islands under the governorship of Lieutenant-Colonel Loganathan, and it is thought he had little involvement in the administration of the territory.

After the war Loganathan said that he only had partial authority over the islands, as the Japanese retained control of the police force and large areas of the government. He emphasized that he was powerless to prevent the worst atrocity of the occupation, which was the massacre of 44 members of the Indian Independence League in January 1944.

By the time the British regained control in 1945, it is estimated that as many as 30,000 of the 40,000 population of Port Blair had been brutally murdered, and the islands of the Andamans were a scene of complete devastation.

Death Railway

——————1942–43——————

*O*ne of the most famous tourist attractions in Thailand is the bridge on the River Kwai, which was made famous by the 1957 film, starring Alec Guinness, William Holden and Jack Hawkins. However, the bridge you see standing today is not the bridge that cost the lives of hundreds of thousands of prisoners of war and it is hard to imagine the suffering these people went through in order to build what became known as the Death Railway. The railway is not only testament to the cruelty of the Japanese during World War II, but also man's bravery and determination, with approximately one in five prisoners dying during the construction.

WORKERS	NO. EMPLOYED	TOTAL DEATHS
Asian labourers	200,000	+/- 80,000
British POWs	30,000	6,540
Dutch POWs	18,000	2,830
Australian POWs	13,000	2,710
American POWs	700	+/- 356
Korean and Japanese	15,000	1,000
soldiers	15,000	1,000

REASON FOR CONSTRUCTION

One of the main reasons for the construction of the railway was to overcome the reliance on sea transport as the only means of supplying Burma during Japan's occupation in 1942. The sea route through the Strait of Malacca was prone to submarine attack and the Japanese decided an alternative method of transport was needed. The British had already considered a railway connection between Thailand and Burma, but it was considered to be too large a project. The Japanese, however, felt that it was possible and planned to start the project in June 1942, to connect Ban Pong with Thanbyuzayat. Engineers carried out a survey of the 415-km (258-mile) route and expressed considerable doubt about the economics of the project. However, with so much free labour at their disposal, in the form of Allied prisoners of war, the Japanese arranged for the construction to start immediately from both ends using metre gauge single track.

The route ran along the east bank of the Mae Klong River from Bangkok until it reached the Khwae Noi River. From there it had to cross the Mae Klong and run along the east bank of the Khawe Noi until it reached the mountains. It would cross the mountains at Three Pagodas Pass and then snake down towards Thanbyuzayat. Using this route meant they could utilize the rivers to help transport materials and men to the necessary sites.

The first prisoners arrived on 23 June, 1942, and started work by moving the tracks and sleepers from the disused yards of the Federal States of Malaya Railways (FMSR). The first bridge to be constructed was a wooden trestle across the Mae Klong. It was 220 m (240 yd) in length and was completed in February 1943. A second bridge, of concrete and steel construction, used semi-eliptic spans brought from Java, and this innovative piece of engineering was finished in July 1943. The two lines met at Konkuita on 17 October, 1943 after only 18 months of extremely hard work by both teams. The Burma teams built 152 km (95 miles) of track, while those from the Thailand end, a total of 263 km (163 miles).

RAILWAY OF DEATH

The Japanese were so concerned with getting the railway track completed that they gave little or no concern for the welfare of their prisoners. They pushed them to their limit on a project that had been estimated to take over five years to complete, and death became commonplace.. Many of the prisoners were little more than teenagers, and the cruelty and callousness shown to those working in the jungle camps was unimaginable. By early 1943, disease, starvation and sheer overwork had killed so many of the prisoners that the Japanese were forced to hire 200,000 Asian coolies to help finish the railway. The men worked from dawn until after dark and often had to trudge many miles through the jungle to return to base camp where conditions were appalling and often steeped in mud, particularly during the rainy season. There was little, if any, medical treatment available to the prisoners and many suffered terribly before they died. A hospital for malaria, dysentery, pellagra and beri-beri patients existed in name only. It was a basic, dilapidated bamboo-framed structure with a thatched roof, where the sick were placed to wait their eventual death. Occasionally, a man would recover from his sickness, but he was rewarded by being sent straight back to work.

The men's diet consisted of rice and salted vegetables, which they were allowed to eat twice a day, but this diet was not enough to sustain them for the 16 hours a day they were forced to work, under atrocious conditions. Many of the prisoners were tortured, even for the smallest offence, and beatings became a regular part of their daily routine. If the Japanese guards felt a man wasn't working to his full potential, he would be beaten savagely and was made to kneel on sharp sticks while holding a boulder for hours on end. Others were tied to trees with barbed wire and left there for several days without food or water.

One of the jobs given to the prisoners was to fell rubber trees and carry the logs back to the camp to fuel the cookhouse and the locomotives. The men worked in teams of three – an axeman and two carriers. Occasionally the men were able to buy food from passing native vendors, but if they were caught trying to smuggle it back into the camps by the Japanese they were severely punished.

After work each day the men would be told how many deaths had occurred while they were away. For each body, four prisoners would be enlisted to wrap the body in straw matting and carry it to the cemetery. This was sometimes a very difficult task because beri-beri caused a kidney malfunction, which resulted in fluid retention. Often a victim would have ballooned in size by as much as 136 kg (300 lb), which made them heavy and difficult to carry.

The only item of clothing they were allowed to wear was a Japanese-style loin cloth, and out of respect for the dead the men would try to cover their naked bodies with leaves. Others prisoners had the unenviable task of digging the endless graves and bury-ing the bodies, most of the time not knowing the identity of the man they had buried. All of these men probably had families back home, but all were buried in unmarked graves.

Right from the start the Japanese acted without compassion, and they could turn into sadistic execu-tioners at the slightest provocation. It has been estimated that for every sleeper laid it cost one human life – a total of 120,000 sleepers where laid while constructing the Death Railway.

RAILWAY DESTROYED

After the railway was completed, the remaining 30,000 prisoners were housed in six camps along the railway track, so that could carry out any maintenance that was necessary. These camps were placed close to the bridges and other strategic positions along the line, so the prisoners became targets of Allied attacks. Many of the prisoners lost their lives in the subsequent bombing raids.

Both bridges were bombed by the Royal Air Force in February 1943. The prisoners of war made repairs and by April the wooden trestle bridge could be used again. It was damaged again in April 1943 by the US Air Force, which meant that repair work had to be carried out for a second time. Both bridges were back in operation by the end of May 1943. Another raid by the Royal Air Force on 24 June finally put the railway out of commission for the remainder of the war.

Following the surrender of the Japanese army from Burma, the British army took out 3.9 km (2½ miles) of the track on the Thai–Burma border. The railway was in a poor state and when the British carried out a survey it showed that, due to poor construction, the bridge was not strong enough to support commercial traffic. The track was subsequently sold to Thai Railways and the 130-km (80-mile) section from Ban Pong to Namtok was rebuilt. It is still in use today.

The wooden trestle bridge, which was actually blocking the river, was removed, while the steel bridge was repaired by the Japanese. Beyond Nam Tok the line is still abandoned, and parts of it have been converted into a trail for walkers. There have been many plans put forward to rebuild the entire railway, but so far this has not been carried out.

MEMORIALS

There are several memorials that have been erected to remember the people who lost their lives during the original construction of the track. Right next to the steel bridge is a plaque and an old locomotive, and part of the original wooden bridge is housed in the World War II museum, also beside the modern bridge. Two other museums are in Kanchanaburi, the Thailand–Burma Railway museum, which opened in 2003, and the JEATH War museum. The best memorial is at Hellfire Pass, which was a land cut where a large majority of the prisoners lost their lives. The main cemetery is in the city of Kanchanaburi, with 6,982 prisoners of war buried there, mainly British, Dutch, Australian and American. There is a smaller cemetery with 1,750 graves a few miles outside of the city of Chong Kai.

The Japanese, who were wrong to have pushed their prisoners so far, openly admitted after the war that they were 'overwhelmed by their tenacious spirit'.

China and the
Yellow River Flood
————1938————

The Great Yu once said, 'Whoever controls the Yellow River controls China', and taming its water has proved to be a major undertaking for centuries. Even without the intervention of man, the river has cost millions of people their lives. When the Japanese blew up the flood dykes in 1938, the resulting flood engulfed three provinces and 44 counties resulting in the loss of 893,303 lives and the displacement of a further 3.9 million people.

BRIEF HISTORY

The Yellow River, or Huanghe, is the second longest river in China and gets its name from the muddiness of its water. Its source comes from the northern area of the Bayanhar Mountains in the Qinghai Province and finally empties out into the Bohai Sea in the Shadong Province. Over the centuries its changes of course have been spectacular and catastrophic, with 26 major changes in the past 2,000 years. As China became more populated, the floods of the Yellow River became increasingly dangerous and many attempts were made to control its flow. After a devastating flood in 1917, the Chinese government sought outside advice on flood management, but the discussions never really found a solution.

In 1931, the flooding of the Yellow River, due to the broad expanse of flat land around it, was described as one of the world's deadliest natural disasters. It has been estimated that as many as 4 million people lost their lives, either by drowning, disease and resultant famine, although the precise figure is probably far higher.

Political turmoil, war with Japan and civil war prevented any further large-scale projects. After the onset of the Second Sino-Japanese War in 1937, there was a man-made disaster that was to surpass any of the previous floods.

JAPANESE ADVANCES

In 1937, the Imperial Japanese Army were making advancements in the heart of the Chinese territory, and by 1938 they had taken control of all of North China. They took control of Kaifeng, the capital of Henan, on 6 June and then threatened to capture Zhengzhou. Because Zhengzhou was part of a major railway network between the Long Hai and Jing Guang railways, the Chinese feared that it would endanger the cities of

Wuhan and Xi'an if the Japanese takeover succeeded. The Chinese government decided to take drastic action and the Guomindang Authority burst the dyke at Huayuankou, near Zhengzhou City, in order to stop any further advancement by the Japanese.

The flood waters started pouring out of Huayuankou early in the morning on 9 June, 1938. The river, which was close to its peak annual flood, swept over 14,500 sq km (9,000 sq miles) of the plain, drowning thousands in its path. Millions of people were made homeless and all the devastation was for nothing – it didn't succeed in stopping the Japanese army.

The situation was made worse by the fact that the Chinese government decided not to inform the public before destroying the dyke, for fear of the news leaking out to the Japanese. This meant that as the flood water submerged millions of homes, the people had no time to flee. Had they had prior warning it is possible that many lives would have been saved.

The dykes on the Yellow River were rebuilt in 1946 and 1947 and the water returned to its original course. Today, the Chinese are managing to control the floods on the Yellow River, but this could be only a temporary measure. The authorities are aware that another '100-year' flood like the floods of 1761 or 1843, would be unstoppable.

PART FIVE

GREAT WAR
CRIMES TRIALS

Nuremburg War Crimes Trial

1945–49

*T*he Nuremberg Trials were a series of trials designed to bring the perpetrators of the Nazi holocaust in World War II to justice. Over 100 defendants took the stand in 12 major trials, revealing an extraordinary picture of what Hannah Arendt later called, 'the banality of evil'. What emerged was that the men and women who committed hideous acts of cruelty on a grand scale in the name of the Third Reich were, in their private lives, often ordinary people: who were responsible, respectable citizens, loving family members and kind neighbours.

The Nuremberg Trials showed that, despite these qualities, the defendants were completely unable to empathize with their victims, or, indeed, regard them as human beings; and that, further, they were able to put aside what moral qualms they may have had by thoroughly identifying with the ideology of Nazism and conforming to what the authorities demanded of them. What also emerged from the trials was just how horrifically cruel, to the point of insanity, the Nazi regime had been: the dreadful stories of what had gone on in the concentration camps traumatized Germany, Europe and the rest of the world, and remind us just how barbaric 'modern' civilization continues to be.

HORRIFIC EXPERIMENTS

As World War II came to a close, the United States President, Franklin D. Roosevelt, raised the question of how to bring the leaders of the Third Reich to justice as war criminals. The Allies had discovered that atrocities in the concentration camps went beyond the scale of what anyone had imagined, and that the Nazis had been involved in the full-scale genocide of the Jewish people, not only gassing them to death in great numbers but torturing and brutalizing them as well. In addition, people with mental and physical disabilities, homosexuals, communists, gypsies, twins and others, had been abused, as Nazi doctors conducted horrific experiments on them.

Roosevelt felt that the captured Nazi leaders should be tried in a court of law, but there was some disagreement about this. Churchill favoured immediate execution of the Nazi leaders, and Stalin wanted to execute thousands of officers. According to some sources, Roosevelt initially thought that Stalin was joking about this, but soon realized his mistake. The US Treasury Secretary, Henry Morgenthau Jr, then came up with a plan to punish the Germans with a series of crushing economic and other sanctions. However, when Roosevelt died in April 1945, his successor Harry S. Truman rejected the Morgenthau Plan, realizing that it would create problems for the future (as had the previous agreement, The Treaty of Versailles, at the end of World War I), and he went on to devise a plan for a judicial war crimes review with the head of his War Department, Henry L. Stimson.

DEFEAT AND SUICIDE

In the meantime, several leading Nazi figures had committed suicide once it became clear that their cause was lost. Hitler, as is well known, shot himself in his Berlin bunker when news of the Allied victory reached him, shortly after marrying his mistress Eva Braun, who also killed herself. Heinrich Himmler, the head of the notorious SS and Gestapo, which had been responsible for the deaths of millions of Jews and others, also took his own life, poisoning himself with cyanide when he was captured. Joseph Goebbels, who became chancellor for one day after Hitler's death, also committed suicide, along with his wife, Magda, who had earlier drugged and poisoned their six children. Martin Bormann, Hitler's private secretary, escaped; some believe that he died while doing so, others that he went on the run for many years after the war.

BRUTALITY AND SADISM

Eventually, it was agreed that the war criminal trials should take place in the German city of Nuremberg, at the Palace of Justice. The first of the trials, in which 24 prominent members of the Nazi administration were charged, took place from 20 November, 1945 to 1 October, 1946, and became the most famous, attracting worldwide attention.

During the trial, evidence of the extreme brutality and sadism of the Nazi regime came to light as the prosecution presented their case. In one instance, prosecutors produced a tattooed piece of human skin, which had been tanned for use as a lampshade. Apparently, the wife of the Commandant of Buchenwald, Isle Koch, liked to have the skin of concentration-camp victims made into decorative household objects for her home. She even used the shrunken head of one victim as a paperweight. In another instance, the prosecution read out descriptions of experiments performed by Nazi doctors on camp inmates. For example, Dr Sigmund Rasher forced victims at Dachau to strip naked before being thrown into tanks of iced water, then threw them into hot water to see how rapidly they warmed up. All the while, the victims had thermometers thrust into their rectums. Dr Rasher's notes also reported how, in most cases, the victims went into convulsions and died during the experiments.

BURNING LIVE CHILDREN

Inmates who had survived the concentration camps also gave their testimony. In one case, a Frenchwoman, Marie-Claude Vaillant-Couturier, described her ordeal at Auschwitz. According to her, Nazi soldiers had gone through the crowds of inmates, sizing up which were to be gassed and which could be forced to perform slave labour on the basis of their physical condition. In another instance, she described how the Nazi soldiers ran out of gas in the chambers, so begun to hurl live children into the furnaces instead. In total, 33 witnesses and hundreds of exhibits were produced, confirming that the Nazi regime had perpetrated some of the worst crimes in human history, and on a scale much larger than ever before.

One of the most interesting aspects of the trial was the evidence of psychiatrists, such as Leon Goldensohn, who was charged with caring for the mental health of the defendants during the trial and detailed the personality traits of those involved. (His notes describing his conversations with the former Nazi officers were later published as *The Nuremberg Interviews*.) In most cases, the defendants alleged that they knew nothing about the concentration camps and what had been going on in them, although this was hard to believe. For example, Joachim von Ribbentrop alleged that he knew nothing of the concentration camps, even though several of them were located near his homes. In other cases, they reported what they had done without seeming to understand that it was wrong. For instance, Colonel Rudolf Hess, speaking as a defence witness for SS head Ernst Kaltenbrunner, described how in an average day at the concentration camp, 10,000 inmates could be gassed to death. His matter-of-fact tone of voice and demeanour shocked many people in the courtroom to the core.

GUILT AND REPENTANCE

In some cases, those accused admitted their guilt and expressed repentance for their heinous crimes. For example, Albert Speer, who had been Minister of Armaments, expressed his regret for participating in the genocide, calling the Nazi regime a disaster, and saying, 'A thousand years will pass and still Germany's guilt will not have been erased.' However, there were others, such as Hermann Goering, who refused to accept that they had committed crimes and continued to maintain that what they had done was right. Shortly before his conviction, Goering made a statement saying that it had been his pleasure to work under Hitler, 'the greatest son which my people produced in a thousand-year history'.

Among those convicted was Martin Bormann, who was tried in his absence and sentenced to death. Hermann Goring, the Head of the Luftwaffe and several sections of the SS, also received the death sentence, but he committed suicide the night before he was due to be executed. Others sentenced to death were: Joachim von Ribbentrop, the Nazi Minister of Foreign Affairs; Wilhelm Frick, the Minister of the Interior and architect of Nazi race laws; Hans Frank, Head of the Poland under its occupation; Wilhelm Keitel, head of the Wehrmacht; Ernst Kaltenbrunner, the highest-ranking SS officer to survive the war; and Julius Streicher, editor of the weekly newspaper, *Der Sturmer*, which had incited hatred and murder of the Jews.

AFTERMATH

Among those who received a life sentence was Rudolf Hess, Hitler's former deputy. Hess later died in Spandau Prison at the age of 93, apparently having committed suicide. (However, some believe he was murdered, questioning the motivation and ability of a 93-year-old to hang by an electrical extension cord from the ceiling.) Since his death, Hess has become a cult figure in Neo-Nazi circles and is regarded with reverence by many contemporary anti-Semites.

Trials of former Nazi officials continued in Nuremberg for the next two years, generating an enormous amount of discussion and controversy. The aim of the trials, besides bringing the culprits to justice, was to ensure that mass genocide of the kind that took place in the Third Reich would never happen again – but sadly, that did not turn out to be the case. However, the Nuremberg trials did bring the hideous crimes of the Nazi war leaders to light, ensuring that they could never become war heroes or martyrs in their country and helped to establish racial tolerance and democracy in modern-day Germany.

Tokyo War Crimes Tribunal

———— 1946–48 ————

*T*he Tokyo War Crimes Tribunal, formally known as the International Military Tribunal for the Far East (IMTFE) was modelled on the Nuremburg Trials and was convened on 3 May, 1946. The aim was to bring prominent figures in the Japanese government to justice after the defeat of Japan in the World War II. In many people's view, Japan's aggressive stance during the war, and its inhumane treatment of prisoners of war and civilians, were comparable with the behaviour of the Nazis during the war, and in some cases worse. For this reason, it was felt by the Allies that the Japanese leaders should pay for what they had done, rather than continue to hold office once the war was over.

The Japanese leaders were tried for a variety of crimes, including starting and waging the war (Class A), committing war crimes (Class B), and committing 'crimes against humanity' (Class C). The trials were more controversial than those at Nuremberg; as many commentators pointed out, the Allied powers themselves had, during their history, all been guilty of such crimes themselves, and it was only because they had won the war that they were in a position to accuse the losers. (For example, the Soviet Union was not the subject of an investigation, even though the abuses of Japanese prisoners of war there had been appalling.) The Japanese, moreover, argued that they had not been signatory to the Geneva Convention, which specified the proper treatment of prisoners of war and civilians, and that therefore they had broken no international law. Moreover, they pointed to the fact that the Allies themselves were not on trial for some of the worst episodes of the conflict, such as the bombing of Nagasaki and Hiroshima, which killed millions of civilians in the most horrifying way and caused lasting sickness and disease in the population as well as untold ecological damage.

A CULTURE OF CRUELTY

However, despite the criticisms, the Tokyo trials went ahead. The Japanese emperor, Hirohito, was not tried, but major figures in his government were charged, including the foreign minister, Baron Hirota Koki, the war minister, General Itagaki Seishiro, and the commander of the Burma Expeditionary Force, General Kimura Heitaro.

The Japanese military had the reputation of being extremely cruel to prisoners of war, and this was indeed borne out by the trial. Japanese military culture was such that soldiers were expected to be unquestioningly obedient to their superiors and to be completely without mercy to their enemies. Since the days of the samurai, Japanese citizens had been taught to be loyal to the emperor, and the Japanese government and people saw it as Japan's right to expand its power and enlarge its empire. Moreover, the Japanese religion, Shinto, which had been adopted as the state religion in the late 19th century, had further reinforced this ideal of obedience to the emperor, who was held to be divine, a descendent of the sun goddess Amaterasu.

REIGN OF TERROR

However, this general cultural influence alone could not explain the sadistic acts of barbarism that took place during World War II in Japan and its occupied territories. What emerged was that during the 1930s, a military dictatorship had taken control in Japan whose reign of terror was similar, in many ways, to that of the Nazis. Japan's secret police, the Kempeitai, ruled the country by fear, while military personnel were required to beat their subordinates for any perceived failure. The further down the ranks the beatings went, the more severe they got, so that during the war, the prisoners taken captive in the camps received the worst treatment of all.

SADISTIC EXPERIMENTS

In such a harsh, militaristic climate, it was hardly surprising that, when Japan joined the Axis powers, their forces would commit dreadful atrocities. However, no one was prepared for the scale of their barbarism, and just as at Nuremberg, the courts were shocked by survivors' accounts of what had gone on the Japanese prisoner-of-war camps. Besides everyday ill-treatment, such as starvation, there were many instances of murder, torture and rape that went unpunished by senior officers. In addition, the Japanese conducted experiments on the prisoners of war, as had the Germans. In one instance, at Unit 731, victims were taken outside in freezing weather, stripped and soaked in water until they had frozen solid. Their arms were amputated, and then their legs. This, apparently, was so that doctors could discover how frostbite affects the human body. Afterwards, the torso was used for other experiments, including researching the effects of diseases such as plague.

The cruelty of such experiments was hardly credible, but there were also other horror stories: of vivisection without anaesthetic on prisoners, and of using them to test for biological and chemical weapons such as poison gas. There were also many tales of torture, which was used on a daily basis to gather military intelligence. After their ordeal, the torture victims were often executed.

'COMFORT WOMEN'

As well as this, the Japanese forced thousands of civilian women into prostitution. They set up military brothels in occupied countries and forced local women to become sex slaves, or 'comfort women' as they were more politely known. In this way, women from the Philippines, Taiwan, Korea, Thailand, Vietnam, Singapore and China became prostitutes in a system that was authorized by the Japanese military officials. However, some commentators allege that this system was not as abusive as it looked, and that many of the women agreed to become prostitutes voluntarily. Whatever the truth, it seems that around 200,000 women became 'comfort women' during the period of World War II.

FORCED LABOUR

Besides this, many civilians and prisoners of war became victims of forced labour camps, in which they were made to work so hard that they died from disease and exhaustion. According to reliable sources, more than 10 million Chinese civilians were forced to become labourers for the Japanese, under a scheme implemented by the Koa-in (the so-called Japanese Asia Development Board'). Today, it is well known, for instance, that over 100,000 civilians and prisoners of war, including British, Australian, Dutch and American servicemen, died while building the Burma Railway from Thailand to Myanmar, known as the 'Death Railway'.

THE VERDICT

In all, seven officials were hanged at Sugamo Prison, Ikebukuro, on 23 December, 1948, and 16 others were sentenced to life imprisonment. Of those serving life sentences, 13 were paroled in 1955, and one, Shigemitsu Mamoru, went on to become Foreign Minister in a later government.

After the trials, prosecutions of other Japanese officials for war crimes continued, and over 4,000 of them were convicted. The largest single trial was that of 93 Japanese officials, who were accused of perpetrating the Laha Massacre, in which 300 Allied prisoners of war were chosen at random and executed in revenge for defeat in battle. In 1946, an Australian tribunal passed the death sentence on Captain Kunito Hatakeyama, who had been in direct command of the massacres, and he was hanged for his crime.

COMPENSATION TO VICTIMS

While the Japanese government has never fully recognized its legal and moral responsibility for the crimes of World War II, individual prime ministers such as Tomiichi Murayama and Kakuei Tanaka have offered their apologies for the suffering caused by the

Japanese military in the past, especially as regards their treatment of the Chinese. However, many political commentators feel that these apologies have not gone far enough, and that Japan should take the example of Chancellor Willy Brandt, the German premier, who in 1970 knelt down at a monument to the victims of the Warsaw Ghetto.

No Japanese leader has so far agreed to make this kind of apology. Instead, in its defence, the Japanese government points to the monetary compensation it has made to the victims of war crimes, in compliance with the Potsdam Declaration of 1945, which specified the terms of Japan's surrender to the Allies. They also point to the setting up of the Asian Women's Fund in 1995, an organization that aims to compensate women forced into prostitution during World War II.

THE ROLE OF HIROHITO

Interestingly, although there is a general view in Europe and the USA that the Japanese refuse to speak about what happened during the war, in recent years there has been a great deal of debate about the issue of war crimes within the country. The view that the Japanese military were only acting in the way they had been trained to do, and were part of a highly authoritarian culture that demanded cruelty towards the enemy as a mark of obedience and loyalty to the emperor, has come under attack. Many critics, both on the left and right, now argue that the Japanese leaders of the time acted in a criminal manner, against the moral and legal constraints of the time, and that the Allies were right to pursue the matter in the courts after the war.

The actions of Emperor Hirohito during World War II have also come under scrutiny, with some commentators arguing that he should have abdicated. Others believe that it was not his moral duty to do so, and that as a figurehead, he was forced to abide by decisions of his ministers. According to the majority view, the real culpability for the war crimes lay with the leading figures in the Japanese Cabinet and military High Command, most of whom were tried and convicted at the Tokyo trials.

The Trial of
Dusko Tadic

———————— 1995–99 ————————

*T*he case of Dusko Tadic is an important one in that it was the first case to be brought before the International Criminal Tribunal for Yugoslavia (ICTY). The ICTY was set up in May 1993 by the UN Security Council for the sole purpose of bringing to trial those responsible for violations of international humanitarian law in the territory of the former Yugoslavia. Its main aim is to bring justice to the victims of the Bosnian war, which saw ethnic cleansing, genocide and many other serious war crimes.

It is probably hard for people to digest, but the 20th century has seen four times as many civilian victims of war crimes and crimes against humanity than there were soldiers killed in all the international wars combined. When the world cried 'never again' after the atrocities of the Nazi holocaust, it was hoped that the prosecution of the Nazi leaders for their monstrous actions at Nuremberg, would put a stop to such barbarity – but this was not to be the case. Between the years 1992 and 1995, atrocities were committed by all sides against all sectors of the population in Bosnia–Herzegovina. Worst of all these atrocities was the gender-selective mass executions of civilians and systematic brutality, particularly against the Muslim population. This is the trial of just one man who was guilty of breaching international law and his complete disregard for his fellow human beings.

BRIEF BACKGROUND

Dusko Tadic was born on 1 October, 1955, in the town of Kozarac. He was born into a military family, his father having been a hero in World War II. His mother had been a detainee at Jasenovac, which was the largest concentration and extermination camp in Croatia during World War II. Tadic became a member of the Serbian Democratic Party (SDS) in 1990.

The SDS attacked the town of Prijedor on 30 April, 1992, with the aid of both the police and military forces. This resulted in the party taking control of Prijedor and Kozarac, which was approximately 10 km (6 miles) to the east. The attack on Kozarac lasted for two days and killed approximately 800 civilians, which was a large proportion of the 4,000 inhabitants of the town. Once the SDS were in control of the town, they started to raid any homes of the non-Serb population and expelled them from the area. They were made to leave with whatever possessions they could carry and walk to camps at Omarska, Keraterm and Trnopolje, and they were subjected to harsh treatment on their already arduous journey. When they arrived at the camps their hardships were to continue as they faced the most appalling conditions.

Tadic was accused of not only having supported the troops in their attack, but being an active member of the SDS and the paramilitary forces and having actively taking part in all stages of the attack on Kozarac. He was further held responsible for the mistreatment of the civilians in the camps, particularly at Omarska. Before the conflict started there were approximately 50,000 Muslims and 6,000 Croats living in the district, but following the ethnic cleansing their numbers were reduced to around 6,000 and 3,000 respectively. Any who remained in the area were forced to live under the most abject conditions.

BROUGHT TO TRIAL

After the cleansing campaign, Tadic was elected president of the local council of the SDS on 15 August, 1992. The following year he was sent to the war zone near Gradacac, but he lasted only one day before going into hiding to avoid being drafted into military service. In August 1993, Tadic went to Nuremberg and then on to Munich where he lived until 12 February, 1994. He was arrested by the Germany police and held in custody until April 1995, when he was transferred to the ICTY in The Hague to face trial.

The trial by the ICTY was the first international war crimes trial since Nuremberg. Security was tight, and the state-of-the-art courtroom at The Hague was sealed off from the spectators' gallery by bulletproof glass. Television crews were given licence to film, and were placed around the room ready to beam the proceedings to closed-circuit monitors in the building and outside in the press tent. To avoid any language problems there were simultaneous video and audio translations into English, French and Serbo-Croat, and a nearly instantaneous transcript of the proceedings appeared on a monitor that was available to everyone taking part in the trial. The same monitor was used to show any available documentary evidence.

Tadic first appeared before the court on 26 April, 1995, and pleaded not guilty to the 34 counts of crimes against humanity. Three of the counts were withdrawn shortly after the trial started, which brought more than 150 witnesses to give evidence. Tadic, who claimed he was a victim of mistaken identity, knew his fate rested with a three-judge panel headed by Gabrielle Kirk McDonald, a former US federal judge from Texas. He faced a maximum life sentence if found guilty.

Almost two years later, on 7 May, 1997, Dusko Tadic was found guilty of crimes against humanity on six counts and of violations of the laws or customs of war on five counts. The prosecution made it clear that despite the fact that Tadic's victims had already suffered the horrors of a two-day artillery bombardment, he still sent them to camps where he was fully aware of the horrific conditions that awaited them. They felt that Tadic had a flagrant disregard for human life and the suffering of others and that he should bear full responsibility for the deaths and the extremely violent and cruel way in which the detainees were treated.

When the sentence was read out it said:

> *. . . that the crimes consisted of killings, beatings and forced transfer by Dusko Tadic as principal or as an accessory, as well as his participation in the attack on the town of Kozarac in opstina Prijedor, in northwestern Bosnia.*

The sentences pronounced by the Trial Chamber ranged from 6 to 20 years. Tadic and his defence team appealed against the sentences.

When the trial went to the Appeals Chamber in July 1999, it proved beyond reasonable doubt that Tadic was responsible for the crimes with which he had been charged, and it found him guilty on ten counts. In November, Tadic was given revised sentences ranging from 6 to 25 years for each of the additional charges.

Tadic appealed for a second time and, although the Appeals Chamber partially reversed their decision, he was finally sentenced to 20 years imprisonment and the case was closed. He was transferred to Germany to serve his term of imprisonment with a mandatory minimum sentence of ten years.

As with all crimes against humanity, it is hard to understand how a person, who probably grew up without any ethnic prejudices, could end up being accused of genocide and violations against his own neighbours. Ironically, the very groups of people who were accused of these crimes were often seen to be sitting together at The Hague either sharing meals, jokes or simply playing cards with their former rivals.

The Trial of
Slobodan Milosevic

———— 2002–2006 ————

The trial of the former Serbian president, Slobodan Milosevic, started on 12 February, 2002, and has been called one of the most important war crimes trials since the Nazi leaders were prosecuted in Nuremburg after World War II. It was being held by the International Criminal Tribunal for the former Yugoslavia in the Hague, and it was hoped that it would force the man who had been nicknamed the 'Butcher of the Balkans' to face the brutality of his crimes committed under the guise of war. Many believed that they would never actually see Milosevic stand in the dock, as the trial had been delayed by his ill health, so when the trial actually commenced there were great sighs of relief among those who believed he was the architect of all the bloodshed.

THE CHARGES

Milosevic was facing three indictments – one relating to atrocities carried out in Kosovo in 1999, another for crimes in Croatia between 1991 and 1992 and the third – the most serious of the three – alleged genocide in Bosnia between 1992 and 1995.

In brief, the **Bosnia** indictment accused Milosevic of the following offences:

Genocide
Crimes against humanity
Grave breaches of the Geneva convention
Violations of the law or customs of war

The Tribunal gave as one example the 1995 massacre at Srebrenica, where several thousands of Muslim men and boys were captured and transported away for execution.

The **Croatia** indictment included:

Crimes against humanity
Grave breaches of the Geneva convention
Violations of the law or customs of war

Under this indictment, Milosevic was held responsible for the murder of hundreds of civilians and the expulsion of over 170,000 non-Serbs who were forced to leave their home towns.

For the atrocities at **Kosovo**, Milosevic along with four of his associates faced:

Crimes against humanity

Violations of the law or customs of war

According to this indictment, Milosevic and his colleagues were directly responsible for the deportation of 800,000 Kosovo Albanians and the murders of about 600 individuals. As commander-in-chief of the Yugoslav army, Milosevic had direct responsibility for the behaviour of of the Serbian security forces under his jurisdiction. The four other people charged alongside Milosevic were, the Serbian president, Milan Milutinovic, former Yugoslav deputy prime minister, Nikola Sainovic, the Yugoslav's army former chief-of-staff, General Dragoljub Ojdanic and the former serbian minister of the interior, Vlajko Stojiljkovic.

Prosecutors at the trial accused Milosevic of 'medieval savagery', stating that it was his search for power that motivated him to commit such atrocities.

MILOSEVIC MAKES A MOCKERY

Milosevic, right from day one, made a mockery out of the court proceedings. He strongly refused to recognize the legitimacy of the UN court and showed no respect whatsoever towards the residing judge. After Milosevic refused to enter a plea or indeed appoint a lawyer on his behalf, the Trial Chamber entered a plea of 'not guilty' for him. They also appointed three international lawyers as 'friends of the court' to make sure that Milosevic's legal rights were not violated.

Milosevic, speaking in English, told the court that he was intending to call 1,631 witnesses in his defence, including the former US president, Bill Clinton, and the British prime minister, Tony Blair. However, it was very uncertain that these influential people would actually turn up. The trial showed that Milosevic still had many loyal supporters among the Serbs and Yugoslavs. During the trial, Milosevic had a team in Belgrade that helped him, often sending information from secret police files.

The complex trial lasted for more than four years and involved scores of documents, photographs, graphic videotapes showing mangled bodies and mass graves, and intercepted audio communications. Forensic teams from around the world managed to exhume 4,000 bodies, although the estimated death toll is considered to be far higher. Milosevic was careful and did not leave any direct trails that would connect him to any of the crimes or even to the commanders and units that carried out the atrocities, so the prosecution had a difficult job ahead of them. In fact, it took the prosecution two years to presents its case in the first part of the trial, which covered the wars in Croatia, Bosnia and Kosovo.

The whole trial was a thoroughly controversial affair, and it produced many conflicting and often strange testimonies. For example, a controversial statement was made by Rade Markovic, who was the former head of the Department of State Security of the Serbian Ministry of the Interior (the Serbian Secret

Service). Prior to being brought to The Hague, Markovic had been held in a Belgrade jail for 17 months. When he was asked to testify he told the court that he had been tortured in jail to force him to agree to give false testimony against Milosevic. He told them that he was offered a change of identify and a comfortable new life if he was prepared to lie.

A BREAKTHROUGH

In October 2001, the investigators involved in the Milosevic case had a major breakthrough. They released the names of several Serbian officials, who had been under close scrutinization, as members of Milosevic's 'joint criminal enterprise'. Rather than face criminal indictments, it was believed that these men would rather cooperate with the investigators. By the end of the year, literally dozens of former Serbian officials, some of whom had been close associates of Milosevic, had agreed to testify against him. Many of these men were considered to be the former backbone of Milosevic's 'secret' state and could therefore be influential in the outcome of the tribunal. It was felt that if these men would name and shame the people who actually ordered the killings, it would help the prosecution convict Milosevic. However, Milosevic proved to be quite a formidable force when it came to attacking the prosecution. He skilfully manipulated the witnesses and he seemed to have a natural ability to throw his opponents off the scent.

Towards the end of his trial Milosevic started to complain of health problems and demanded that he be given a provisional release to Russia for treatment. His request was denied and the tribunal's own doctor was ordered to examine him. His ill health caused many intermissions and prolonged the trial by at least six months. The trial wasn't resumed until October 2004 and the former Soviet premier, Nikolai Ryzhkov, became the first high-profile witness to testify for the defence. Had Milosevic been able to complete his defence, it was believed that he would have gone down the route that NATO's attack on Yugoslavia was aggressive, thus making it a war crime under international law. For example, the bombing of a Serbian state television building in April 1999, in which 16 people died, was a deliberate attack on a civilian target.

THE WORST POSSIBLE OUTCOME

The death of Slobodan Milosevic on 12 March, 2006, brought both shock and disappointment to all who were associated with his ongoing war crimes trial. He was found by guards in his prison cell at the detention centre for the International Criminal Tribunal, and although there were rumours that he had poisoned himself, this was later disproved. His wife and family blamed the tribunal for his death, saying that they had refused him medical treatment.

Although the outcome was not what the prosecutors had hoped for, and many felt Milosevic's death was his ultimate victory over justice, the trial in itself was quite a milestone for justice. No other head of state had ever been tried for such crimes in modern history, so the fact that he was brought to trial is ultimately more important than its final outcome. The fact that Milosevic was forced to come face to face with his actions should pave the way for an individual's right to freedom from fear. Hopefully the trial is just a stepping stone to bringing other brutal dictators before the scales of justice.

FURTHER INDICTMENTS

In addition to Milosevic, eight former Serbian policemen, including former senior police commanders, went on trial in October 2006, on charges relating to the worst massacres of the Kosovo war. They were accused of executing 48 ethnic Albanian citizens, all, with the exception of one, from the same family. The killings took place in Suva Reka in March 1999. The victims included 14 children, two babies, a pregnant woman and a 100-year-old woman. Their bodies were all discovered several years later in a mass grave at a police training camp near Belgrade.

In the same week that the trial started, Serbia's deputy prime minister, finance minister, health minister and energy minister all resigned from the government of Prime Minister Vojislav Kostunica. This was due to the ongoing inability to arrest the fugitive Ratko Mladic, who was the Bosnian Serb leader Radovan Karadzic's army chief throughout the Bosnian war. Mladic has been indicted by the UN war crimes tribunal on charges of genocide and other crimes against humanity, including the massacre of some 7,500 Muslim men and boys in Srebrenica in 1995. Mladic disappeared from view when Slobodan Milosevic was arrested in 2001 and it is believed that he is being protected by sympathizers within Serbia.

PART SIX

WAR CRIMES AND ATROCITIES 1950–2000

No Gun Ri Massacre and other Korean Atrocities

1950–53

During the Korean War, which lasted from 1950 to 1953, the Korean people were subjected to the most atrocious war crimes, which resulted in the loss of about 6 million lives. Of these, it is estimated that as many as 4 million were civilians, not even soldiers in the bloody war between North and South. These people were exposed to immoral massacres and indiscriminate napalm or germ-bombing.

The principal combatants in the war were the North Koreans, later joined by the People's Volunteer Army (PVA) of the People's Republic of China and advisors, aircraft pilots and weapons from the Soviet. South Korea fought alongside the USA, the UK, Canada and the Philippines, with many other nations joining in under the flag of the United Nations. Soldiers from all the armies seemed to target civilians and/or prisoners of war and there were reports of many massacres taking place during the three-year war.

However, one thing is clear: US troops were certainly under orders, following a total defeat at Taejon, to treat any approaching Korean civilians on the battlefield as hostile and were instructed to 'neutralize' them before they could inflict any harm. This order led to fear among the US military and led to the indiscriminate killing of hundreds, if not thousands, of Korean civilians. One such atrocity occurred at a village called No Gun Ri.

UNNECESSARY SLAUGHTER

The village of No Gun Ri is a remote and mountainous region, about 160 km (100 miles) south of Seoul. From 26–29 July, 1950, around 400 Korean refugees fled from their villages and headed towards the small hamlet of No Gun Ri. Many rode on ox carts, while others walked, carrying their children. All were in fear of what lay behind them – the North Koreans. The invasion was in full force and members of the Seventh Cavalry Regiment, First Cavalry Division of the US army, had positioned themselves at either end of a bridge. There were fears that the North Koreans had already infiltrated the refugees, and that if they were allowed to cross the US line, the Koreans would then be able to attack from the rear.

The US soldiers ordered the refugees to leave the road and follow the railway track until they were underneath the bridge. The refugees were forced to stay under the bridge, and at dusk on the third day the soldiers heard sporadic gunfire coming from the direction of the enemy. Next the battalion runner came by with orders to shoot and kill anyone standing under the bridge. Unsure of where the order came from, one of the soldiers asked exactly who had given such an instruction. He said it had come from the executive officer who was assigned to the Second Battalion of the Seventh Cavalry. All of a sudden, machine guns started firing randomly into the crowd of people under the bridge. Bodies fell everywhere and terrified parents dragged their screaming children into a narrow culvert beneath the tracks. The refugees resorted into pulling the already dead bodies around themselves for protection. Mothers wrapped their children with blankets and hugged them with their backs turned towards the entrance.

Some of the US soldiers refused to shoot what one of them described as 'civilians just trying to hide'. Another soldier at the scene described the event as 'unnecessary wholesale slaughter'. Both veterans and survivors of the horrendous event are haunted by the memories of those three nights. They say they can still hear the sound of the little children crying and the screams of their desperate parents. The haunting sight of the children clinging desperately to their blood-sodden mothers is a nightmare that will possibly never leave them.

OTHER INCIDENTS

When the Associated Press (AP) started investigations into the killings at No Gun Ri, they uncovered other incidents. On 3 August, 1950, a US general and other army officers ordered the destruction of two bridges just as South Korean refugees started to cross, killing hundreds of civilians.

Earlier the same day, just 40 km (25 miles) down-river at Tuksong-dong, a steel-girder bridge was blown up, while it was crowded with women, children, old men and ox carts carrying their belongings. Many of the refugees drowned when they jumped into the river and tried to swim to the shore.

Unfortunately, these were not isolated incidents. Instead, they were rather characteristic of one of the bloodiest wars in the chapters of history. Although the survivors of the No Gun Ri massacre sought compen-sation for the unprovoked attack in 1960, the US claims office pointed out that they had left it too long, and that prosecution so many years later was prac-tically an impossibility. On top of that, Korean officials warned against the survivors speaking to anyone about what had happened.

NORTH KOREAN WAR CRIMES

On the other side of the coin, there are many reports of war crimes committed by the North Korean armies during the Korean War against captured United Nations military personnel and innocent civilians. From the onset of the war in 1950, the North Koreans committed a series of war crimes that constituted one of the most heinous and barbaric epochs of recorded history.

In an effort to get detailed evidence on what had occurred during the Korean War, a War Crimes Division in Korea was set up. It was divided into several branches – the Case Analysis Branch, the Investigations Branch and the Historical Branch – each one having their own important role to play in the investigations. The evidence produced before the committee conclusively proved that US prisoners of war, who were not deliberately murdered at the time of capture, were beaten, wounded, starved, tortured, molested, displayed in public and openly humiliated before Korean civilians. On top of this, they were forced to march long distances without food, water, shelter, clothing or adequate medical attention. In specially set-up Communist prison camps, there were further acts of human indignities, as well as massacres on an extremely large scale.

The following cases, which were presented to the War Crimes Division, represent just a few of the atrocities commited by the North Korean and Chinese Communist armies:

THE HILL 303 MASSACRE
A group of 26 US soldiers were captured by the North

Koreans on 14 August, 1950. The soldiers were stripped of their combat boots and personal belongings and their hands were tied behind their backs. The following day a further 19 soldiers joined their group, bringing the total number to 45. On the third day the prisoners were led to a ravine and, with their hands still tethered, were shot in cold blood. One by one the soldiers fell, and only four managed to survive the ordeal to tell exactly what had happened.

THE SUNCHON TUNNEL MASSACRE

In October 1950, when the fall of the city of Pyongyang seemed imminent, the North Koreans loaded about 180 US war prisoners into open railway carriages to be transported to the north. These men were already weak from lack of food and water, having been survivors of the Seoul-Pyongyang death march. For five days they were exposed to the raw Korean climate, and on 30 October they arrived at the Sunchon tunnel.

Late in the afternoon, the prisoners were taken from the railway carriages in small groups and marched towards some nearby ravines, under the pretext of being given their first food for several days. Instead, they were ruthlessly shot, using Russian burp guns.

A total of 138 US soldiers lost their life on that fateful occasion – 68 were murdered, seven died of malnutrition and the remainder of pneumonia, malnutrition and dysentery on the horrendous ride from Pyongyang.

TAEJON MASSACRE

On 27 September, 1950, approximately 60 US soldiers who had been imprisoned at Taejon had their hands wired together and were taken in small groups out into the prison courtyard. They were forced to sit hunched together in previously dug ditches, and then shot at point-blank range by North Korean soliders. Only one soldier lived to tell his gruesome tale.

In addition to this slaughter, a number of Korean civilians, believed to be as many as 5,000–7,000, together with soldiers of the Republic of Korea, were killed at Taejon between 23 and 27 September, 1950.

BAMBOO SPEAR CASE

In December 1950, five US airmen were killed when their convoy of trucks was ambushed by North Korean forces. When their bodies were later discovered by a South Korean patrol, it showed that their flesh had been punctured in as many as 20 different places. The instrument of severe torture was a heated bamboo stick, and the soldiers were literally left to bleed to death from their perforations.

MURDER AT NAEDAE

On 13 October, 1950, a dozen US soldiers were held captive in a Korean hut in a village near Naedae. Without any warning the North Koreans opened fire, killing all but five. One of the survivors said that he heard the first shot and one of his companions, who had been hit in the chest, slumped forward. He said he reacted quickly and hid under a nearby desk, playing dead. A little later he felt someone kick him, still he remained inactive and, even after being shot in the leg he continued to play dead. Eventually, the Korean soldiers left and he lived to tell the tale.

CHAPLAIN-MEDIC MASSACRE

North Korean forces surprised and slaughtered approximately 20 US soldiers on 17 July, 1950. At the time of the killings, the soldiers were being tended to by a regimental surgeon wearing a Red Cross arm-band. Also present was an army chaplain, who could easily be identified by his Christian cross; neither of these men carried a weapon. The chaplain was killed with the soldiers, but the surgeon, despite being badly wounded, managed to survive the ordeal.

JEJU MASSACRE

The Jeju massacre was a suppression against an armed rebellion on Jeju island, South Korea, during the period of 3 April, 1948 to 21 September, 1954. A number of elements led to the massacre, including a complex co-operation between guerilla forces, police, youth groups, local and national armies with a strong US influence. The South Korean right-wing government decided to carry out nationwide campaigns in an effort to flush out communists and their sympathizers.

Communist influence was strong on Jeju island and the campaign led to nationwide unrest. Many decided to resort to armed resistance against the actions of the government.

When the US government backed out of helping to organize the Korean elections, labour party leaders staged massive rallies to demand reunification. In the first of the rallies, police killed six protestors. On 3 April, 1948, rebels relaliated by attacking police stations and government offices, killing an estimated 50 policemen.

When the trouble first started, rebels were given the label 'communist' purely for political reasons, when in truth their motives had nothing to do with communism. The trouble had really started when there was a major crackdown on the islanders' smuggling activities, which was their main source of income. Locals, who were accused of being either smugglers or Communists, were subjected to torture, rape, killings and random incarcerations. This resulted in an angry attack by the locals on all the police stations on the island. The rebels broke into the police stations, freed their relatives and stole arms before retreating. This gave them the upper hand until support arrived from the mainland. Stripped of both arms and ammunition, the police were left in a vulnerable state. The Korean's 9th regiment who, although they were armed, had not been allowed any ammunition as the USA still held power over the island.

The government invasion began on 25 June, which resulted in thousands of people being detained in four separate groups. These groups were divided on their perceived security risk – A, B, C and D. On 30 August, a written order was received by a senior intelligence officer in the South Korean Navy, which instructed the Jeju police to kill all those held in groups C and D by firing squad.

The rebellion continued until the end of the Korean War and it is estimated that as many as 30,000 to 80,000 islanders were killed during this period.

My Lai Massacre

————1968————

The villages of central Vietnam are known collectively as 'My Lai' (literal translation 'Son My'), and have been subjected to the most horrific acts of war. The so-called My Lai massacre, took place on 16 March 1968, and was a turning point in the public's view of the Vietnam War. In a period of just three hours, over 500 Vietnamese civilians, many women and children, were slaughtered in cold blood at the hands of US soldiers.

My Lai lay in the South Vietnamese district of Son My, an area that had been heavily mined by the Vietcong. Many soldiers of Charlie Company, a unit of the US Division's 11th Infantry Brigade, had been maimed or killed in the area, which had left them angry and frustrated. Led by Lieutenant William Calley, Charlie Company entered My Lai, expecting to be confronted by the elusive 48th Vietcong Battalion.

Unsure of what was ahead of them, Charlie Company had been given the order to 'search and destroy'. There were reports that all the civilians had left the village and that the remaining people were either Vietcong or their sympathizers.

As they entered the village, Calley gave the instruction to his men to go in firing, even though they were met with no opposing fire. In the carnage that followed, old men were bayoneted, women and children, including babies, were shot in the back of the head and several young girls were gang raped before being killed. Soldiers went beserk, showing no mercy, even to the families that were huddled together in their huts. The Vietnamese, who tried to show a sign of respect to the soldiers by bowing, were greeted with torture, either by first, clubbed with rifle butts or stabbed with boyonets. Those who emerged with their hands raised in surrender, were simply mowed down. Some victims were mutilated with the signature 'C Company' carved into their chests. Wounded villagers simply stood frozen on the spot, shock and disbelief in their eyes as they watched what was going on around them. Not one of the victims was an armed Vietcong fighter – all were innocent civilians. There was not one US soldier killed or injured in the period of the entire massacre, with the exception of one soldier who shot himself in the foot while cleaning his own pistol.

The total death toll was over 500 in a period of just a few hours. Calley, himself, was reported to have killed 60 civilians who were crouching down in a ditch, after his men balked at his order to shoot.

MILITARY RESCUE

By late morning the word had reached a US army helicopter crew, who came to the assistance of the villagers. The pilot, Hugh Thompson, landed his helicopter in between the terrified villagers and the soldiers, who seemed to be totally out of control. He ordered his men to fire on any US soldiers who continued to threaten any villagers and radioed for help. Two more helicopters arrived and managed to airlift a dozen villages to safety.

AFTERMATH

In the aftermath of the massacre, soldiers on the scene made every effort to cover up their misdeeds, in the hope that the true number of victims would not be revealed. When the news of what had happened at My Lai reached the American public, they were outraged and demanded the immediate withdrawal of troops from Vietnam. The My Lai massacre had simply opened the eyes of people who had previously paid no particular attention to the war.

Despite the fact that the massacre was recorded on film by an army photographer who accompanied Charlie Company, the incident could possibly have gone by without investigation if an army officer by the name of Ron Ridenhour, hadn't written a letter directly to President Nixon. He also sent copies to the

Pentagon, the State Department, the Chief of Staff and several members of Congress. He told the story he had heard from his fellow soldiers, ending the letter with:

I feel that I must take some positive action on this matter. I hope that you will launch an investigation immediately and keep me informed of your progress. If you cannot, then I don't know what other course of action to take.

General William Westmoreland, who also received a copy of the letter, was appalled at its content and immediately ordered an investigation. Calley was told to return immediately to the USA and was subsequently charged with 109 counts of murder, well below the actual numbers who had died. However, it would be another two months before the American public heard the full extent of the atrocity. In 1969, an investigative journalist, Seymour Hersh, broke the news. Already horrified by news that had been leaking through about the horrors of the Vietnam War, hundreds of other witnesses were eventually called to the stand. The charges included murder, rape, sodomy and general mayhem. Investigators suggested that there should be a further 30 prosecutions for the atrocities and another 30 for the cover up that went on after the event. Even though the US army was already under intense pressure for its conduct in Vietnam, only one man was every prosecuted, the unit's commander,

William Calley. He was sentenced to life imprisonment, but he was released in 1974 after many appeals.

In many ways the My Lai massacre represented a major turning point in the public's attitude towards Vietnam. Not only were they horrified when the images were released but they were also appalled at the way the prosecutions were handled. It was evident that the army wanted to downplay the event and the punishment given to the scapegoat, Calley, never really matched the magnitude of the crime.

Ireland: Bloody Sunday

————1972————

*T*he term 'Bloody Sunday' has been used to describe an incident that occurred on 30 January, 1972 in Londonderry, Northern Ireland – and bloody it was. Londonderry, itself, is an old city that is famous for its resistance over the years to various sieges. However, today it bears the scars of sectarian violence.

On the morning of Bloody Sunday, a number of paratroopers were bussed into Londonderry as they expected rioting. They were told to arrest any trouble-makers and the paratroopers knew there was a possibility they could be shot at by snipers.

On the afternoon of 30 January, a Northern Ireland Civil Rights Association (NICRA) march had been planned in protest against the continuation of intern-ment without trial in Northern Ireland. It is estimated that between 10,000 and 20,000 men, women and children took part in the march and, at the onset, the participants were in high spirits. The planned route of the march should have taken them past the guildhall, but they were prevented from entering the city centre by members of the 1st Batallion of the British Parachute Regiment. The main body of the march then proceeded towards a place called Free Derry Corner. However, a small group of teenagers broke away from the main march and goaded the soldiers by constantly pushing the barriers, shouting insults and throwing stones at them. The soldiers' response at this time was to use a water cannon, tear gas and rubber bullets to try and disperse the troublemakers, but it wasn't long before matters deteriorated rapidly.

At 16.10 p.m. the paratroopers were given orders to move in and arrest as many civil rights marchers as possible. They advanced down Rossville Street into the Bogside, but what happened next is still uncertain. It is alleged that at some point in the proceedings the British command centre had received instructions that there was an IRA sniper in the area, and the paratroopers were given instructions to use live ammunition. They placed snipers on the city walls above the Bogside and started to shoot unarmed civilians. John Duddy, the first man to be killed, was actually running away from the troops when he was shot in the back.

Aggression against the British troops escalated at this point and, despite a ceasefire from headquarters, the soldiers fired over 100 rounds directly into the fleeing crowds. During the next 30 minutes the British soldiers killed 13 men and injured a further 13, mainly by single shots to the head and trunk. Another man died from his wounds after being admitted to hospital, bringing the total dead to 14.

WITNESS REPORTS

The picture of Father Daly waving a blood-stained handkerchief was captured on film by a BBC cameraman and appeared on the front pages of the national press. The 39-year-old curate from St Eugene's Cathedral in Londonderry joined the march as it passed by his cathedral, just after he had finished conducting a funeral. He was standing close to 17-year-old John 'Jackie' Duddy when he was shot. Father Daly and other members of the march tried to help him, but realised that they needed to get him to a hospital. They decided to make a dash for it, and Father Daly ran in front with his blood-stained handkerchief in his hand while some other men carried John behind him. The soldiers were firing everywhere and the men were frightened, particularly as they were all unarmed. Father Daly gave the last rites to many of the dead and severely injured on Bloody Sunday. John Duddy unfortunately died while the men were trying to carry him to safety.

Although the soldiers responsible for the shootings insisted that they had come under sustained gun attack from members of the IRA, evidence from witnesses ran to the contrary. All the eyewitnesses, apart from the soldiers themselves, who included marchers, local residents and journalists, all confirmed that the soldiers had fired into an unarmed crowd who were in fact running away from them. Even people who had stopped to help the wounded were shot at. No British soldier was wounded by gunfire, and there was no proof whatsoever that they had been fired on by anyone. In the aftermath, irate crowds burned down the British Embassy in Dublin on 2 February, 1972, and Anglo-Irish relations hit an all-time low.

The shock and anger caused by the events on that day was responsible for provoking many young Catholic men to enlist in the IRA and join in the fight to try and end British control.

FIRST INQUIRY

As soon as the British government learned of the killings, they appointed Lord Widgery, who was Lord Chief Justice at that time, to open an inquiry into the events of that day. The Irish people were wary about the impartiality of Widgery, and even more sceptical when he decided to hold the Tribunal in Coleraine, which was about 51 km (32 miles) away from scene of the killings. Some considered boycotting the inquiry, when they learned that many key witnesses, including some of those who had been wounded on that Sunday, were not even to be called to take part in the Tribunal. Widgery's report, which was issued less than three months after the event, exonerated the British soldiers, stating that they were justified in using live ammunition as there was a strong suspicion that some of the people killed had been firing weapons or handling nail bombs. There was nothing to back up his report, and further forensic evidence proved that any trace of explosives on the clothes of 11 of those killed was negative. The clothes of the remaining men could not be tested as, for some unexplainable reason, they had already been washed.

SAVILLE INQUIRY

After considerable pressure to reopen the inquiry, on 29 January, 1998, Tony Blair, then British Prime Minister, announced there would be a new investigation under the chairmanship of Lord Saville. The ensuing inquiry, which ran between March 2000 and January 2005, turned out to be one of the longest and most expensive in British legal history. The new inquiry was the result of the frustration of the relatives of those killed and injured on Bloody Sunday, claiming that the first tribunal had been a 'whitewash'.

Because a number of soldiers felt their lives would be in danger if they had to testify in Ireland, the inquiry was moved to London. There were disruptions right from the start of the inquiry, when a number of police officers told the tribunal that they would only testify from beind screens in order to protect their identity.

Colonel Derek Wilford, who was the officer in charge of the Parachute Regiment on Bloody Sunday, never wavered in his testimony that his soldiers were fired on first. However, he did go on to say that the regiment had disobeyed his orders by driving deep into the Bogside in a number of armoured cars.

By the time the inquiry retired to study its findings, it had cost a total of £155 million and interviewed over 900 witnesses, including leading politicians, civilians, policemen, soldiers and members of the IRA. Even Sir Edward Heath, the prime minister at that time, was called to take the stand.

However, vital helicopter video footage and army photographs were never made available to the inquiry and, on top of this, guns used on the day by the British soldiers, which should have been produced as evidence, have since been destroyed. Because of the enormous amount of information to be studied, the Saville inquiry has not published its report to date. Christopher Clarke QC, counsel to the inquiry, said that he hoped the proceedings had played a part in enabling people to come to terms with the events of the day, but some people feel that it raised more ghosts than it put to rest.

Bokassa: the Devil Emperor

———————1921–96———————

*I*t is little wonder that Jean-Bédel Bokassa was nicknamed the 'Ogre of Berengo' and 'Cannibal Emperor'. Apart from reportedly murdering members of his own army and poisoning his own grandchild, Bokassa also personally participated in the massacre of over 100 schoolchildren who protested against paying for school uniforms bearing his picture.

MILITARY BACKGROUND

Jean-Bédel Bokassa was born on 22 February, 1921, in the village of Bobangi in the Moyen-Congo, in the present-day Central African Republic. His father, Mgboundoulou, was a tribal chef of the M'Baka, which was a small tribe in the forest south of Bangui. In 1927, when Bokassa was only six, his father was murdered by French colonial occupiers. His mother never got over the loss of her husband and committed suicide one week later, leaving Bokassa and his 11 siblings, to be raised by Catholic missionaries.

As soon as he was old enough, Bokassa enlisted in the army, fighting for the French in World War II in Indo-China and Algeria, and heended the war as sergeant major. He was awarded the Legion d'Honneur award, which was created by Napoleon, and also the Croix de Guerre, a military decoration of both France and Belgium. Bokassa left the French army in 1961 and joined the military ranks of the Central African Republic. Bokassa rose quickly through the ranks, becoming both colonel and chief of staff of the armed forces.

SELF-PROCLAIMED EMPEROR

In 1966, with his country in a state of economic confusion, Bokassa decided to overthrow the autocratic David Dacko (who was his cousin), in a *coup d'état*, after a threatened nationwide strike. Bokassa immediately assumed power as the President of the Republic and head of the *Mouvement pour l'évolution Sociale de l'Afrique Noire*, which was the only political party at that time. In 1972, Bokassa declared himself president for life, and in 1974 he survived an attempt on his life and a coup attempt later that same year.

Bokassa decided to convert to Islam after a meeting with Muammar al-Qadhafi of Libya and also changed his name to Salah Eddine Ahmed Bokassa. It is thought that this was simply a ploy to try and obtain funds from Libya, and when no financial aid was forthcoming, Bokassa abandoned his newly acquired faith.

In September 1976, Bokassa dissolved the government and replaced it with the Central African Revolutionary Council. In December of that year, Bokassa declared the republic a monarchy, giving it a new name, the Central African Empire. So that he could legally crown himself Emperor Bokassa I, he quickly converted back to Catholicism, and he almost ruined his country financially with his overly-extravagant coronation, costing an alleged $20 million. For the next 14 years that he was in power, he abused his position and looted his country of any riches that it contained. Many of his subjects thought that he was totally insane, and they compared his egotistical extravagance to that of the other well-known dictator, Idi Amin. Bokassa even bragged that Pope John-Paul II had made him an apostle of the Catholic Church. Rumours of torture were rife, and it has even been suggested that Bokassa himself took part in the thrashings. In 1979, everything was to change.

THE LAVISH PALACE

Bokassa's once lavish palace rose out of a palm grove, approximately 80 km (50 miles) from the capital of Bangui. Inside the palace was a garish Italian bathroom and a luxury kitchen. The bedroom, where the emperor slept, had a gold-plated bed surrounded by piles of gold and diamonds. Next to the palace was an airstrip, and one terrified neighbour reported that Bokassa used to simply pick up beggars and drop them into the Obangui River. In the grounds were once ornate cages containing lions and crocodiles, and today natives make money selling the tall grasses growing inside to inquisitive tourists. What is even more strange, are the late emperor's 62 children, once the elite of the country, now dressed in tatters and living in derelict outhouses in the grounds of the palace.

THE GRIM DISCOVERY

The French remained loyal supporters of Bokassa and the French president, Valéry Giscard d'Estaing, became a close friend. He often accompanied Bokassa on hunting trips in Africa and was given uranium, which was a vital ingredient for the manufacture of France's nuclear weapons. D'Estaing was frequently given personal gifts of gold and diamonds by Bokassa, but eventually these tokens of friendship became an embarrassment for the president. The French grew increasingly critical of the friendship, and after a riot in Bangui in 1979, which led to the massacre of many civilians, French support ran out.

Bokassa was ousted from his luxurious home when it was stormed by French troops in 1979, after they arranged a coup in order to remove him from power. Bokassa fled to the Ivory Coast. When the authorities searched his palace, Villa Kolongo, a strange smell came from the freezer. When they opened it they found the bodies of some of his political opponents, and some children, not only in the walk-in freezer, but in the bottom of his swimming pool, too.

Apparently, in 1979 Bokassa had declared that all the nation's schoolchildren should wear uniforms and, ironically, the only producer in Bangui happened to be one of his wives. The families of the children were exceptionally poor, and they couldn't even begin to pay for the uniforms. One day they gathered in the streets and threw rocks at Bokassa's car as it drove past. Bokassa was furious and rounded up approximately 100 children, both innocent and guilty, and had them all murdered. Bokassa killed many himself and kept many of their remains in his freezer at his palace. In the same freezer, he kept the corpses of some of his political enemies he had eliminated, and he was said to have frequently snacked on their brains and hearts.

In 1980, Bokassa, *in absentia,* was condemned to death not only for mass murder but also for cannibalism. Bokassa remained in exile in the Ivory Coast for four years and then fled to France, who gave him diplomatic immunity due to his past history with the French Foreign Legion.

In 1986, Bokassa came out of exile and returned to Bangui, where he was immediately arrested and tried for treason, murder, cannibalism and embezzlement. The trial lasted for several months and, although he was cleared of the cannibalism charges, Bokassa was again sentenced to death on 12 June, 1987. In February 1988, however, his sentence was commuted to life imprisonment and then reduced further to just 20 years.

Bokassa was released from prison in 1993, when the country returned to a democratic state. Bokassa lived the rest of his life in the ruins of his former palace in Bangui. It is thought he had at least 17 wives and concubines and as many as 62 children. Bokassa died of a heart attack on 3 November, 1996.

LEGACY OF CORRUPTION AND GREED

Even today Africa remains a continent that is tangled up with poverty and corruption. Selfish leaders, such as Jean-Bédel Bokassa, have done nothing to raise the population out of a state of deprivation. He took advantage of impoverished Africans to further his own wealth, using public funds to fund his own lavish lifestyle. On top of that he was a ruthless murderer, annihilating anyone who got in his way or didn't kowtow to his demands. His regime was most definitely characterized by many human rights atrocities.

The Butcher of Africa
————————1971–79————————

*I*di Amin was President of Uganda from 1971 to 1979, but his term of office was witness to one of the bloodiest dictatorships in the history of Africa. Under his rule as many as 400,000 people are believed to have been killed and many more were imprisoned and tortured. Although Amin gave himself the exalted titles of 'His Excellency President for Life', 'Field Marshal Al Hadji Doctor Idi Amin, VC, DSO, MC', 'Lord of All the Beasts of the Earth and Fishes of the Sea' and 'Conqueror of the British Empire in Africa in General and Uganda in Particular', to the rest of the world he was known as the 'Butcher of Africa'.

HIS EARLY YEARS

Idi Amin was born, Idi Awo-Ongo Angoo, between the years of 1923 and 1925, into the Kakwa tribe in Koboko, in the north-west corner of Uganda. Shortly after Amin was born, his father, a farmer and a follower of Islam, abandoned the family, leaving his son to be raised by his mother, Assa Aatte, a self-proclaimed sorceress. He was the third eldest of eight children and received only a rudimentary education, excelling in sports and reciting the Qur'an. He converted to Islam at an early age, which is when he changed his name to Idi Amin. In 1946, he joined the King's African Rifles as an assistant cook and laundry assistant. In 1947, as a private, he transferred to Kenya for infantry service, and he was promoted to corporal in 1948.

By 1954, Amin had made the rank of *effendi* (or warrant officer), which is the highest possible rank for a black African in the colonial British army. He allegedly got his nickname 'Dada' while serving in Kenya, because every time he was caught with a woman in his tent, to avoid being punished, he pleaded that she was his *dada*, which is Swahili for 'sister'.

During his service in the army Amin trained as a boxer and took the title of Uganda's light heavyweight boxing champion, which he held from 1951 to 1960. Amin returned to his homeland of Uganda in 1954, and by 1961 he had become one of the first two Ugandans to be appointed commissioned officers, with the rank of Lieutenant. He was described by a former officer as 'an incredible person who certainly isn't mad – very shrewd, very cunning and a born leader'.

FIRST SIGNS OF BRUTALITY

The first signs of the brutality that Amin became famous for appeared in 1962, when troops under his command committed the Turkana massacre. It was during an operation to try and stop tribesmen from stealing cattle from the neighbouring region of Turkana in Kenya that his true character came to the fore. Investigations carried out by British authorities in Kenya, later revealed that the victims of the massacre had been tortured, beaten to death, had their genitalia removed and, in many cases, were buried alive. However, with Uganda's independence only a few months away, the authorities decided against court-martialling Amin for what they described as his 'over-zealous' methods.

Uganda gained its independence from the UK on 9 October, 1962, and the king of the Baganda tribe, Sir Edward Mutesa became the first president. Milton Obote became the country's first prime minister and received the full support of Amin. Overlooking the rumours of torture, Obote rewards Amin for his loyalty by promoting Amin to major in 1963, and to colonel and deputy commander of the army and air force in 1964. Shortly after Uganda's independence, Amin was sent to Israel on a paratrooper training course. During this period he became a favourite with the Israelis when he acted as a go-between for the supply of arms and ammunition to Israeli-backed rebels fighting a war in southern Sudan.

In 1965, both Obote and Amin were involved in a scandal involving the smuggling of gold, coffee and ivory out of what is now the Democratic Republic of Congo. When President Mutesa demanded a parliamentary investigation into the financial scandal, Obote decided to take defensive action. He suspended the constitution, arrested almost half of his cabinet and installed himself as president for life. He drove Mutesa from his palace in a military operation led by Amin, which forced him into exile in the UK, where he remained until his death in 1969. Obote formed a new constitution that abolished all of the country's previous kingdoms. Amin, who was now in charge of the army and air force, starts to build a strong base by recruiting members of the Kakwa, Lugbara and other ethnic groups into his army. However, his relations with Obote began to turn sour when Amin was charged with misappropriation of millions of dollars of military funds.

AMIN SEIZES POWER

When Amin learned that Obote was about to have him arrested, he organized a military coup while Obote was out of the country attending a Commonwealth seminar in Singapore. Amin's new military government accused Obote and his regime of corruption, economic mismanagement, failing to maintain law and order and suppressing democracy. Initially, the coup was fully supported by the Ugandans and welcomed by the British, with Amin's promise of abolishing Obote's secret police, freeing of all political prisoners, introducing economic reforms and also pledging to return the country to civilian rule as quickly as possible.

After taking power, Amin said, 'I am not an ambitious man, personally, I am just a soldier with a concern for my country and people.' Little did people realize that giving Amin a free rein would be the worst thing possible for Uganda. No sooner was he in charge than he ordered the mass executions of officers and troops who he believed to be loyal to the overthrown Obote. Forming his own 'State Research Bureau' he sent death squads out to eradicate military leaders and intelligentsia who Amin believed would oppose his rule. An explosion in a prison cell at the Makindye Prison in Kampala killed 32 army officers, and it is believed that as many as two-thirds of the army's 9,000 officers were executed during Amin's first year in power, many by beheading.

Obote, who had taken refuge in Tanzania, tried to regain control through a military invasion in September 1972, but his attempt failed. Amin immediately retaliated by bombing Tanzanian towns and getting rid of any Acholi and Lango officers in the army.

Amin becomes more and more paranoid, fearing a coup within his own government, and he started his own system of ethnic cleansing. Determined to make Uganda 'a black man's country', Amin started to expel the country's 40,000 to 80,000 Indians and Pakistanis from Uganda, giving them just 90 days to leave. They were only allowed to take what they could physically carry with them and were warned by Amin, 'If they do not leave, they will find themselves sitting on fire'. Any

possessions they left behind, along with their businesses and homes, were divided among Amin's favourites
within his army.

Aware of the true nature of Amin's regime, the
British and Israel governments started to remove their
support and refused to sell him any more arms or
ammunition. Amin then looked to other countries for
support and turned to Libya for aid, with the promise
to their leader, Colonel Muammar Gaddafi, that he
will turn Uganda into an Islamic state. Amin broke any
relations with the UK, the USA and Israel, and gave his
support to the Palestinian liberation movement. All
British property in Uganda was seized and business
relations between the two countries was severely restricted. Any Britains still living in Uganda were threatened with banishment. By 1973, the USA had closed
its embassy in Kampala, followed by the UK closing its
High Commission in Uganda in 1976.

CAMPAIGN OF PERSECUTION

Still paranoid that his regime was under threat, Amin
started a campaign of persecution against rival tribes
and Obote supporters. It is alleged that as many as
500,000 people died under Idi Amin's regime, including ordinary citizens, former and serving cabinet ministers, the chief justice, judges, diplomats, academics,
teachers, prominent Roman Catholic and Anglican
clergy, senior bureaucrats, doctors, bankers, tribal

leaders, business executives, journalists and a number of foreigners living in Uganda. In certain cases, entire villages were wiped out, and there are reports that so many bodies were thrown into the Nile that workers had to continually drag them out to stop the dam from clogging up. There are also reports that he threw corpses to crocodiles and then held 'conversations' with the decapitated heads of his victims, which he kept in his freezer. On top of this there are also allegations that he committed cannibalism.

As a result of all the terror and the displacement of the country's economic backbone, Uganda starts a rapid downhill spiral. Always having to look over his shoulder for fear of being assassinated, Amin doubled his presidential guard and increased the size of his army. Meanwhile, the remainder of the world was disgusted by Amin's policies and use of extreme tactics.

AMIN AND THE ENTEBBE RAID

Amin had strong ties with the Palestine Liberation Organization (PLO), and in 1976 he became personally involved in hostage negotiations with Israel. It all started on 27 June, when four pro-Palestinian guerrillas hijacked an Air France flight, flying from Israel to Paris via Athens, with 250 passengers on board. Amin, on hearing about the hijack, invited the guerrillas to stop at Entebbe International Airport in the city of Entebbe, just 32 km (20 miles) outside of Kampala. The hijackers, two from the PLO and two from Germany's Baader-Meinhof gang, diverted the plane to Entebbe, where it landed on 28 June. Here they were joined by three more colleagues, where they demanded the release of 53 PLO and Red Army Faction prisoners in return for the hostages on the plane. Idi Amin arrived at the airport to give a speech in support of the PLO and even supplied the hijackers with extra troops and weapons.

On 1 July, the hijackers agreed to release a large number of the hostages, but they decided to hold captive the remaining 100 passengers who were either Jewish or Israeli. Amin arranged for a transport plane to take the freed hostages to Europe. The crew were offered their freedom but decided to stay with the plane, while the remaining hostages were transferred into the airport building. Then the hijackers set a deadline for 11.00 p.m. for their demands to be met, and if they weren't, they threatened to blow up the aeroplane and passengers. However, their plan was foiled when Israeli commandos stormed the the airport at midnight on 3 July. They managed to free all the hostages, with the exception of two, one of whom was killed by the Israeli forces and another, 75-year-old Dora Bloch, who had been taken to a hospital shortly before the raid, was killed under the direct orders of Amin.

During the 35-minute shoot-out, 20 Ugandan soldiers were killed along with all the hijackers. The leader of the assault force, Lieutenant Colonel Yonatan

Netanyahu, was also killed by an Ugandan sentry. The Israelis managed to destroy 11 Russian-built MiG fighters, which amounted to a one-quarter of the Ugandan air force. From this time onwards, partly due to the success of the Israeli operation, the Amin regime started to crumble.

DEPOSITION AND EXILE

In the last few years of his regime, Idi Amin became increasingly erratic, bordering on madness. He became more outspoken and had his tunics specially tailored so that he was able to wear many World War II medals, including the Military Cross and Victoria Cross. He gave himself a number of different titles, including 'King of Scotland'. When his diplomatic relations broke down with the UK, Amin decorated himself with the title of CBE or 'Conqueror of the British Empire'.

It wasn't until 1977 when the first indepth exposé of his murderous rule really became known. In an attempt to try and divert the world's attention from his country's internal problems, Amin launched a major attack on Tanzania. However, Tanzanian troops, with the help of armed Ugandan exiles, quickly put a stop to Amin's army and he was forced to flee to Libya, taking with him four of his wives, several of his mistresses and about 20 of his children. After being asked to leave Libya, Amin found final asylum in Saudi

Arabia, where he was told he would be allowed to stay as long as he remained out of any political activity. The Saudis provided him with a monthly stipend of about US$1,400, domestic servants and cars enabling to end his last few years in comfort.

Meanwhile, he left behind him a trail of destruction in Uganda. Not only had he eradicated a large majority of the population, but he also left his country with a massive annual inflation rate of 200 per cent and a national debt of US$320 million.

In 1980, Obote returned to power to try and put right some of the harm that had been done, but his re-election proved to be a big mistake, as his second administration seemed to have been as violent as Amin's. His reign only lasted until 1985 when he was ousted once again.

Amin tried to return to Uganda in 1989, always believing that his country still needed him. He never expressed any remorse for the pain and suffering he had inflicted on the Ugandan people, and his attempted return set alarm bells ringing. He was intercepted at Zaire, where the president forced him to return to Saudi Arabia.

On 23 July, 2003, one of his wives pleaded with President Museveni to allow her dying husband to return to his homeland. The reply from the president was that if he returned he would have to 'answer for his sins' and face a trial for war crimes.

Idi Amin died in Saudi Arabia on 16 August, 2003,

at the age of 79. He was buried in Jeddah against the wishes of his family, who wanted his body returned to Uganda. Amin was a man who wanted power at all costs and who was prepared to obliterate anyone or anything that stood in his way. His methods were unconventional and harsh, leaving his country in a shambles. Despite his atrocious acts of crimes against humanity, there are still some who say that after several years of national torture that 'life was actually better under Amin!'

The Killing Fields
of the Khmer Rouge
————1975–79————

*T*he Khmer Rouge were a radical group of Marxists who had an aggressive control over Cambodia for four hellish years, from 1975 to 1979. Saloth Sar, better known as Pol Pot, was the leader of the communist guerilla group, which cost the lives of an estimated two million Cambodians, who died from either starvation, torture or execution. The Khmer Rouge were a ruthless organization who killed without reason and ruled on the basis of instilling fear.

CLEARING THE CITIES

When the Khmer Rouge first came to power on 17 April, 1975, thousands of Phnom Penh residents came out onto the streets to rejoice. This was not because they were supporters of the new group, but because they were relieved that a five-year civil war had come to an end. In fact the majority of the citizens of Cambodia were unaware of who was running their country as the Communist Party of Kampuchea (CPK), the political force behind the Khmer Rouge, felt that furtiveness was the best way of controlling the population. As the people of Phnom Penh celebrated the fact that Cambodia was at last at peace, the Khmer Rouge started planning their campaign of terror.

The Khmer Rouge troops, who were already hardened and embittered by the years of brutal fighting, marched through the streets of the capital with stern faces, making their presence known. They started to order people to leave their homes and abandon the city, and by the end of the day hundreds of thousands of men, women and children were on the move. When the people asked why they had to leave, they were told 'The Americans are going to bomb the city!' Of course, there were going to be no attacks; it was simply a ploy on the part of the Khmer Rouge to cleanse the city of unwanted residents in order to create the ideal communist society.

Evacuation of the cities was only the first of many radical moves taken by the Khmer Rouge. As the people were forced out of the cities to live in the rural districts, they soon learned of the new, harsh rules that were being imposed by the Angka (The Organization). This organization were a clandestine group of Khmer Rouge leaders who dictated exactly how Cambodian citizens should conduct their lives. All institutions were banned, including banks, shops, hospitals, schools, religion and families. Everyone was compelled to work between 12 and 14 hours a day, seven days a week. Children were forced to live away from their families, and they had to work either in mobile groups or train as soldiers. Their diet consisted of one bowl of watery soup which, if they were lucky, contained a few grains of rice.

The Khmer Rouge killed young and old indiscriminately – babies, children, adults – all were killed without reason. If the Khmer Rouge didn't like them, if they didn't work hard enough, if they came from different ethnic groups, if they were educated or even if they showed signs of distress when their children were taken away – all of these were the excuses behind the slaughter. Everyone had to pledge total allegiance to the Angka for fear of losing their life. Communications with the outside world were forbidden and all the previous rights of the Cambodian citizen were cruelly taken away. The people of Cambodia soon realized that they had to live by the rule of the new, barbaric dictators.

LIFE IN THE WORK CAMPS

One of the main reasons for resettling the urban population into the countryside was to build a new country based on agricultural success. Pol Pot, together with his Khmer Rouge leaders, put together a four-year campaign in which the people of Cambodia were expected to produce an average yield of 3 metric tons of rice per hectare (1.4 tons per acre) annually. The average national yield up until that time had only been about one metric ton per hectare. To try and meet these new, impossible demands, the people were forced to work for 12 to 14 hours a day, with little food and inadequate periods of rest. Many of whom were born and raised in the cities were not used to manual labour and soon fell sick, and many died. Those who survived, but who were not considered well enough to go back to work, simply disappeared. They were taken away from the camps, forced to dig their own graves and then hit on the back of the head with a shovel. Regardless of whether the knock to the head killed them, the victims were still buried and left to suffocate.

On the one hand, peasants or previous land workers were known as the 'old people' by the Khmer Rouge and were seen as ideal communists for the new state. On the other hand, however, city dwellers were seen as the 'new people' and they were considered to be the root of all capitalist evil. For this reason, the lives of the new people were seen as having no real value for the Khmer Rouge campaign, and so even the most minor violation of rules was enough reason to send them to the killing fields. For example, if they were seen to be trying to get extra food, this was seen as a sin, despite the fact that the rations were so low hundreds of thousands of Cambodians starved to death. As family relationships were banned, if they were seen talking to any relative they would die, if they wore glasses they would die, if they were educated they would die, and so it went on. Even those people who worked themselves into the ground for the Khmer Rouge, would eventually be charged as associate enemies of the state and taken off to the killing fields. Living under these incredibly harsh conditions, the Cambodians did everything they could in their power to stay alive, cutting off all ties with their past and pretending to be an illterate peasant or one of tthe 'old people', just on the off-chance they might manage to stay alive.

TUOL SLENG

As if the conditions weren't harsh enough in the work camps, a number of political prisoners and their families met their fate inside the Khmer Rouge interrogation centres. The most famous of these was Tuol Sleng, meaning 'hill of the poisonous trees', the site of an abandoned Phnom Penh high school and code-named S-21. The people who were taken inside Tuol Sleng were simply known as *konlaenh choul min dael chenh* – 'the place where people go in but never come out'. Tuol Sleng was part of a sophisticated network of prisons where people were systematically imprisoned, tortured, interrogated and murdered by a group of sadistic guards who would do anything to extract fictitious confessions to imaginary crimes. Many of the prisoners were selected from all around the country and were often former members of the Khmer Rouge who had been arrested for supposed espionage.

The Khmer Rouge became a killing machine of frightening proportions. In just under four years, an excess of 1.7 million Cambodians died under the regime of Pol Pot and his Khmer Rouge. In Tuol Sleng, alone, an estimated 17,000 people were executed.

On arrival at the detention centre, the prisoners were photographed and forced to give personal information. All their possessions were removed and they were ordered to remove all their clothes. They were then taken down to the detention cells, where they were shackled to the walls. In the larger cells, where as many as 50 to 100 prisoners were held, they were collectively shackled in leg irons to long pieces iron bar. There were no beds so the prisoners were forced to sleep on the concrete floors, and there was just one solitary latrine box. Food was served twice a day at 8.00 a.m. and 8.00 p.m. and consisted of two or three tablespoons of rice porridge but nothing to drink. Every few days the guards would hose the prisoners down but the insanitary conditions led to sickness and skin diseases. Many people died during the night and guards would come each morning and take the bodies away.

From the moment of detention the captives had to adhere to a strict set of rules, which were pinned to a notice board outside the cells, written in both Khmer and English. These rules, ten in total, dictated how they could act, how they had to respond to questioning and how, in fact, they had to accept the fact that they were traitors and would be treated as such.

THE SECURITY REGULATIONS

1. You must answer accordingly to my questions – don't turn them away.
2. Don't try to hide the facts by making pretexts this and that. You are strictly prohibited to contest me.
3. Don't be a fool for you are a chap who dare thwart the revolution.
4. You must immediately answer my questions without wasting time to reflect.
5. Don't tell me either about your immoralities or the essence of the revolution.
6. While getting lashes or electrification you must not cry at all.
7. Do nothing, sit still and wait for my orders. If there is no order, keep quiet. When I ask you to do something, you must do it right away without protesting.
8. Don't make pretexts about Kampuchea Krom in order to hide your jaw of traitor.
9. If you don't follow all the above rules, you will get many lashes of electric wire.
10. If you disobey any point of my regulations you shall get either ten lashes or five shocks of electric discharge.

The methods of torture were both cruel and barbaric. Prisoners were forced to confess by using battery-powered electric shocks, searing hot metal prods or knives or having their head constantly ducked under water. Outside in the prison courtyard was a wooden frame that was once used by gymnasts, which the Khmer Rouge had converted into gallows. The majority of the prisoners were innocent, but the Khmer Rouge main objective was to extract whatever confession they felt was suitable. Although many of the prisoners died from the severity of the torture, the plan was not to kill them before they extracted the necessary information. The dubious nature of these confessions mattered little to the Khmer Rouge who built up a massive dossier of names allowing them to prove to themselves that there was indeed a massive web of traitors against them.

After the prisoners were interrogated, they were taken along with their family to the Choeung Ek extermination centre just outside Phnom Penh. Here, they were killed by being battered with iron bars, pick-axes, machetes and other forms of makeshift weapons. It was rare for a prisoner to be shot because the Khmer Rouge considered bullets to be a precious commodity to waste on their contrived traitors. Mass graves containing 8,895 bodies were discovered at Choeung Ek after the fall of the Khmer Rouge regime. Many of the dead were former inmates in the Tuol Sleng prison.

Today thousands of these confession files have been uncovered, including 5,000 photographs that give an insight into the brutal and inhumane treatment of prisoners at the hands of the Khmer Rouge. Out of the approximate 17,000 prisoners taken to Tuol Sleng, there are only seven known survivors. These men were kept alive because the Khmer Rouge believed they had special skills. One survivor, Vann Nath, who had trained as an artist, was put to work painting pictures of Pol Pot. After his internment, Nath continued to paint 15 scenes, including a self-portrait, which depicted the harsh realities of life and death at the detention centre.

THE FALL OF THE KHMER ROUGE

While the Khmer Rouge were intent on destroying what remained of the Cambodian society, there were stirrings of unrest with their old enemy, Vietnam. Although it was expected that the two new communist governments of Vietnam and Cambodia would eventually come to some kind of political agreement after years of conflict, their hatred and mistrust of each other ran too deep. Pol Pot, who showed signs of having an inferiority complex as far as the Vietnamese were concerned, was concerned that his neighbours were about to attack Cambodia. He decided to make a pre-emptive assault by invading Vietnam and looting the villages that were close to the border. The Soviet Union had ceased supporting Cambodia as soon as Pol Pot came into power; however, without their aid, China and the USA stepped in and pledged their support to the Khmer Rouge.

In 1978, Vietnam amassed thousands of troops

along the border with Cambodia. At the same time, a friendship treaty was signed between Vietnam and the Soviet Union, which was a direct result to Cambodia's now close relationship with China. On Christmas Day, 1978, 100,000 Vietnamese troops poured across the border, and they quickly gained a strong foothold in the north-east of Cambodia. Within a matter of weeks the Vietnamese had managed to capture Phnom Penh and forced the Khmer Rouge to flee. Pol Pot, himself, escaped by helicopter as the Vietnamese took control of the city.

As order started to return to Phnom Penh, the Vietnamese formed a new government known as the People's Republic of Kampuchea (PRK), led by a young prime minister by the name of Hun Sen. Despite the inborn fear of Vietnamese domination, many defectors of the Khmer Rouge helped to form the core of the new government.

Relieved that the harsh rule of the despotic Khmer Rouge was over, hundreds of thousands of Cambodian families started the long march home in the hope of finding some of their relatives. In most cases, however, they returned to find that nothing was left of their former lives – no homes, no possessions and, most tragically, no family. In reality, the Khmer Rouge came close to their dream of eradicating all memories of the old Cambodia. The country had literally been turned upside down by the Khmer Rouge years, and the new government had the daunting task of trying to not only heal the mental and physical wounds, but also rebuild the country economically.

NO CHANCE FOR WAR CRIMES TRIBUNAL

Owing to the fact that neither Pol Pot nor any of his followers were ever held accountable for the atrocities committed during his years in power, the weight of their crimes fell on the last of the Khmer Rouge leaders, General Ta Mok. Although Hun Sen permitted many of the high-ranking Khmer Rouge officials to return to Cambodian society without any form of recrimination, he decided that Ta Mok, nicknamed 'The Butcher', was to be the scapegoat. He was arrested on 6 March, 1999, in an effort to make him pay for the sins of the Marxist excesses. Ta Mok was regarded by many people as the most brutal of all the Khmer Rouge leaders, and he was known to have played a key role in a series of massacres and purges. He was the leader of the forces that destroyed the former royal capital of Oudong in 1974, killing many officials and government soldiers and forcing thousands of citizens to leave their homes.

Ta Mok died on 21 July, 2006, thereby evading any form of trial. His death left a Khmer Rouge prison boss, Kaing Khek Iev, more commonly known as Duch, as the organization's only surviving member in prison. Pol Pot died in April 1998 from an apparent heart condition, while in his hiding place in the jungles of northern Cambodia. Although there was much relief at his death, many felt that this relief was tainted with frustration that the mastermind of the killing fields died before he could be brought before a tribunal. Like Adolf Hitler before him, Pol Pot did not survive to take the brunt of his actions, and consequently he was unable to bring anyone else down with him. Many Cambodians feel deprived that one of the most sordid episodes in their lives will never be truly revealed, as the deaths of the leaders of the Khmer Rouge have taken the secrets with them.

Atrocities in East Timor

———————1975–89———————

*E*ast Timor is in Southeast Asia, just north-west of Australia in the Lesser Sundra Islands at the eastern end of the Indonesian archipelago. It is comprised of half of the island of Timor, the nearby islands of Pulau Atauro and Pulau Jaco and the Oecussi-Ambeno region on the north-west side of the island of Timor. It is a small country of just 14,609 sq km (5,376 sq miles) and is located approximately 640 km (400 miles) north-west of Darwin, Australia.

East Timor's struggle for independence has been long, hard and traumatic, with the small nation suffering some of the worst atrocities of modern times. They eventually achieved their independence on 20 May, 2002, but it is estimated that as many as 100,000 Timorese died as a result of Indonesia's 25-year occupation, which ended in 1999. A further 300,000 people were forced into West Timor as refugees, and the majority of the country's infrastructure, including homes, irrigation systems, water supply, schools and the country's national grid, were all destroyed. It wasn't until the Australian-led peacekeeping troops of the International Force for East Timor took the matter into their hands, that the period of violence and terror was brought to an end.

LIFE UNDER THE MILITIA

For over 24 years the people of East Timor suffered at the hands of the Indonesian militia, through torture, starvation and arbitrary executions and massacres. It is impossible to know exactly how many civilians have been killed since the invasion by the Indonesian army and militia in 1975. This is mainly due to the fact that the Indonesian President Suharto banned journalists and human-rights activitists from entering the area from 1975 to 1989. Five Australian journalists who did manage to get through the blockades were killed by the army in Balibo. The information that has been gathered about the atrocities comes mainly from just a handful of journalists, activists and aid workers who actually made it into East Timor and out again in the past 25 years.

The Indonesian militia were formed in the 1970s, before the invasion of East Timor, and appeared to be funded mainly by the Indonesian military. One of the most brutal groups of militia is known as the Mahidi, who are known to have employed underhand tactics of intimidation and fear, which included abduction, torture, rape and murder.

The main objectives of the militia was to extract information about the location and planned strategies of the resistance movement in East Timor. They used whatever perverse method they thought would be most effective to achieve their goals. Photographic evidence has been released of militia hanging up the Timorese by chains, shoving steel poles down their throats, forcing them to eat dirt, applying electric shocks to their genitalia and finally burying their bodies in unmarked graves. Other favoured methods of torture by the militia were the pulling out of finger and toenails, crushing people's fingers under the legs of chairs, ducking them under water, or partially suffocating them by placing bags over their heads. Known resistance leaders were forcibly beaten about the head, many being left with severe brain damage.

The militia seemed to take pride in their torture tactics, and it is through their own photographic records that the atrocities eventually came to light. Their killing methods were also extreme to the point of perversion. Not only did they kill with bullets, they dropped people from helicopters into the sea with rocks tied round their bodies to ensure they sank. There is also evidence of them running people over with bulldozers and swinging babies around by their feet and slamming their heads into rocks. Many of their victims were disembowelled with body parts left as grim reminders to warn others of a similar fate.

TORTURE OF WOMEN AND CHILDREN

The atrocities committed by the Indonesia militia were not just confined to the men of East Timor. The women and children also felt the brunt of their aggression and human-rights violations. They were constantly raped in front of other family members, forced to marry Indonesia soldiers, subjected to torture by electric shocks, sexually abused and, in some cases, forcibly sterilized in an effort to reduce the East Timor population.

The militia used rape and sexual assault as a tool of war, in an effort to extract information from the women as to the whereabouts of members of the resistance. In addition to this, the militia forced women to serve as their sex slaves, often making them pregnant in an effort to, as they describe it, 'depurify' the Timorese population.

'FENCE OF LEGS'

One of the most harrowing abominations of the Indonesian occupation was their 'Fence of Legs' campaign, which was carried out in 1981. The militia rounded up a large number of civilians, regardless of their age and state of health, and made them march across the island. They made them march in lines with the intention of flushing out resistance fighters and, most importantly, Xanana Gusmao, who was the nation's most recent leader.

One section of the human fence began walking westwards from Tutuala in the far east of East Timor, while another marched along the Viqueque corridor. The two fences met at Mount Matebian and then spread out to Lacluta. However, the militia's plan went terribly wrong as one after another of the Timorese dropped either from sickness or starvation. Those that didn't die were tied up and stabbed to death, ending the march with the most horrendous massacre. Although there are no figures as to how many actually died during those marches, it is thought that as many as 60,000 civilians were forced to take part.

Rather than uncovering guerilla fighters, the operation merely found villagers cowering in the bush. The marches took place during the main planting season, which meant that most of the subsistence farmers who were forced to take part were unable to plant their crops, which led to a major famine. This, on top of an already weakened population, led to further hardships for the long-suffering Timorese.

Unfortunately, the 'Fence of Legs' was not an isolated case, and the militia routinely used civilians in their campaigns. They were known to recruit children as young as ten, who were savagely punished if they failed in their duties.

SANTA CRUZ MASSACRE

On 12 November, 1991, Indonesian troops fired on an

innocent group of people taking part in a peaceful memorial procession to the Santa Cruz cemetery in Dili. More than 271 Timorese were killed, 278 were wounded, 103 were hospitalized and 270 people simply 'disappeared'.

This massacre, unlike many others that had taken place during Indonesia's occupation, was filmed and photographed by international journalists Amy Goodman and Allan Nairn, both of whom were badly hurt. Allan Nairn was beaten with the butts of rifles, which fractured his skull.

Just prior to the massacre, the Indonesian army were sweeping through villages and towns in East Timor, rounding up anyone who they believed might be planning to talk to a UN-sponsored delegation that was due to arrive from Portugal. The Indonesians threatened people throughout the country, warning them that if they talked to the delegation they would be killed. Ironically, the delegation never actually arrived in East Timor, but the Indonesians decided to carry out a massacre anyway. Just after the announcement that the delegation was to arrive, the Indonesians stormed the San Antonio de Motael church and seized a young man by the name of Sebastiao Gomes. He was shot at point-blank range, and it was his funeral at Dili on 12 November that attracted such a large crowd of mourners.

As the funeral procession wound its way through the streets of Dili, many other people joined in. Some went to stand beside the newly dug grave, while others waited outside, hemmed in by the walls of the cemetery. They stood around talking excitedly and nervously, but one of the crowd noticed that the exit had been blocked by an Indonesian army truck. As they turned to look down the road, the crowd noticed a long, slowly-marching column of uniformed soldiers. The crowd grew nervous, as the seemingly endless line of soldiers advanced closer and closer. They were right to be nervous, and it wasn't long before the inconceivable happened. The soldiers broke ranks, raised their rifles and fired in unison into the crowd of people standing in the cemetery. People fell where they stood, too stunned to move; others tried to flee, gasping in horror, only to be gunned down. The street was soon awash with blood, with the bodies of schoolgirls, young men and older Timorese lying to left and right. It was a deliberate mass murder of unarmed, defenceless people with no provocation whatsoever.

A SLOW RECOVERY

The Santa Cruz massacre was actually the turning point for the people of East Timor, as it set in motion a chain of events that led to the country becoming independent. Even though the people of East Timor now have their freedom and independence, it will probably be many more years before they see justice for the decades of abuse inflicted on them by the Indonesian military.

The rebuilding of East Timor has been one of the United Nation's biggest success stories, but the continuing state of poverty and unemployment means that the country will need to rely on outside assistance for many years to come.

War Crimes in Sri Lanka

————1980s–2006————

*S*ri Lanka (meaning 'resplendent island') is a lush, beautiful place that is located just off the south-eastern coast of India. However, its white beaches and beautifully scented flowers are just a backdrop to an island that has been the scene of one of the world's most violent and merciless conflicts.

The island of Ceylon (as it was once known), which is located off the coast of India, is the home to two major ethnic groups – the Sinhala and the Tamils. The Sinhala call their country Sri Lanka, while the Tamils call theirs Tamil Eelam. In the early 1800s, the British took control of Ceylon and installed a form of government which, in theory, gave the Sinhala control of the whole island. The Tamils, who were not pleased by the situation, to say the least, claimed that the Sinhalese subjected them to constant harassment, persecution and even torture. The Tamils formed a group called the Liberation Tigers of Tamil Eelam (LTTE) and started a civil war against the Sinhalese in 1983. The war has swung to the advantage of both sides over the years, and it is estimated that as many as 60,000 people have been killed and more than one-and-a-half million more displaced.

With a population of approximately 18 million, the losses that Sri Lanka has experienced can be compared to those suffered by France and the UK in both World War I and World War II. The war is between the Sri Lankan forces, who represent the Sinhalese Buddhist majority, and the LTTE, who want a separate state in the north and east of the island for the predominantly Hindu Tamil minority.

Both sides have committed serious war crimes and over the years, despite numerous assurances, they have continued to eliminate defenceless soldiers and committed atrocities against innocent civilians time and time again. For example, in 1993 alone, at least 200 Tamil civilizians were killed when the Sri Lankan army bombed villages, destroying churches, hospitals, schools, houses and factories – none of which were legitimate targets of war. Almost one-quarter of Sri Lanka's Tamil population have fled the country during the years of active warfare, which has created a dispersion of around 600,000 and 800,000 worldwide.

THE TAMIL TIGERS

From the start of the 1970s, the Liberation Tigers of Tamil Eelam (LTTE) developed into a formidable and frightening fighting force. They are said to be about 10,000-strong and their soldiers consist of men, women and children. By either abducting or using threatening tactics on their parents, the Tigers have managed to recruit thousands of underage child soldiers, some as young as eight years old. Tamil families in the north and east of Sri Lanka have literally been press-ganged into letting their sons and daughters leave home for military service. When the families refused, the Tamils simply abducted the children from their homes at night or waited until they came out of school. Even since the ceasefire began in 2002, the Tamil Tigers have still continued to recruit children, taking advantage of the refugees who were found homeless after the catastrophic tsunami in 2004. Since the start of February 2002, the Tamil Tigers have recruited over 3,516 children, but the United Nations Children's Fund (UNICEF), states that this probably only represents a small proportion of the total number.

Apart from fighting the conventional war, the Tamil Tigers have also targeted civilians and deliberately attacked villagers. In one early morning attack in 1999, the Tigers were accused of literally hacking to death women and children in a majority Sinhala village. The Tigers have been accused of trying to ethnically cleanse Jaffna, when they asked all the non-Tamils to leave in 1990.

The Tamils are also notorious for their suicide attacks, which are conducted by highly motivated men and women. These people literally turn themselves into human bombs.

1983 GENOCIDE

The anti-Tamil riots that took place in July 1983 in Sri Lanka changed the course of the nation's history. The riots, which were vicious and bloody, lasted for several days and left over 3,000 Tamils dead and a considerable amount of property destroyed. Instead of trying to stop the genocide, Sri Lankan politicians, police and armed forces, as well as several members of the Buddhist clergy, actually took an active part in many of the murders and rapes. The Tamils were targeted by the Sinhalese, who subjected them to untold misery. They were beaten or hacked to death in a frenzy of racial hatred, and their homes and businesses were razed to the ground. The riots caused fear in the Tamil society, and created a movement of refugees within the island. Thousands of Tamils fled to Tamil Nadu, Europe and North America. Even the Sri Lankan President, Jayawardene, refused to condemn the riots and refrained from issuing any form of statement until a few days after the riots were over.

Perhaps one of the most brutal and obviously well organized part of the riots, took place within the confines of a prison in the city of Colombo. Although it was supposed to be a place of maximum security, not just one, but two massacres took place there in the space of just one week.

In the first incident 35 inmates were killed in the Welikada gaol on 25 July, and just two days later a further 17 were killed. The attack is thought to have taken place because two supposed guerilla leaders, Sellarasa Yogachandiran, leader of the LTTE, and Ganeshanathan Jeganathan were being held under the death sentence for the murder of a policeman. When the assailants came across the two men, it is reported that they were forced to kneel while they had their eyes gouged out with iron bars. Then they were stabbed to death and their testicles were wrenched from their bodies.

After these killings, nine prisoners were moved to a padlocked hall, upstairs in the same block. Among these men were Dr Rajasunderam, Sir Lanka's Gandhian leader, two Catholic priests and a Methodist minister. The nine men were convinced that there would be a further attack, and they were given assurances that they would be protected, but no further measures were taken.

It was about 2.30 p.m. on 27 July, when the nine men heard whistling and jeering coming from outside. One of the priests looked out of the high window and saw prisoners breaking in from a nearby compound. They were wielding axes, iron bars, pieces of firewood and sticks, and there was not one prison guard in sight. The mob had already killed 16 people in the cells on the floor below and they ran up the stairs and started to try and break open the padlocked door. Dr Rajasunderam cried out to the men, 'Why are you trying to kills us, what have we done to you?' At that moment the door burst open and he was hit on the side of the neck with an iron bar and blood literally spurted several feet. The remaining eight men decided that they had better defend themselves and started to break up the tables and chairs and, using the legs, they managed to defend themselves. The mob threw bricks and the eight men retaliated by throwing them back. Pieces of firewood and an iron bar were thrown as weapons and this continued for about half an hour. The mob shouted, 'You are priests, we have to kill you!' Eventually the violence was ended when the army intervened using tear gas.

Although the official report says that the killings at Welikade gaol were the result of a prison riot, the story does not really ring true. If this were the case, then how did the prisoners get out of their cells without the aid of the guards, and where did they get their weapons? According to sworn statements, the assailants claimed that they were given the instructions by the prison authorites, who ordered them to kill all those prisoners being held at the young offenders ward, which is where the Tamil prisoners were kept.

The families of those murdered on those two days only learned about their death via a news broadcast on the radio. What is worse, they were not even given the chance to say a final goodbye as the men were buried before their families got to see the bodies.

TIMELINE OF CONFLICT

Since the beginning of the conflict, the blood of innocent civilians has stained the hands of the Sri Lankan forces. In many cases, the attacks have been the result of the forces suffering some form of setback in their fight for power. Below is a list of just some of the atrocities that have been carried out between the years 1986 and 1997.

1986
30 November: In attacks on villages in the north-east border, 127 people, mostly Sinhalese, are killed.

1987
21 April: LTTE detonate a car bomb at Colombo bus station, killing 113 people.

7 May: A bomb destroys central telegraph office, killing 14 people.

14 May: 150 killed when the LTTE attack the city of Anuradhapura.

2 June: LTTE stop bus and shoot 33 people, including 29 Buddhist monks.

1988
11 February: Shootings at Duluwewa result in the killing of 34 Sinhalese.

28 February: Further 37 Sinhalese killed at Borawewa.

1 May: Bus is blown up by a landmine in Trincomalee, killing 22 passengers.

14 November: Bus attacked in Trincomalee, killing 27 Sinhalese.

1989

13 April: Car bomb explodes in Trincomalee, killing 51 shoppers.

1990

3 August: When praying at a mosque in Kattankudy, 140 Muslims were killed in machete, gun and hand grenade attack.

12 August: Another 120 Muslims killed at Eravur.

1991

2 March: Deputy Defence Minister Ranjan Wijeratne is killed in a car bomb explosion in Colombo.

21 April: In south-east Moneragala, 21 villagers are killed.

8 July: 27 civilians killed in Batticaloa.

1992

1 September: In Batticaloa 22 Muslims are killed by a bicycle bomb.

15 October: In Palliyagodella 166 Muslims are killed.

1993

23 April: Former Security Minister, Lalith Athulath-mudali is killed at a rally in Colombo by LTTE terrorists.

1994

19 January: At Anuradhapura, 15 bus passengers are killed in a bomb blast.

21 March: 22 fishermen killed in Puttalam.

24 November: Opposition leader, Gamini Dissanayake, and 51 others killed by a suicide bomber.

1995

26 May: at Kallarawa, 42 villagers are killed.

7 August: Suicide bomber explodes bomb hidden in coconut cart in Colombo, killing 24 and wounding 40.

20 October: Terrorists blow up two oil depots in Colombo, killing 20 security personnel.

1996

31 January: A truck packed with explosives rams into the Central Bank building, killing 100 and injuring 1,400 people.

4 July: Woman suicide bomber kills 21 civilians and soldiers and wounds 50, including a cabinet minister.

24 July: LTTE explode two bombs on a commuter train, killing 57 people and injuring at least 257.

1997

9 September: Civilian ship attacked in the port of Trincomalee; 32 people killed in a gun battle between terrorists and Sri Lankan navy.

15 October: In Colombo, 11 people killed in terrorist bomb blast and ensuing gun battle.

This is by no means a complete list of all the atrocities that have occurred during the war years in Sri Lanka. One of the latest, and possibly the most horrifying, occurred on 14 August, 2006, when four Kfir jet bombers of the Sri Lanka Air Force dropped 16 bombs on the Chencholai children's home in Vallipunam. More than 400 schoolgirls were staying overnight at the Chencholai home, and 61 were killed in the unprovoked attack on a nonmilitary location. Another 129 severely wounded girls were rushed to nearby hospitals.

MASS GRAVES UNCOVERED

A former soldier by the name of Somaratne Rajapakse, who had been sentenced to death in June 1998 for the rape and murder of a Jaffna teenager, alleged that the army had buried many 'disappeared' Tamil civilians in mass graves near Jaffna town. Exhumation began straight away and the first grave uncovered contained the skeletons of two males. The victims, one with his hands tied with rope and the other blindfolded, were identified as two men in their twenties who had simply disappeared in 1996 after the army took Jaffna. An additional 24 grave sites were uncovered around Chemmani village near Jaffna, which contained a total of over 100 bodies. Forensic experts from both Sri Lanka and abroad reported that the remains showed signs of physical assault and murder. This only accounts for a small proportion of the tens of thousands of people who have been reported as missing at the hands of the security forces, but it proves that major acts of inhumane conduct have occurred over the years of the conflict.

ONGOING HORRORS

The cost to human lives continues day by day, not just those killed in battlefield combat as a result of a 'take-no-prisoners' tactic, which has been adopted by both sides, but also to civilians and their exodus from the war-torn areas. Despite planned peace talks the clashes continue, and in October 2006 reports came in of one of the deadliest suicide bombings of the war, when nearly 100 people, mostly Sri Lankan sailors, were killed by suspected Tamil Tiger rebels. The sailors died in a suicide blast, when the rebels drove a lorry loaded withe explosives into a convoy of naval buses. The attack happened near the town of Dambulla and a spokesman who described the attack as despicable said, 'All these people were without weapons and were simply going on leave.' In 2006 alone, as many as 2,000 people have been killed, and this is since the ceasefire settlement of 2002, which raised hopes of the war coming to an end. In October heavy battles on the Jaffna Peninsula left hundreds dead, despite commitments by both the government and the rebels to return to the negotiating table. The Tamil Tigers, from their secret jungle base in the north-east of Sri Lanka, show no signs of being defeated by the military of the Sri Lankan army, even though they are vastly out-numbered. All the time the military control the peninsula – which the Tamil Tigers claim to be their cultural heartland – it appears the conflicts will never come to an end.

Israel and the
Occupied Territories

————2000–2006————

*U*nder the terms of the Geneva Convention, article number 54:

> *Starvation of civilians as a method of warfare is prohibited.*

As is:

> *. . . to attack, destroy, remove or render useless objects indispensable to the survival of the civilian population.*

According to the above, the Israeli army's latest offensive in the Occupied Territories amounts to them having committed serious war crimes. We all have a general idea of what we think a war crime is, but there are many different degrees of heinousness with which they are carried out. War crimes are among the most serious crimes under international law and represent offences against humanity as a whole. Perhaps the prime example of crimes against humanity is what

Hitler and the Nazis did to the Jewish people during World War II, and that is what the UN Human Rights Commission have determined the Israelis are currently doing to the Palestinian people.

Since the start of the Al-Aqsa Intifada, which is the wave of violence that began in September 2000 between Palestinian Arabs and Israelis, the world has witnessed almost on a day-to-day basis, the injustices against the Palestinian people living in occupied Palestine. During this period the Israeli army have killed more than 700 Palestinians, including as many as 150 children. Nearly every one of these killings was unlawful – either by shooting, shelling or air raids on civilian residential areas; unauthorized executions; or as a result of the use of excessive force.

Following the harsh restrictions imposed by the Israelis on the movement of Palestinians within the Occupied Territories, the Palestinians have suffered widespread poverty and unemployment, and access to health and educational facilities has been hampered. On top of this, the Israelis have destroyed hundreds, if not thousands, of Palestinian homes, a large majority of their agricultural land and much of the basic foundations of their society.

LIVING IN THE SHADOW OF A WALL

The Israelis have continued to expand their territory and illegal settlements, and they restricted the

Palestinians' movement even further by the erection of the Israeli West Bank barrier in June 2002. The majority of the barrier was constructed of a network of fences with vehicle/barrier trenches and up to 8-m (26-ft) high concrete walls. In addition to the concrete wall and fencing materials used in the construction of the structure, sections of the barrier included electrified fencing, 2-m (6½-ft) deep trenches, roads for patrol vehicles, electronic ground/fence sensors, thermal imaging and video cameras, unmanned aerial vehicles, sniper towers and razor wire. It is located partly within the West Bank and partly along the border between the West Bank and Israel proper.

The barrier is a controversial project, with supporters claiming on the one hand that it is a necessary tool for protecting Israeli citizens from Palestinian terrorism. On the other hand, opponents claim that it is an illegal attempt to expropriate Palestinian land under the guise of security.

In 2006, the building of the wall in the Occupied Territories reached a critical stage. The completed sections of the wall have already caused considerable suffering to the Palestinian population. Homes have been demolished, thousands of olive trees uprooted, acres upon acres of land have been expropriated and roads have been destroyed to make may for the construction. If the Israelis are permitted to continue building the wall, much greater hardships and undue suffering lie ahead for the Palestinian population.

ATTACK ON THE GAZA STRIP

Following the abduction of Israel Defence Forces (IDF) soldier, Galid Shalit, by the Palestinians, the Israelis once again violated humanitarian law and attacked the Gaza Strip on 28 June, 2006. They fired six missiles at the only electrical power plant operating in the Gaza Strip, aiming at the plant's six transformers. Two of the missiles missed their target on the first attempt, but a few minutes later two more missiles completed the mission.

This attack has had major and long-term humanitarian consequences for the 1.5 million inhabitants of the Gaza Strip. The majority of the inhabitants have been forced to live without electricity in the fierce summer heat, and the harsh effects of the attack continue to be felt in all areas of their life. As a result of the lack of electricity, medical services provided by clinics and hospitals have declined drastically. Most of the people only have access to water for two to three hours a day and the sewage system is on the verge of collapse. Those residents with limited mobility have struggled due to the fact that the majority of the lifts in the buildings do not function and the lack of refrigeration has exposed many people to the risk of food poisoning. Small businesses, who rely on a steady supply of electricity, have been hit hard and the economy is now in a poor state.

The Israelis launched 'Operation Summer Rain'

overnight in the southern sector of the Gaza Strip, with the primary mission of finding the captured soldier, Shalit. They began house-to-house searches in the area, and bulldozers moved in to clear the way of mines and bombs. The IDF moved into the area, taking up strategic positions at the now nonfunctional Gaza International Aiport in the south-eastern corner of Gaza. The Israelis scoured the Gaza–Israeli border for more tunnel entrances like the ones used to adjuct Shalit, and an IDF spokesman said, 'We will stay here as long as necessary until we return with the kidnapped IDF soldier'.

In an effort to have some bargaining power, the Israeli military detained more than 64 Hamas officials and parliamentary officials in overnight raids across the West Bank. The detained ministers included Finance Minister Omar Abdel Razeq, Social Affairs Minister Fakhri Torokma, Prisoners' Affairs Minister, Wasfi Kabha and Deputy Prime Minister and Education Minister Nasser Shair.

The Israeli airforce staged mock air raids over Gaza, causing sonic booms that caused mass panic among the civilians. They also dropped leaflets urging the residents to avoid moving around in the area because of impending military activity. Nervous civilians stockpiled batteries and candles, as well as food and water, expecting the worst. In southern Gaza, at the Rafah crossing with Egypt, which had been closed since the capture of Shalit, militants blew a large hole in the border wall. Palestinian security forces immediately formed a human cordon to stop people from pushing their way through the gap, and a curfew was imposed to further restrict the movements of the inhabitants.

Aiming attacks at civilian objects is forbidden under International Humanitarian law and is considered to be a war crime. The bombing of the Gaza Strip power plant was purely a civilian structure, and it did nothing whatsoever to hamper Palestinian attacks on the Israeli territory. Under international law the Israelis are responsible for the lives and welfare for those people who live on the Gaza Strip, and it is now up to the government of Israel to put things right.

OTHER UNLAWFUL ATTACKS

Over 120 Palestinians have been killed in extrajudicial executions, including more than 30 innocent by-standers, four of whom were children. In September and October 2005, four Palestinian schoolchildren were shot dead by the Israeli army either in their classrooms or walking to school in the Gaza Strip. Raghda Adnan al-Assar and Ghadeer Jaber Mukhaymar, aged ten and nine, were shot dead while they were sitting at their desks in the UN Khan Yunis refugee camp. On 5 October, Israeli soldiers killed 13-year-old Iman al-Hams near her school in Rafab. Witnesses reported that a commander repeatedly shot at the schoolgirl from close range, even though it was obvious she was a child who was obviously scared to death. Although the commander was charge with illegal use of his weapon, he was not charged with either murder or manslaughter.

On 22 March, Hamas leader Sheikh Ahmed Yassin, a 68-year-old paraplegic who was bound to a wheelchair, was assassinated by an Israeli airstrike as he left a mosque in Gaza City. Seven other Palestinians were killed in the attack and at least 17 more were injured. His successor, Abd al-Aziz al-Rantisi, was also assassinated on 17 April.

When Israelis opened fire on a nonviolent demonstration on 19 May, eight people were killed, including three schoolchildren, 10-year-old Walid Naji Abu Qamar, 11-year-old Mubarak Salim al-Hashash and 13-year-old Mahmoud Tariq Mansour. Many other unarmed demonstrators were wounded in the attack.

Palestinians have constantly been used as human shields during Israeli military operations, compelling them to risk their lives, despite the fact that this practice was banned by the Israeli High Court. In April 2005, Israeli soldiers forced 13-year-old Muhammed Badwan onto the bonnet of their jeep, tying him to the front windshield. They used him as a human shield to discourage Palestinian demonstrators from throwing stones at them during a demonstration in the West Bank village of Biddu.

In May 2005, the Israeli army destroyed approximately 300 homes and severely damged 270 other buildings in the Rafah refugee camp in the Gaza Strip.

This left about 4,000 people without homes. When the IDF arrived with their bulldozers, many people were trapped inside their homes and they had to drill holes in the back walls in order to escape. Thousands of residents fled in fear, and UN schools were used as temporarily shelters to house the refugees. Israeli officials claimed the mass destruction was intended to further widen the 'no-go' area along the Egyptian border and to uncover illegal tunnels used to smuggle weapons into the Gaza Strip.

Following the death of two Israeli children in October 2005, the IDF launched a major attack on the Jabalya refugee camp in the northern Gaza Strip. This attack destroyed over 200 homes and buildings, and it also resulted in severely damaged roads and other vital infrastructures.

VIOLATIONS BY PALESTINIANS

Of course human rights violations are not just restricted to the Israeli army, Palestian armed groups have also killed 67 Israeli citizens, eight of which were children. The majority of these attacks were claimed by the al-Aqsa Martyrs Brigade, which is an offshoot of Fatah, and by the the armed wing of Hamas.

RESPECT FOR HUMAN RIGHTS

Until the Israelis and the Palestinians respect the law of

human rights, there will be no peace or settlement in the area of the Occupied Territories. Even in the overwhelming majority of the thousands of cases of unlawful killings and other grave human rights violations, no thorough investigations have been carried out. As the growing tension between Israel and Palestine continues to mount, there is an ever-growing concern for the safety of the civilian population. Instead of improving, the situation looks as if it will deteriorate further in the light of the end of the fragile ceasefire, adding to the already deteriorating health and humanitarian conditions in Gaza and the West Bank.

Sabra and Shatila Massacres

-------- 1982 --------

*S*abra and Shatila were two refugee camps on the outskirts of Muslim Western Beirut. The camps were established when a large number of Palestinians sought refuge from Israel during the 1967 Six Day War against Egypt, Jordan and Syria. The issues leading up to the massacres, which the UN General Assembly condemned as an act of genocide, have been many years in the making and are extremely complex.

EVENTS LEADING TO THE MASSACRES

To put it as simply as possible, the Sabra and Shatila massacres were the outcome of an alliance between Israel and the Lebanese Phalangists. The Phalangists were a Christian political party and militia, who attracted Christian youths from the mountains northeast of Beirut as well as students from Beirut itself. At the start of the Lebanese Civil War, the Phalangists cooperated with Syria, but after 1982, Israel became their most important ally. In their long-standing war against Palestinian nationalism and the Palestine Liberation Organization (PLO), Israel were pleased to have the support of the Phalangists. Even though it was Israel who was responsible for the mass exodus of Palestinians, the hostility felt by the Israelis and the Phalangists against the Palestinians, led to them forming a secret alliance. Under the terms of this alliance, the Israelis supplied the Phalangists with money, arms and equipment to help them fight the PLO in Lebanon.

Although many have suggested that the massacres were a direct result of the murder of President Bachir Gemayel of the Lebanon and leader of the Phalangists, it was not a spontaneous act of vengeance, but a well planned operation. The Israelis were keen to motivate a mass exodus of Palestinians from Beirut and other parts of the Lebanon by means of mass terror. They had used this tactic before in a previous number of massacres, and it was a disturbing pattern of political struggle directed against innocent civilians – women, children and the aged population.

ISRAEL MOVE TO WEST BEIRUT

Initially, the Israeli government announced that its intention was to only penetrate as far as 40 km (25 miles) into the Lebanese territory. However, this was just a ruse, as Sharon had already planned a more ambitious project some months earlier. Having already committed a

466

serious of violations against the civilian population in the south of the country, the Israelis proceeded to penetrate as far as Beirut. By 18 June, 1982, the Israelis had sur-rounded the PLO armed forces in the western part of the capital. The intensive shelling of Beirut resulted in the deaths of 18,000 people and a further 30,000 injuries, the majority of which were civilians.

The fighting went on for a period of two months, after which a ceasefire was negotiated via the US Envoy, Philip Habib. Under the terms of the ceasefire, the PLO was to evacuate Beirut under the watchful eye of a multinational force. The USA told the Palestinians that they would take control of the security of the civilians in the camps after the evacuation was com-pleted on 1 September, 1982, but no such supervision was ever put into operation.

The decision to move to West Beirut was taken by the Israeli Prime Minister, Menachem Begin and Israeli Defence Minister, Ariel Sharon, even though it viola-ted the ceasefire and broke Israel's promise to US President Reagan, not to enter Beirut after the PLO's evacuation. On 10 September, the multinational forces evacuated Beirut and the next day, Ariel Sharon announced that 2,000 'terrorists' had stayed inside the refugee camps around Beirut.

PLANNING THE MASSACRE

On the evening of 14 September, Ariel Sharon and

Israel's Chief of Staff, Rafael Eitan, had a meeting in which plans were made to have the Phalange forces storm the two refugee camps. By dawn, on 15 September, Israel stormed West Beirut and cordoned off the Sabra and Shatila camps.

The following day a high-level meeting was held and the job of carrying out the operation was assigned to a major security official in the Lebanese forces, Eli Haqiba. Also present were the Supreme Commander of the Northern Forces, General Amir Dawri and Fadi Afram, Commander of the Lebanese forces.

The attack on the camps by the Phalangists militia-men started just before sunset on Thursday, 16 September, under the watchful eye of their Israeli allies. The Israeli army surrounded the camps, providing the Phalangists with the necessary support to carry out their heinous crime. They gave them bulldozers and a maps of the insides of the camps. Fired by the death of their Christian president, Bachir Gemayel, and the years of brutality they had suffered at the hands of the Palestinians during the PLO occupation of Lebanon, the Phalangists set about their three-day orgy of rape and slaughter. To give them more light, the Christian militia set off incandescent bombs into the air so that none of the Palestinians would be able to escape. Those who did try to escape the killing and rape – women, children and the elderly – were quickly brought back to the camps by the waiting Israeli soldiers. By Saturday morning, 18 September, the massacre had reached its peak and thousands of Sabra and Shatila camp refugees had been slaughtered.

By the end of the third day, there were bodies everywhere and it was a nauseating scene. Many of the victims had been mutilated by axes or knives; others had their heads smashed, their eyes removed, their throats cut, and the skin had literally been stripped from their body. Severed limbs lay strewn around the floor and others had been disembowelled. It was one of the most indecent acts of genocide that the world had ever witnessed.

NEWS SPREADS

News of the massacre started to spread quickly after a number of women and children had successfully escaped to the Gaza Hospital in the Shatila camp. They told the doctors there exactly what was happening, and before long foreign media had got hold of the news. Journalists who went into the camps after the massacre were nauseated by what they saw. Loren Jenkins of the *Washington Post* described the scene:

> *The scene at the Shatila camp when foreign observers entered Saturday morning was like a nightmare. Women wailed over the deaths of loved ones, bodies began to swell under the hot sun, and the streets were littered with thousands of spent cartridges. Houses had been dynamited and bulldozed into*

rubble, many with the inhabitants still inside. Groups of bodies lay before bullet-pocked walls where they appeared to have been executed. Others were strewn in alleys and streets, apparently shot as they tried to escape. Each little dirt alley through the deserted buildings, where Palestinians have lived since fleeting Palestine when Israel was created in 1948, told its own horror story.

The exact number of victims may never be fully ascertained. At the time the international Red Cross counted 1,500 bodies, but by 22 September, this number had risen to 2,400. The following day a further 350 bodies were uncovered, but because the Lebanese authorities forbade the opening of mass graves, the true number will probably never be known. Realistically, the number of victims is somewhere around 3,000 to 3,500, one quarter of whom were Lebanese, while the remainder were Palestinians.

The Israeli public were sickened when they discovered what had taken place, and on 25 September a huge demonstration of 300,000 Israelis was held in Tel Aviv, demanding the resignation of Prime Minister Menahem Begin and Ariel Sharon. They also demanded the establishment of a judicial commission of inquiry to investigate the circumstances of the massacre.

Even though Sharon insisted that he could not have known that the Phalangists were going to commit the atrocities in the Sabra and Shatila camps, he was still forced to resign his post as Defence Minister. Sharon's reputation worldwide deteriorated to such a degree that it nearly ended his political career.

The Phalangist leader, Elie Hobeika, who was held directly responsible for carrying out the massacres, was under investigation for several years before his sudden death in 1985. Apart from his involvement in the massacres, Hobeika was also linked to several other crimes, including the 1978 assassination of Zghorta MP, Tony Franjieh, and a 1985 car bomb attack that severely injured Sidon MP, Mustafa Saad and killed his daughter, Natasha. It is believed that the Syrians discovered Hobeika's involvement with the CIA and arranged for his death in a part of Beirut that was heavily patrolled by Lebanese security forces. He was killed in a bomb blast on 24 January, 2002, just one day after he said he was ready to testify in a case brought by Palestinians in Belgium accusing Ariel Sharon of sanctioning the Sabra and Shatila massacres.

The secrets of the Palestinian camp atrocities have probably gone to the grave with the death of Hobeika. A Belgian court has now postponed a decision over whether to indict Ariel Sharon for his role, while lawyers for the survivors try to gather more evidence. However, as two more Phalangist militia have been mysteriously murdered since the death of Hobeika, there is major concern that the true events may never be uncovered as the death list continues to grow.

Srebrenica Massacre

——————1995——————

*T*he Srebrenica massacre has become the symbol of Serbian evil and has been described as 'a horror without parallel'. It was a cold-blooded execution of over 8,000 Muslim men and boys, while the international community and UN peacekeepers simply looked on. The massacre took place between 10 and 19 July, 1995, in and around the Bosnian town of Srebrenica, when Serb forces segregated civilian men from the women and killed them *en masse*.

BACKGROUND

The events that took place at Srebrenica mark the climax of a civil war in Bosnia–Herzegovina, a country that lies on the Balkan peninsula of southern Europe. It has an estimated population of around four million people and is the homeland to three ethnic groups – Bosnians, Serbs and Croats. The conflict began in 1992 and has been described as one of the most violent and genocidal periods in the history of the war. Atrocities were committed by all sides and against all sectors of the population, but the Serb strategy of gender-selective mass executions of non-combatant men, was the most severe and systematic atrocity of all.

One of the largest massacres during the early part of the war took place at a gymnasium in the village of Bratunac in April 1992. An estimated 350 Bosnian Muslim men were literally tortured to death by the Serb paramilitaries and special police. Bratunac was not far from Srebrenica, but although they were able to capture Bratunac, the city of Srebrenica was heavily defended by Naser Oric. Oric was a former Bosnian military officer who commanded the army of the Republic of Bosnia forces in Srebrenica with the help of associated squads of civilian *torbari* (or 'bag people'). He has been described as a 'Rambo-like' figure with a reputation for carrying out atrocities on Serb villagers.

In April 1993, the Serb forces managed to close in on Oric and succeeded in overcoming his army, taking control of Srebrenica. The leader of the Serb forces, General Ratko Mladic, had already made it quite clear that he disliked the menfolk of Srebrenica, whether they were involved in the war or not, and in horrific scenes that soon captured the world's attention, he started to segregate the inhabitants of the village. Literally hundreds of women and children were evacuated from Srebrenica before he finally tightened the noose and stemmed the flow of any further refugees.

Worried about what was happening in the village,

the international community declared Srebrenica to be one of five 'safe areas', the other four being Zepa, Gorazde, Tuzla and Sarajevo. However the term 'safe area' was never really defined, and sufficient forces were never supplied to ensure the occupants safety. As the events at Srebrenica two years later proved, they were probably among the most 'unsafe' places in the entire world.

THE MASSACRE

Srebrenica was the home to tens of thousands of civilians who had taken refuge there from earlier Serb offensives in the north-east of Bosnia. They had been placed under the protection of about 600 lightly armed Dutch infantry troops when it had been designated a United Nations 'safe area'. Supplies in the village were running low as nothing had been brought into the enclave since early May.

In July 1995, Serb forces, in an effort to ethnically cleanse the area of the Muslims living in the enclaves, tightened their noose further on the so-called 'safe areas'. Serb forces started shelling Srebrenica, and Muslim fighters in the village asked for the return of their weapons that had been surrendered to peace-keepers. Their request was denied.

The commander of the Dutch forces requested for backup after shells and rockets fell close to the refugee centres, but help was slow in coming.

On 9 July, the Serbs stepped up their bombing and mass panic took hold of the civilian population. Thousands of refugees fled into the village centre ahead of the advancing Serbs, who attacked the Dutch observation posts, taking approximately 30 hostages. By the evening around 4,000 refugees were in the village and large crowds had gathered around the Dutch positions. The Dutch tried to pacify the crowd by telling them that NATO planes would launch massive attacks on the Serbs if they had not withdrawn from the safe area by 6.00 a.m. the following morning.

However, the Serb forces did not retreat, and the Dutch request for backup had been denied, as they said it had been 'submitted on the wrong form'! The promised NATO planes, which had been airborne since 6.00 a.m., had to return to refuel, and the citizens of Srebrenica feared the worst. By midday, more than 20,000 refugees had gathered at the UN base at Potocari.

At 2.30 p.m. two Dutch fighters dropped bombs on the Serb troops surrounding Srebrenica. They responded by saying they would kill their Dutch hostages and continue with the shelling of the refugees. Taking their threat seriously, the Dutch decided not to attack further.

By mid-afternoon the Serb commander, Ratko Mladic, entered the village, accompanied by Serb cameramen. In the evening Mladic demanded a meeting with the Dutch Colonel Karremans, at which he delivered an ultimatum that the Muslims must hand over their weapons to guarantee their safety.

The next day, 12 July, buses arrived to transport the women and children to safety. Meanwhile, the Serbs started to round up all the men aged between 12 and 77 for what they called 'interrogation for suspected war crimes'. In the next 24 hours, it is estimated that as many as 23,000 women and children were deported, while the men were held hostages in trucks and warehouses. Around 15,000 Muslim fighters managed to escape Srebrenica and fled to the hills in their effort to get to Muslim protected territory, but they were shelled in their attempt and the majority were killed.

The first massacre of unarmed Muslims took place in a warehouse in the neighbouring village of Kravica. In return for the release of the 14 Dutch officers, peace-keepers handed over about 5,000 Muslims who had been sheltering at the Potocari base. Following talks between the UN and the Serbs, the Dutch were even-tually allowed to leave the enclave as long as they left their weapons, food and medical supplies behind.

In the five days that the Serb forces occupied Srebrenica, it is believed that more than 7,000 Muslim men were brutally massacred. Many of them were killed in the school gymnasium in Bratunac, the site of an earlier genocide of Muslim men. Many more were slaughtered at a football pitch near Nova Kasaba, which turned out to be the worst killing ground in the period of the massacre. It is alleged that some of the refugees were forced to dig their own graves, after which they were simply lined up in front of them and shot one by one. In a radio broadcast, which was intercepted by westerners, the Bosnian Serb commander, General Radivoj Krstic, told his forces, 'You must kill everyone. We don't need anyone alive'.

Muslims who had fled to the hills had become trapped by the Serb bombardment and, through lack of food, water and sleep, many of them succumbed to hallucinations and paranoia, which resulted in them turning on one another. Some even resorted to shooting themselves, believing that the Serbs would take pity on the wounded. Others simply committed suicide in an attempt to escape the nightmare they found themselves in. Thousands, with the promise of safe passage, surrendered to the Serbs, only to be taken to nearby fields and warehouses, where they were brutally executed and buried in mass graves.

FINAL DEATH COUNT

The estimated number of men killed range from 7,000 to as high as 10,000, but that doesn't account for the 18,406 Muslims, Serbs and Croats who are still listed as missing. It has certainly gone down in history as one of the worst cases of concentrated genocide in Europe during the past 50 years. As to who is responsible – the executions were reportedly carried out under the orders of General Ratko Mladic and Radislav Krstic, who ironically was promoted to general within a few days of the killings.

In 1996, the International Criminal Tribunal indicted both Mladic and Krstic for 'crimes against humanity'. In July 1999, the Tribunal found that the atrocities at Srebrenica had been operating under a 'direct chain of military command' from Belgrade and the Serbian President, Slobodan Milosevic. Before he could be brought to justice, Milosevich died on 11 March, 2006, while on trial at The Hague.

The United Nations should also feel compelled to share responsibility for allowing the massacre to happen right under their noses. They released a self-critical statement in November 1999, which stated:

> *Through error, misjudgement and the inability to recognize the scope of evil confronting us, we failed to do our part to save the people of Srebrenica from the Serb campaign of mass murder.*

The memory of the Srebrenica men has been kept alive by their women, who have organized themselves into a group called 'The Women of Srebrenica'. They continue to press for further forensic investigations, which so far has turned up some 3,000 bodies.

Genocide in Rwanda
———— 1994 ————

*R*wanda is a tiny country in Central Africa and is probably best remembered as being the subject of one of the most intensive killing campaigns ever to take place. In a period of 13 weeks after 6 April, 1994, as many as half a million people perished in a mass slaughter, almost three-quarters of the minority Tutsi population. At the same time, thousands of majority Hutus were also slain because they opposed the killing campaign and the forces that were in control of it.

RWANDAN HISTORY

Rwanda's population is divided into two ethnic groups: the Hutus and the Tutsis. The Hutus make up the larger number and they are by tradition crop growers and farmers. Over the centuries, Hutus have attracted Tutsis from northern Africa to come and work in Rwanda and, for over 600 years, the two groups shared the same language, culture and nationality. Rwanda was first colonized by the

Germans, but during World War I the country was taken over by the Belgians, who upset the balance of the community and caused a rift between the two groups. Using the strategy of 'divide and rule', the Belgians granted preferential status to the minority Tutsis because they were predominantly the landowners, while the Hutus mainly worked on the land. This thoughtless introduction of a class structure unsettled the stability of the Rwandan population. Proud of their new status, some of the Tutsis started to behave like aristocrats, which made the Hutus feel like the underdogs, and a political divide was formed.

To add to the already vulnerable situation, the Europeans introduced modern weapons and modern methods of war. Missionaries also came from Europe, bringing with them a new twist – they taught the Hutus to see themselves as the underdogs – which helped to inspire a revolution. With the backing of the Europeans, the Hutus chose to fight back, resulting in the loss of over 100,000 lives in the 1956 rebellion. Three years later the Hutus had seized power and were stripping the Tutsis of their land and control of Rwanda. Over 200,000 Tutsis retreated to neighbouring countries, where they formed their own army, the Rwandan Patriotric Front (RPF). The Tutsis trained their men and bided their time, waiting for the right opportunity to get their own back on the Hutus.

POLITICAL UNREST

After their initial delight in succeeding to take power and Rwanda's independence in 1962, the inexperienced Hutus started to face turmoil within their own government. Tension built up and, all the while aware that the Tutsis might retaliate, the Hutus started to take repressive measures. In 1990, the RPF rebels seized the moment and attacked, forcing the Hutu president, Juvénal Habyarimana into signing an agreement that sanctioned the Hutus and Tutsis would have equal power. Hutus, however, fiercely opposed any Tutsi involvement in running the government and ethic tensions heightened. The situation was made even worse when a plane carrying Burundi's president, Melchior Ndadaye, was shot down.

Aware that the fragile ceasefire that had been put in place in 1993 was about to crumble, the UN sent a peacekeeping force of around 2,500 multinational soldiers to try and stop the aggression that was building up. The Hutus, who had openly accused the Tutsis of assassinating their president, decided that the only solution was to annihilate the entire Tutsi population. In April 1994, amid ever-increasing threats of violence, the Rwandan president, Habyarimana and the new Burundi president, Cyprien Ntaryamira, held peace meetings with the Tutsi rebels. The final straw in the camel's back took place on 6 April, when a small plane carrying the two presidents was shot down by ground-fired missiles as it approached Kigali airport. Their deaths plunged Rwanda into a frenzied state of political violence and the genocide began.

THE GENOCIDE

Just 24 hours after the plane was shot down, road-blocks started to appear on the roads around Kigali, manned by the Interahamwe militia. The Interahamwe (meaning 'Those Who Stand Together' or 'Those Who Fight Together') was the most important of the militias formed by the Hutus. Tutsis were immediately separated from the Hutus and literally hacked to death with machetes on the side of the road. Victims who could afford to pay were given the option of dying from a bullet. Specially organized death squads, working from carefully prepared lists, went from neighbourhood to neighbourhood in Kigali. Not only did they murder all the Tutsis, but they picked on moderate Hutus as well, including their prime minister, Agathe Uwilingiyimana. The prime minister was protected by Belgian guards, who the Hutus arrested, disarmed, tortured and then murdered, which prompted the Belgians to withdraw the remainder of its UN troops – just what the Hutus wanted.

The violence spread like wildfire, moving from Kigali into the surrounding rural areas. Via the radio, the government urged Tutsis to congregate at churches, schools and stadiums, promising that they would make these safe places of refuge. Little did they realize that by gathering in large groups they actually made themselves easy targets. Surprisingly, some of the helpless civilians were able to ward off attacks by simply using sticks and stones – that is until the joint forces of the Rwandan army and presidential guard were brought in to wipe them out with machine guns and grenades. Against this kind of attack they had no defence. In just two weeks, by 21 April, it is thought that as many as 250,000 Tutsis and moderate Hutus had been slaughtered, making it one of the most concentrated acts of genocide ever witnessed by the world.

What made the genocide even more atrocious is the fact that it was aided and abetted by government officials, who even bribed the killers to do their dirty work. Local officials assisted in rounding up the victims, making suitable places available for the Hutus to carry out their slaughter. Men, women, children and babies alike, were killed in their thousands in schools and churches, in some cases the clergy conspired with the killers. The victims, already frozen by fear, had to bear the fact that they were being killed by people they knew – neighbours, fellow workers, sometimes even relatives by marriage.

The Interahamwe weren't driven by drink, drugs or even mindless violence, but a fanatical dedication to fight for their cause. They were cold-blooded killers who were urged not only by the media, but also by their own government to wipe out the Tutsis. Participants were often given incentives, such as money or food, and were even told they could keep the land of any Tutsis that were killed.

The power of the radio was instrumental in spreading the killing frenzy. It is important to point out that one of the first things Africans buy when they get a job is a radio and even the poorest houses listen intently to catch snatches of government broadcasts. It is not surprising, therefore, that when the Hutus heard the voices coming through the radio to 'kill, kill, kill the Tursi minority', the Hutus responded and literally did as they were told.

One fact that is not widely publicized about the Rwandan genocide is that it was mainly directed at the young, male Tutsi population, fearing they were members of the RPF guerrilla force. However, as the days went by women and children were also victims. Survivors later told stories of being raped either by individuals or gangs, sometimes using sharpened sticks or gun barrels. Sometimes they were sexually mutilated, or they were forced to marry to become nothing more than sex slaves.

THE MASSACRE IS OVER

The killing didn't stop until July when the RPF finally managed to capture Kigali, causing the collapse of the government. They declared a ceasefire and as soon as the Hutus realized that the RPF had been victorious, an estimated two million fled to Zaire (now the Democratic Republic of the Congo). It wasn't until the killing stopped that the UN troops and aid workers arrived to try and restore the basic services.

Why was it that as the killing intensified, the rest of the international community deserted Rwanda? Erratic media coverage while the genocide was taking place conveyed the false notion of two 'tribes' of African 'savages' mindlessly killing each other as they had done for many years. As a result, there was little public pressure in the West for governments to intervene. Controversy has raged ever since over the role of foreign governments and the UN in allowing the genocide to proceed. It wasn't until 7 April, 2000, the sixth anniversary of the massacre, that Belgium's prime minister apologized for the international community's failure to intervene. He told a crowd of thousands at the site of a memorial that, 'A dramatic combination of neglicence, incompetence and hesitation created the conditions for the tragedy'.

At the beginning of the First Congo War in 1996, many Tutsi refugees returned to Rwanda, which instigated the start of the long-awaited genocide trials. The UN formed the International Criminal Tribunal for Rwanda (ICTR) and in September 1998, they issued their first charges on genocide.

In Rwanda itself, approximately 120,000 people were jailed on allegations of having taken part. Many have since died due to the appalling conditions and overcrowding in the jails. By the end of April 2000, about 2,500 people had been sent to trial and of these about 300 received death sentences.

Three journalists from Rwanda went on trial in 2001 for war crimes, because they were the voices behind the radio broadcasts that urged the Hutus to kill. This is reminiscent of the Nazi editor, Julius Streicher, who was sent to the gallows at Nuremberg in 1946.

HAS A LESSON BEEN LEARNED?

The scars of the genocide and the subsequent reprisals will probably always stay with the Rwandans, and even worse it could provoke another round of mass killing. With the economy badly damaged and little hope of a quick recovery, many Tutsis still feel that the only way to rebuild their lives is to repress the Hutus. The Hutus, who once again feel downtrodden, because they have been labelled 'guilty' for the last massacre, feel that no one cares about what happens to them under the latest Tutsi-led government. Extremists on both sides believe that the only solution is complete annihilation of the other side, and many believe they are preparing for another slaughter. It appears despite all the pain and suffering, the Rwandans have not learned an important lesson – that violence simply doesn't pay.

PART SEVEN

21st Century: The War Crimes Continue

Saddam Hussein's Regime
———————— 1974–2003 ————————

Although the Iraqi people have suffered the atrocities inflicted by the US military, possibly the greatest threat to them over the years has been Saddam Hussein's regime. For over two decades he has terrorized, killed, tortured and raped the Iraqi people and their neighbours. Under his regime it is fair to say that many hundreds of thousands have died as a direct result of Hussein's actions, a vast majority of them being Muslims. He has used a wide range of torture methods, including the gouging out of eyes, severe beatings and electric shocks, leaving many of his victims dead or with permanent physical and pschological damage.

It has been estimated that during Hussein's 1987–88 campaign of terror against the Kurds, as many as 100,000 were killed and 2,000 of their villages destroyed. The use of chemical agents, such as mustard gas and nerve agents, have resulted in some 30,000 Iraqi and Iranian deaths. Possibly the worst attack was the one on Halabja which resulted in approximately 5,000 deaths.

Freedom of worship was also restricted, as Hussein's regime curbed their religious practices, including a ban on communal Friday prayer and funeral processions. His oppressive government policies have led to as many as 900,000 Iraqis, mainly Kurds, fleeing to the north of the country to avoid having to renounce their Kurdish identity or lose their property.

During his regime it is also estimated that as many as 400,000 Iraqi children under the age of five, unnecessarily died of either malnutrition or disease. The Oil-for-Food Programme, which was established by the United Nations in 1995 and terminated in late 2003, was intended to allow Iraq to sell oil on the world market in exchange for food, medicine and other humanitarian needs for ordinary Iraqi citizens without allowing Iraq to rebuild its military. However, Hussein's regime blocked the access of international workers, who were supposed to ensure the correct distribution of the supplies. During Operation Iraqi Freedom, coalition forces uncovered military warehouses which were full of supplies that had never reached their intended destination – the Iraqi people.

Saddam Hussein's regime has also been known to carry out frequent executions. For example, in 1984 4,000 prisoners were killed at Abu Ghraib prison; 3,000 prisoners were killed at the Mahjar prison from 1993–98; 2,500 prisoners were executed between 1997 and 1999 in what has been described as a 'prison cleansing programme'; 122 political prisoners were executed at Abu Ghraib prison in February/March 2000; 23 political prisoners were executed at Abu Ghraib prison in

October 2001; and at least 130 Iraqi women were beheaded between June 2000 and April 2001.

THE ANFAL CAMPAIGN

One of the worst campaigns mounted by the regime of Saddam Hussein was the anti-Kurdish Anfal campaign in 1988. This was a 'cleansing' campaign aimed at the Kurdish population, who are considered to be the world's largest nation who do not actually possess a state of their own. Their territory is divided between Turkey, Iran, Iraq and Syria, with as many as 4 million Kurds being concentrated in Iraq.

When Hussein came into power, it appeared to bode well for the Kurds, especially when his Ba'ath Party made an agreement with the Kurdish rebel groups. This agreement granted them the right to use and broadcast their own language, as well as giving them a considerable amount of political independence. However, it wasn't long before the agreement began to break down, when the Ba'ath Party started to evict Kurdish farmers, replacing them with poor Arab tribesmen and women. In March 1974, the Kurdistan Democratic Party (KDP) retaliated, which sparked off a full-scale war. Villagers were forcibly removed from their homes and eventually 130,000 Kurds fled to Iran.

It was these refugees, the Barzani tribespeople, who would fall prey to one of the worst cases of genocide of male members of a population the world had ever seen. In 1983, the Iraqi security forces started to round up all the males of the Barzani tribe from four refugee camps near Arbil. Just as dawn broke the soldiers stormed into the camps, taking captive all the male members of the tribe, including an old, mentally deranged man who was usually tied up for his own safety and a preacher who was on his way to the Mosque to call for morning prayer. The soldiers broke down doors and searched every house. In fact, they searched everywhere – inside chicken coops, water tanks, refrigerators – anywhere that it was possible someone could be hiding. Women cried, desperately hanging onto their sons, as the soldiers rounded up any males over the age of 13 and took them away to face their final fate. None of these men were ever seen again. The women pleaded with the soldiers not to take their men away, as Saddam Hussein had already hinted what he intended to do to the Barzani tribes-men. This earlier operation foreshadowed the tech-niques that would be used on a much larger scale during the Anfal campaign.

In March 1987, Hussein's cousin, Ali Hassan al-Majid, was appointed secretary general of the Ba'ath Party of the northern region, which included the Kurdish dominated area. He had a reputation for brutality and following the Iraqi's army control of the Kurdish insurgents, he took the matter into his own hands. His new campaign of terror became known as 'al-Anfal' (The Spoils), which took place between

23 February and 6 September, 1988. The campaign was broken down into eight different stages, with seven of them directly targeting areas controlled by the Patriotic Union of Kurdistan (PUK), which had been founded in 1975 by Jalal Talabani.

Al-Majid amassed around 200,00 soldiers, supported by air attacks, against a poorly-matched few thousand Kurdish guerillas. They went to work rounding up all the villagers, regardless of gender or age, and transported them to detention centres, where they were subjected to gendercidal selection. Any adult or teenage males (those considered to be of fighting age) were separated from the remainder of the community. Small children were allowed to stay with their mothers, while the elderly or infirm were taken away to separate living quarters.

The men were divided into smaller groups and hustled into large rooms or halls, which soon became grossly overcrowded. Beatings were almost routine and after several days of inhuman treatment, they were trucked out of the centres to be killed in mass executions. Many of the prisoners were lined up in front of pre-dug mass graves and shot from the front. Others were made to lie down in pairs next to mounds of fresh corpses, before they too were killed. Others, who had been bound together, were made to stand on the edges of the graves and shot from behind so they fell face-first into the pits. When they had finished their killing spree, the soldiers used bulldozers to roughly cover the graves of literally thousands of Kurdish males. Some of the men did not even make it as far as the 'slaughter stations'. they were simply lined up and shot at their point of capture, by firing squads.

Although the aim of the al-Anfal campaign was to cleanse the Kurdish population of its males, thousands of women, children and elderly people perished as well. Mass executions of women and children were known to have taken place at a site on Hamrin Mountain, between the cities of Tikrit and Kurkuk. Those who did not die in the executions were trucked off to resettlement camps, where conditions were both squalid and insanitary, resulting in the death of thousands more, the majority of whom were children.

The infrastructure of the Kurdish population was almost destroyed by the al-Anfal massacre. By the time the genocidal frenzy was over, 90 per cent of the Kurdish villages and more than 20 towns and villages had literally been wiped off the map.

APPALLING TREATMENT

In August 1988, with the al-Anfal campaign coming to an end and many months of vicious chemical attacks on civilian populations, the UN Sub-committee on Human Rights voted to condemn Iraq for its human rights violations. It is blatantly obvious that the influence of Saddam Hussein's dictatorship affected all levels of Iraqi society, whether through the influences and actions of the Ba'ath Party or the Iraqi army and security forces. Hussein's use of strong patriarchal control over ministers and senior party officials led to their loyalty and subservience to their leader, resulting in the unthinkable terror and cruelty that existed during his term of power.

How does Saddam Hussein defend his treatment of the Iraqi people? By arguing that he had to use powerful methods in an effort to unite such a large and diverse nation as Iraq, that had Kurds in the north, Sunni Muslims in the middle and Shi'ites in the south. When asked by a very nervous reporter why Hussein had used such extreme measures under his regime, he simply replied, 'Of course. What do you expect if they oppose the regime?'

END OF HIS REGIME AND CAPTURE

In 1998, Saddam Hussein failed to conform to the requests of UN weapons investigators, which instigated the issuing of the Iraq Liberation Act, authorizing the removal of his regime. The USA tried its hardest in 2002 to try and topple the Iraqi leader, but Hussein kept insisting that he didn't possess any weapons of mass destruction. In March 2003, the USA led the war on Iraq to try and oust Hussein and to end his regime once and for all.

On Sunday, 14 December, 2003, the toppled leader was found hiding in a tiny dirt hole by the American

Special Forces. His accommodation was a far cry from his former palaces of unadulterated luxury. When he was discovered, he was sitting among filth and squalor, surrounded by rubbish, plastic bags, empty bottles, rotten fruit and just one broken chair as furniture.

Hussein and his 11 top known associates (dubbed 'Saddam's Dirty Dozen'), faced preliminary charges on July 2003 before an Iraqi Special Tribunal, on charges of war crimes and crimes against humanity. The actual trial started on 19 October, 2005, in Baghdad, and Hussein was charged with killing 148 people in Dujail, following an attempted assassination on him when he visited the village. On 5 November, 2006, the tribunal reached its decision and Hussein was sentenced to death by hanging. On top of this it is thought that he will be charged with further atrocities against the Iraqi people. Below is a list of his alleged crimes that will be raised by the tribunal.

1974
Five known, and possibly many more, Shia religious leaders are killed.

1970–2003
After the discovery of 270 mass graves, Hussein faces being charged with killing tens of thousands people.

1982
Following a failed assassination attempt on Hussein,

148 people were killed in the village of Dujail.

1983
About 8,000 male members of the Kurdish Barzani tribe were arrested and deported to southern Iraq, but no trace of them has ever been found.

1988
Up to 182,000 people were killed or died from cold and hunger when Hussein attempted to depopulate Kurdish regions. About 5,000 people were killed in a chemical attack on the village of Halabja in just one day.

1990
When Iraq was invaded in 1990, hundreds of citizens of Kuwait were rounded up and tortured. 700 oil wells were set alight, which polluted the Persian Gulf.

1991
In the aftermath of the Gulf War thousands of people died when Hussein's regime suppressed uprisings by Kurds and Shias.

HUSSEIN ON TRIAL

The trial of the dethroned Iraqi dictator Saddam Hussein was flawed right from the start with lawyers and witnesses being murdered, judges dismissed because they were deemed to be biased, and consider-

able outside political interference. The trial began on
19 October, 2005, and the following day a defence
attorney was kidnapped and later killed. On 8
November a lawyer for a co-defendant was killed. The
trial reconvened on 28 November and on 4 December
one of the five trial judges stepped down. Defence
lawyers walk out of the court the following day when
they are denied the right to challenge the trial's
legitimacy. On 7 December, Saddam refused to attend
court proceedings and on 21 December claimed that
he had been tortured by Americans whilst being held
in detention. The chief judge, a Kurd, resigned on 15
January, 2006 and another Kurd is named to replace
him. On 21 June another lawer for Saddam Hussein is
kidnapped and killed. Hussein goes on hunger strike
and is force-fed through a tube and on 23 July he is
hospitalized. The first trial is adjourned on 27 July and
the new trial does not reconvene until 21 August.

Hussein, his half-brother, Barzan al-Tikriti and Iraq's
former chief judge Awad Hamed al-Bander were being
charged with crimes against humanity following a
wave of revenge killings in 1982 in the northern city of
Dujail, after an assassination attempt on Hussein. On 5
November, 2006, celebratory gunfire was heard across
parts of Baghdad and other Iraqi cities, as Hussein and
his two former top Iraqi officials were sentenced to
death by hanging.

On the day of the sentencing Hussein walked calm-
ly into court wearing his usual dark suit and white

shirt, with his Koran in his hand. Judge Rauf Abdel Rahman ordered him to stand as he read out the verdict, but Hussein refused and had to be forcibly removed from his seat by court attendants. As the judge read out the death sentence, Hussein shouted, 'Allahu Akbar! (God is Great). Long live Iraq! Long live the Iraqi people! Down with the traitors!'

The celebrations in Baghdad were in defiance of a 12-hour curfew that had been placed on city, because of expected retaliatory violence from Hussein's Sunni Arab supporters. Since the trial began, there has been soaring sectarian violence which has brought Iraq on the brink of civil war. Few Iraqis believe that the verdict will help to ease the conflict in any way, while US President, George Bush, welcomed it as a 'milestone . . . to replace the rule of a tyrant with the rule of law'. The question, however, that is in the back of many peoples' minds, is will his death really bring justice for his hundreds of thousands of victims?

Invasion of Iraq:
A War Crime in Itself?

2003–2004

$\mathcal{T}$he invasion of Iraq in 2003, codenamed 'Operation Iraqi Freedom', will always remain a controversial subject and, as more and more hideous pictures and stories were released by the media worldwide, it exposed the horrors that were being inflicted under the name of 'war'. The invasion of the century officially started on 20 March, with the objective of 'disarming Iraq of weapons of mass destruction, to end Saddam Hussein's support for terrorism and to free the Iraqi people'. All good reasons to go to war – but it has since been deemed a violation of international law, breaking the UN Charter. Since the horrific attacks of 11 September, 2001, on the Twin Towers in New York, it is easy to see why the USA wanted to take action in its fight against global terrorism. The wrong weapons in the wrong hands can threaten people worldwide, but what is inconceivable is the treatment of Iraqi civilians and soldiers in the effort to rid the world of these weapons. Pictures that were broadcast on Australian television showed pictures of Iraqi soldiers – naked, wounded, covered with blood, women's underwear draped over their heads – in painful and degrading positions. Is this really how prisoners of war should be treated? Other footage revealed soldiers brutally assaulting a group of youths, dragging them into a compound and beating them with batons and kicking them until they lost consciousness.

Estimated civilian deaths at the end of the war amounted to 50,000, and many more were made homeless. The subsequent environmental consequences as the result of malnutrition and other serious health problems caused further civilian devastation. This, and the fact that no 'weapons of mass destruction' were actually uncovered, has opened arguments that attacking Iraq may have involved committing not only war crimes, but crimes against humanity as well.

WAR CRIMES FROM ABOVE

According to the terms of the Nuremberg Convention:

The crimes hereinafter set out are punishable as crimes under international law: wanton destruction of cities, towns or villages, or destruction not justified by military necessity.

The Geneva Convention quite clearly states that it is a war crime to launch indiscriminate attacks affecting the civilian population or their property. If this is the case, why do the ordinary people of Iraq still have nightmares about the constant air attacks on their homes during the Iraqi War. Time and time again, US planes bombed peasant villages where they knew full well that there were no military bases. Added to this, the use of depleted uranium causes poisoning by radiation, and this too has destroyed the lives of untold numbers of civilians and soldiers alike. For example, 13 members of staff at the Basra Training Hospital, who were all present when the building was bombed with armour-piercing shells covered with uranium, are now all suffering from cancer. The use of depleted uranium is most certainly a war crime, the horrific consequences of which are still to run their course.

The cluster bomb is one of the most heinous, unpredictable and deadly weapons of modern warfare. It is a 4-m (14-ft) weapon that weighs about 453 kg (1,000 lbs). When it explodes it sprays literally thousands of smaller bomblets over a large area. These were dropped on populated areas, not only maiming and killing civilians, but also farm animals and wildlife – in fact, anything they came into contact with. In addition, the small bombs are bright yellow and, because they look like playthings, thousands of children have been killed by dormant bomblets, which then explode spraying shards of metal that can tear through a 6-mm (¼-in) sheet of steel. Under the Geneva Convention, it is a war crime to use weapons in the knowledge that they 'will cause an excessive loss of life or injury to civilians', which definitely makes cluster bombs criminal weapons.

The Iraqi War was the deadliest campaign for non-combatants since the Vietnam War. Reports that have been gathered from hospitals and morgues show a level of civilian casualties that far exceeds the First Gulf War, which in itself cost more than 5,000 civilian lives.

FALLUJAH MASSACRE

In November 2004, there was a major assault on the Sunni city of Fallujah when US and Iraqi military forced out the town's residents, bombed hospitals and buildings, attacked whole neighbourhoods and then denied the entry of relief workers into the area. The attack was so severe it made the Mai Lai massacre that took place in Vietnam seem pale by comparison. Using the deadly Lockheed Ac-130 'Spectre', which is a deadly weapon that pumps out thousands of rounds of high-explosive ammunition every minute, US forces destroyed 10,000 buildings, and as a result made over 100,000 residents homeless.

The day started peacefully when approximately 200 demonstrators turned up outside a school that had been taken over by about 100 US soldiers the previous day. The demonstrators had come in peace to ask the soldiers to leave so that they could reopen the school. The US soldiers claimed that they were fired upon and acted accordingly, but there is absolutely no evidence to corroborate their story. Witnesses have described a scene of complete mayhem, as the soldiers fired on unarmed demonstrators who were fleeing in fright. The road was stained with large patches of blood, and shoes lay discarded as the people ran to get away from the massacre.

There have also been reports that the USA used white phosphorous as a weapon in the Fallujah attack. This would be consistent with the stories that the refugees related afterwards, describing the phosphorous weapons, horribly burnt bodies and fires that were impossible to put out with water. Almost one year after these allegations came to light, a new harrowing documentary entitled *Fallujah: The Hidden Massacre* was produced, which provided fresh evidence of the use of chemical weapons.

It is believed that the death toll of the Fallujah massacre was 600, with another 1,000 injured. Local hospitals reported that the majority of the victims were women, children and the elderly, and that more than 60,000 women and children fled the city in panic. After the attack many of bodies were buried in the city's football stadium because the US forces had blocked the road leading to the cemetery.

Unfortunately, the Fallujah massacre was not just an isolated incident and the atrocities committed there will never be forgotten by the Iraqi people. The words of the US government that they were there to help 'liberate' the Iraqis seems to be slipping away into oblivion to reveal the crude reality of foreign occupation and violent oppression.

THE WEDDING MASSACRE

In the remote village of Mukaradeeb, wedding celebrations had only just finished on 19 May, 2004, and at 10.30 p.m. the guests were hurrying back to their homes at the end of a lovely day. The wedding was the biggest event to take place that year in the small village of just 25 houses, and it had brought a lot of people together. The bride and groom, Ashad and Rutba Rakat, had already settled in their tent for the night when they heard the first sound of a fighter jet in the sky above. Then some of the guests saw the headlights of what appeared to be a military convoy heading their way.

The bombing started at about 3.00 a.m. and the first place to be hit was the tent that had been used for the ceremony. People started running out of the main house where the wedding took place as bombs fell, destroying the entire area. By this time, the armoured vehicles had reached the village and started firing machine guns at the people outside the house.

Just before dawn, two large Chinook helicopters dropped off many more soldiers. They set explosives in the main wedding house and the building next door. Just a few minutes later, the two buildings exploded, leaving just a pile of rubble. Everywhere lay bodies of women, children and men, all badly mutilated. By sunrise the death toll was 42, with 27 of them being members of the now extended Rakat family. Remarkably, the bride and groom were among the survivors because they had been sleeping in tents away from the main house.

The explanation by the US military was that they had been targeting a 'suspected foreign fighter safe house', during which time they had come under hostile fire. Despite the fact that there was no evidence to back their story, the US military continued to claim that the Mukraradeeb was a legitimate military target. At the end of the day, 27 small mounds of dirt and one crudely cut marble headstone bearing the words 'The American Bombing' are grim reminders of what once again appears to have been a pointless attack on innocent civilians.

AND SO IT GOES ON . . .

Previously, in early April, night-time raid on a farm in the Al Janabin suburb on the edge of Baghdad killed 20 civilians, including 11 children. The following day Al Jeezera television showed footage of a predominantly Christian town, Bartallah, having received heavy civilian casualties after a night of intense bombing.

Just three weeks into the war, the Americans dropped bombs on a residential area of Baghdad. This killed 14 civilians, most of them members of a Christian family. The wanton destruction of cities and villages went on and on, leaving a trail of carnage behind them.

In a way it was an unusual war because US President George W. Bush announced on 1 May, 2003, that it was all over – the American mission had been accomplished – and yet three years on it is obvious that the conflict is far from over. It is obvious that the struggle is losing credibility if it is used to justify acts that would otherwise be deemed as offensive, such as the killing of innocent people who are in no way involved in the hostilities.

Camp X-Ray: Guantanamo Bay

2001

The US Naval base at Guantanamo Bay is the oldest and only detention centre in Cuba. The primary job of Guantanamo Bay is to serve as a stratetic logistics base for the Navy's Atlantic fleet and to support counter drug operations in the Caribbean. In 1991, the base was expanded as some 34,000 Haitian refugees passed through Guantanamo Bay. The refugees fled Haiti after a violent coup brought on by political and social upheaval in their country. In May 1994, Operation Sea Signal began and the naval base was given the job of supporting Joint Task Force 160, providing humanitarian assistance to thousands of Haitian and Cuban migrants. In late August and early September 1994, 2,200 family members and civilian employees were evacuated from the base as the migrant population climbed to more than 45,000 and the Pentagon began preparing to house up to 60,000 migrants on the base. Separate camps were erected on the south side, each one being given a name to correspond with the phonetic alphabet used for official military radio communication – Camp Alpha, Camp Bravo, right up to Camp Golf. When additional sites were added on the north end of the base, they were named using letters from the opposite end of the alphabet, and this included Camp X-Ray.

Following the attacks on the Twin Towers on 11 September, 2001, and military operations in Afghanistan, numerous individuals who were alleged to be members or fighters associated with al-Qaeda were taken captive. It was decided to transfer these detainees to Cuba to the Camp X-Ray facility. The base was to serve as a temporary holding prison under the jurisdiction of the USA during their war on terrorism.

Since Camp X-Ray was closed on 29 April, 2002, it has drawn strong criticism both in the USA and worldwide for its alleged mistreatment of the detainees. Although officials from the Department of Defence stressed that the holding conditions at Guanatanamo Bay would be humane and in accordance with the Geneva Convention, the validity of this claim has since been in dispute. Foremost among the issues raised was the question of the detainees legal status. While the majority of the people felt that they should be given the status of prisoners of war, which gave them certain rights under the Geneva Convention, the USA refused to give them that designation, preferring instead to hold them as 'illegal combatants'.

ALLEGED MISTREATMENT

When the detainees arrived at Guatanamo Bay they were given jumpsuits to wear made out of reddish cloth, which, in the Arab world, is a colour reserved for condemned men. It is alleged that the US guards at Camp X-Ray played on the men's fear and took advantage of their 'freedom from restrictions' to abuse basic human rights.

After their arrest, prisoners were taken to the camp, blindfolded, ear-muffed and gagged. Their arms and legs were tethered, their hands covered with mittens, their beards shaved off and their heads covered by masks. The US Army later stated that these measures were 'for the prisoners' own safety and well-being'.

Two accounts of Afghanistan arrests given to Amnesty International read as follows:

They were beating us on the head and back and ribs. They were punching us with fists, kicking me with their feet. They said: 'You are a terrorist! You are al-Qaeda! You are Taliban!'

I was down on my knees, bent over, and they kicked me in the chest. I heard my ribs crack. Then I was lying on my side and they kicked me in the back, in the kidneys and I fainted.

The prisoners were allegedly detained in conditions

that amounted to cruel, inhumane and degrading treatment of a fellow human being. The open-air cells were
approximately 2 m (6 ft 8in) by 2.4 m (8 ft), and surrounded by barbed wire. This at least afforded the
inmate the luxury of being able to lie down. They were
given a bucket for their toilet needs, a paper-thin foam
mat to sleep on, a single blanket, one bucket for water,
two red/orange jumpsuits, one pair of flip-flops and a
towel for bathing. According to British newspapers,
more than 30 of the inmates were driven to pathetic
lengths to commit suicide, even to using a plastic
spoon to slit their wrists.

CAMP DELTA

When the detainees at Camp X-Ray reached
maximum occupancy, i.e. 320, it was necessary to
build a larger enclosed long-term detention facility.
The construction of Camp Delta was started on
9 April, 2002, about 8 km (5 miles) from Camp X-Ray.
When Camp X-Ray was officially closed down on
29 April, the detainees were moved to the new camp.

Although the conditions at the new camp were
supposed to be superior to Camp X-Ray – with running
water, flushing toilets and a bed raised off the floor – by
10 June, 2006, three Guantanamo Bay detainees had
committed suicide. The military reported the men
hanged themselves with nooses made of sheets and
clothes. One of the men was first detained when he was

a juvenile, and each had been imprisoned for the past four years but never charged with a crime.

When 24-year-old Murat Kurnaz was released from the base on 24 August, 2006, he claimed to have been exposed to water torture, sexual harassment and desecration of Islam while staying on Guantanamo.

The detainees are kept in isolation for the majority of the day, blindfolded when moved about the camp, and forbidden to talk in groups of more than three. There have been many allegations of torture, including sleep deprivation, the use of truth drugs, beatings, being locked in cold, inhumane cells and also being forced to maintain uncomfortable positions for long periods of time.

A US soldier who once worked as an interpreter at Camp Delta during the interrogation sessions, talked openly to the press about what went on inside the camp. He told of fake interrogations to try and impress visiting administration and military officials. Prisoners that had already been subjected to interrogation were placed behind one-way mirrors and asked the same questions again in front of the visitors. He also talked of interrogators resorting to sexual techniques to get what they wanted out of the prisoners. One female interrogator was supposed to have removed all her clothes and rubbed her naked body up against the prisoners. Pornographic magazines and videos were also used as rewards to confessing.

WORLDWIDE CRITICISM

The use of Guantanamo Bay as a military prison has received much criticism from human rights organizations worldwide, who state there is strong evidence of mistreatment of prisoners. In response, the Bush administration argued that the Third Geneva Convention does not apply to possible al-Qaeda or Taliban fighters, it is only for uniformed soldiers of a recognized government. The UN and Amnesty International have called the whole situation a 'human rights scandal', questioning the legal status and physical condition of the detainees at Guantanamo.

Since 2002, hundreds of the detainees have been released or handed over to their national governments. Reports have been put together from the prisoners who have been released from Guatanamo, describing in detail the treatment they received while being detained. Out of the approximate 750 detainees, only 10 have ever been tried and none has ever been proven guilty. The camp still holds about 460 detainees from 40 different countries, and is said to include terrorist suspects picked up in Eastern Europe and Africa. It wasn't until March 2006 that the US defence department actually released the names and nationalities of the people being held.

To date, the only organization that has been allowed full access to the camp is the International Red Cross. There has been constant pressure from organizations around the world to have the prison camp closed down as more and more allegations of torture come to light. One inmate, who had been on hunger strike, complained of being force-fed through nasal tubes and that he had been the constant victim of unfair interrogation techniques, including solidary confinement and exposure to extreme temperatures, noise and light. There are also reports that many of the inmates have suffered from mental breakdowns, and Amnesty International described the camp as 'the gulag of our times'.

There have been no new inmates since September 2004, but the department of defence has fought against the closure of the camp, stating that 'many of the detainees are still dangerous and would attack the USA if they were released'. The status of inmates is reviewed each year through a system of military administrative review boards, which recommends whether the detainee should remain in captivity or is eligible for release. Finally on 17 October, 2006, a law was passed that set the standard for the interrogation and prosecution of foreign terror suspects, but although many reports have been issued regarding the alleged mistreatment of prisoners at Guatanamo Bay no one has ever been prosecuted.

Many of the practices developed by the USA since 11 September, 2001, in relation to detainees captured in the 'global war on terror' appear designed to evade judicial or other scrutiny. The prime example of this is the creation of offshore prisons, the most well known of which is at Guantanamo Bay. It is thought that the US authorities deliberately chose Guantanamo as a detention centre in an attempt to put the detainees beyond the jurisdiction of the US courts and consequently courts in other parts of the world as well.

It is evident that prisoners held under the label of 'terrorism' need to be treated more humanely as anti-Americanism in nations all over the world has surged to an all time high. The atrocities that have occurred at Guantanamo Bay and Abu Ghraib have done more harm than good in cementing relationships between the USA and Muslim-speaking countries, or indeed in lessening the threat of attack from terrorists.

Torture, Rendition and the CIA's Secret War

―――――― 2001–2006 ――――――

Since the terror attacks on New York on 11 September, 2001, there have been many allegations regarding the CIA's secret detention of terror suspects. The fact that they have used European countries as regular stopping places for their transfer to other countries has become a major political issue between the USA and Europe. According to the media, US president, George W. Bush, signed a document as the result of an inquiry that gave the CIA the authority to either kill or capture any al-Qaeda members anywhere in the world. Since the signing, the Bush administration has done everything in its power to keep the CIA operations a secret, thereby avoiding any legal implications.

THE USE OF RENDITION

To avoid scrutiny, the CIA has been transferring detainees to countries in the Middle East known to practise torture as a matter of routine. Captured al-Qaeda suspects have been taken from US custody to other countries, such as Syria, Uzbekistan, Pakistan, Egypt, Jordan, Saudi Arabia and Morocco, where they were tortured or otherwise mistreated. This practice is called 'rendition', which, in law, literally means the 'surrender' or 'handing over' of persons or property, particularly from one jurisdiction to another. Although the practice of rendition is not new, the way the CIA are apprehending suspected terrorists but not bringing them before a court of law, is. What is disturbing about this latest 'tool' in the fight against terrorism is that not only have innocent citizens been detained, but many detainees have also simply 'disappeared' while in US custody. It is alleged that the CIA have conducted more than 1,000 secret flights over European territory since 2001, many of which were used to transfer terror suspects.

According to a former CIA agent, he told reporters:

If you want a serious interrogation, you send a prisoner to Jordan. If you want them to be tortured, you send them to Syria. If you want someone to disappear – never to see them again – you send them to Egypt.

Rendition is not the same as deportation. Under US immigration laws a person may be deported for a variety of reasons, including charges of terrorism. Rendition, however, is a covert operation in which an innocent person can be forcibly removed to another country or state where he has committed no crime.

Under rendition, the person handing over the suspect is knowingly passing his 'package' to a country who is far less scrupulous about human rights than the country from which they are being transferred. As the practice has grown, the CIA is finding it harder and harder to keep it under cover, and criticism of the rendition system has grown. Under the current law, rendition is strictly prohibited if the rendered person is subjected to any kind of torture, and human rights groups are working on legal challenges to try and stop the practice from continuing.

Rendition was developed by the CIA back in the 1990s for the purpose of tracking down and disrupting the militant Islamic organizations in the Middle East, in particular al-Qaeda. For fear of jeopardizing their own intelligence methods, the CIA wanted to avoid the normal procedure of trying suspects under US law and came up with the alternative of transferring them to Egypt. In Egypt they would be handed over to the Mukhabarat (Arabic for 'intelligence'), which was well known for its brutality. This arrangement suited both countries as the Egyptians had been trying to track down Islamic extremists, some of whom were Egyptian, and for the USA, because torture is illegal under US and international law.

The first person to be the subject of rendition was Talaat Fouad Qassem, one of Egypt's most wanted terrorists. He was arrested in Zagreb by the CIA in September 1995, with the cooperation of the Croatian police. He was taken on board a US ship somewhere on the Adriatic Sea, interrogated by US agents and then returned to Egypt. He has never been heard of or seen since and is believed to have been executed without having been given a trial.

Another operation that has come to light took place in Albania in the summer of 1998. Five Egyptians were known to be in contact with Osama bin Laden's deputy, Ayman al-Zawahiri and, over the course of several months, four militants along with Shawki Salama Attiya were captured by Albanian security forces, who collaborated with the CIA. The five men were flown to Cairo – where they were interrogated using harsh torture methods. On his release Attiya said that he had electric shocks applied to his genitals, that he was kept in a cell that was filled with dirty water and that he had been hung up by his limbs for hours on end.

Despite the fact that they are being constantly questioned about the practice of rendition, the CIA and the White House strongly resist any in-depth investigation. They refuse to release any information about the suspects that have been detained in other parts of the world.

'REVERSE' RENDITION

Another variation, which has become known as 'reverse rendition', is when US agents abduct suspects on foreign soil, or assumed custody of detainees from other countries, in transfers that completely bypass any legal process or human rights protections. Some of the victims of reverse rendition have later turned up in Guantanamo, but the most sinister and least well-documented cases are those of the detainees who have simply 'disappeared' after being detained by the USA or turned over to US custody.

One example of this practice was the case of a Yemeni businessman Abd al-Salam Ali al-Hila, who was handed over to the US authorities and then disappeared for a year and a half before turning up at Guatanamo Bay detention centre. Although there have been many reports in the media regarding the renditions of suspects to third countries, this case was different – in fact, it was the 'reverse'. Foreign authorities picked up the suspect in a non-combat situation and handed him over to the USA without the basic protection afforded to criminal suspects.

Al-Hila was literally kidnapped from the streets of Cairo and disappeared when under US custody. When al-Hila was picked up on 19 September, 2002, during a business trip to Cairo, he was taken to Baku in Azerbaijan and later to the Bagram air base in Afghanistan. After his disappearance, his family did not hear from him until April 2004, when they received a letter, which was smuggled out of Afghanistan. Al-Hila has sent subsequent letters to his family to let them know he is still alive via the International Committee of the Red Cross and, most recently, from Guatanamo.

Unfortunately, the al-Hila case is not unique. It appears that the Bush administration feels it is within its legal rights if the detainees come under the label of 'terror suspects'.

BLACK SITES

The term 'black sites' is a military term that literally means 'secret jails in foreign countries', which are operated by the CIA. Recently the term has gained notoriety when the *Washington Post* published a controversial article claiming the existence of black sites, which was vehemently denied by many European countries. The secret facilities for detaining and interrogating suspected terrorists are believed to be in Thailand, Afghanistan and several other democracies in Eastern Europe, on top of the already notorious Guatanamo Bay prison in Cuba. This hidden network of internment is all part of the illicit war on terrorism at present being carried out by the CIA. It relies on the assistance of other foreign intelligence agencies, and the concealment of any details is paramount to the success of their operations. Due to what the CIA and the White House consider the clandestine nature of these black sites, virtually nothing is known about who is kept where and the exact locations. This information is only available to a handful of people to protect national security and because of the fear that the information could be leaked out. Although the CIA has issued reports and testimonies regarding the alleged abuse carried out at Guatanamo Bay, it strongly denies the existence of any black sites.

THREE MEN DISAPPEAR

In 2003, three Yemeni nationals all disappeared. When their whereabouts was eventually disclosed it appeared they had been kept in a series of secret locations run by US agents. The reason for the clandestine operation was so that it put the victims beyond the protection of the law, while at the same time concealing any violations from external scrutiny. The three men were Salah Nasser Salim 'Ali, Muhammad al-Assad and Muhammad Faraj Ahmed Bashmilah.

The nightmare started on the night of 26 December, 2003, in Dar-es-Salaam, Tanzania, where Muhammed al-Assad had lived since 1985. Al-Assad had just sat down to dinner with his Tanzanian wife, Zahra Salloum, and her brother and uncle, when he heard a knock at the front door. The three men at the door were an immigration officer and two state security officials, who ordered al-Assad to surrender his passport and mobile phone. As al-Assad walked away from the men to get his passport from his study, he was grabbed from behind; his hands were handcuffed behind his back and his head was covered with a hood. He was forcibly pushed into the back of a car, which sped away from the house, leaving al-Assad in a state of shock.

He was frightened and kept asking his captors what was happening to him and where were they taking him, but they gave him no reply. He was taken back to a flat and questioned for several hours, before being taken to a waiting plane. All the time al-Assad was wearing a hood, so he had no idea where he was. However, he was aware of the roaring of the plane engines. Again he asked his captors where he was being taken, and this time they responded, 'We don't know, we are just following orders, there are high-ranking ones who are responsible.'

The tenuous link under which al-Assad seems to have been held for so long was his supposed dealings with a black-listed charity. He ran a small business importing car parts and also rented out offices in a small building that he owned. Just prior to his arrest, al-Assad had leased one of the offices to the Al-Haramain Islamic Foundation, which was a Saudi Arabian charity that the USA believed was involved in terrorist funding. The arrest of the other two men Salah 'Ali and Muhammad Bashmilah seemed to have been triggered off purely because they had recently visited Afghanistan.

Al-Assad's flight lasted for about three hours and when they landed he stepped out onto the tarmac into hot sunshine. From the airport al-Assad was taken to a cell where his hood and handcuffs were removed. It was a large, dirty room with a foam mattress and two small windows up near the ceiling. His food was passed to him through a small hole in the door and he thought he was kept there for about three weeks. The only person that spoke to him was his interrogator and translator, who kept asking him about his associations with the Al-Haramain charity. Judging by the accent of his jailers he thought he had probably been taken to East Africa.

After this period of internment, al-Assad was cuffed, hooded and taken to an airport, and this time the flight lasted a lot longer, possibly about eight hours. At his new destination the weather was considerably cooler, and again he had no idea of where he had been taken. He was held in a cell with no windows and nothing but a piece of matting on the floor. He remembers feeling cold but wasn't even given the luxury of a blanket. For a number of days he was left completely on his own, and after what he thinks was about nine days, he was interrogated once again, this time in English.

Next he was taken by car to a smaller, and what seemed to be a much older, cell. He was held here for several months and was occasionally questioned by the same interrogators and always about the same thing, his connection with the charity.

Al-Assad's next move was by helicopter, and his description of his next detention centre is the same as that given by the other two men. He said that the guards were all dressed in black and their faces were permanently covered. The only way they communicated with him was by hand gestures and the cell, which had no windows, meant that he never knew whether it was day or night, or what the conditions were like outside.

All three men were subjected to the same regime of interrogation – constant white noise played through loudspeakers and artificial light 24 hours a day. They were forbidden to speak to anyone with the exception of the interrogators and were only taken for a shower once a week. Salah 'Ali also reported that he had been suspended from the ceiling and had the soles of his feet beaten so badly that he was unable to walk when he was finally released from the hooks. On another occasion he was stripped and beaten by a circle of masked soldiers bearing sticks.

In May 2005, all three men were taken to a secret detention centre somewhere in the Yemen and today they are still being held without having received an official trial or charges. Yemeni officials said they had been given explicit instructions by the US government to continue to detain the three men until they receive further instructions.

Zahra Salloum was told that her husband had been deported to the Yemen because his passport was not valid, and this story was repeated by the media. Salloum was suspicious about the story and phoned al-Assad's 75-year-old father who lived in the Yemen. He travelled to the capital to see if he could find his son, but he was assured by the Yemini government that al-Assad had never entered the country. Determined to find out what had happened, he continued his journey to Dar-es-Salaam, where he filed a *habeus corpus* petition with the Tanzanian courts. Al-Assad's father was later to learn from Tanzanian officials that his son had been handed over to US custody, but no one knew where he had been taken.

It appears that two months earlier the same thing had happened to Salah Nasser Salim 'Ali and Muhammad Faraj Ahmed Bashmilah. All three men had entered the USA's covert network of illegal detentions and had simply 'disappeared'. The aim of the network is to try and collect as much information as they can through the use of long-term interrogation, without any judicial oversight. What is also worrying is the fact that is was a high-ranking official like an immigration officer who made the original arrest. This would suggest that the CIA are placing considerable reliance on foreign security and intelligence services to aid them in their rendition operations. The detainees are denied their legal right to speak to a lawyer, their families, doctors or even to be given a fair trial.

What these three cases have brought to light is the fact that the rendition system is not just for 'high category' detainees, and it is feared that the network is far more complex than originally believed. The three ordinary men mentioned here detained in at least four different secret locations, which were most likely to have been in different countries, judging by their descriptions of the length of their flights.

In September 2005, the Minister of the Interior

Rashad Al-Alimi reported that the three men had been accused of being members of terrorist groups. They said their trial would commence as soon as they received the files from the CIA, but as yet no information has been forthcoming.

Muhammad Bashmilah stated, 'If there are really charges we are ready to defend ourselves . . . we are Yemenis in Yemen, so why is the minister waiting for the Americans to decide?'

Following mounting investigation in Europe, it is believed that the US Senate will soon approve a rule that will necessitate the director of national intelligence to provide regular and detailed updates about any covert detention centres that are maintained by the USA overseas. This would also require an in-depth report on the treatment and condition in which the detainee is held.

EUROPE FIGHTS BACK

On 17 February, 2003, an Egyptian cleric by the name of Hassan Mustafa Osama Nasr (also known as Abu Omar) was allegedly abducted by the CIA as he walked to his mosque in Milan to take morning prayers. He had been living in asylum in Italy after his Islamic organization was declared illegal by the Egyptian government. Omar literally vanished off the face of the earth and nothing was heard of him until 13 months later, when he was able to make several phone calls to his friends and relatives. He claimed to have been abducted by US agents and taken to a joint US/Italian base, from where he was flown to Egypt. In Egypt he was subjected to aggressive torture tactics, such as beatings and electric shocks applied to his genitals. At the time of the phone calls, Omar had been released from detention on the orders of an Egyptian judge due to lack of evidence against him. However, a short while later he was again arrested and his whereabouts are no longer known.

Unhappy with the misuse of European soil during rendition operations, an Italian judge, Guido Salvini, issued a warrant for the arrest of 22 people believed to be agents or operatives of the CIA in June 2005. By November, the Justice Ministry in Italy requested for the extradition of the 22 suspects from the USA, and in December European arrest warrants were issued. These warrants were enforceable in all the 25 EU member countries and did not require the approval of any government.

The 22 agents have been accused of abducting Abu Omar without Italian permission and flying him to Egypt for interrogation. Italy claims that the abduction of Omar not only hampered their own investigations into Italian terrorism, but also violated Italian sovereignty. The arrests of these agents by Italy are part of a retaliation against the rendition policies used by the CIA. Many Italian citizens have voiced quite openly that they are not happy about the prospect of people being taken away from their own country to be tortured elsewhere. Sweden has also been looking into the activity of rendition, and Canada has set up hearings after one of its citizens was captured by US agents and flown to Syria for questioning without the knowledge of the Canadian government.

There is no doubt that the rendition controversy has damaged the United States' working relationship with the EU in the war on terrorism. However, despite the fact that Europe's governments have repeatedly denied their collaboration in the US programme of renditions, as evidence of the practice has come to light it has become clear that many European governments have adopted a 'see no evil, hear no evil' approach when it comes to rendition flights using their territory.

Genocide in Kosovo

——————1998-99——————

$\mathcal{K}$osovo is a province in southern Serbia that borders Montenegro, Albania and the Republic of Macedonia. It has an ethnic population of about two million people, predominantly Albanians, with smaller proportions of Serbs, Turks and Bosniaks. The province has been under United Nations administration since 1999, and it has been the subject of long-running and territorial disputes between the Serbian government and Kosovo's Albanian population.

In the late 1980s, a new, authoritarian leader emerged, a Serbian named Slobodan Milosevic. He was a former communist who had turned to nationalism and religious hatred in his efforts to gain power. As the Yugoslav federation started to collapse, Milosevic saw the opportunity to take control by inciting the long-standing tensions that were already present between the Serbs and Muslims in Kosovo. The Orthodox Christian Serbs, who were in the minority, claimed they were being downtrodden by the Albanian Muslim majority and Milosevic played on the dissent within the population. Under Josip Tito, the Muslims had enjoyed considerable independence, however, under the power of Milosevic, this autonomy would soon be taken away.

THE START OF ETHNIC CLEANSING

In 1989, Milosevic closed down the regional assembly and government and imposed a police state on Kosovo. Tens of thousands of Albanians lost their positions in government and private institutions alike, and Serbs were put in their place. Milosevic, who was trying to ethnically 'cleanse' the province, encouraged the migration of young Albanian men. Fearing for their own safety and now finding it difficult to earn a living, this is exactly what happened. Literally hundreds of thousands of Albanians fled Kosovo for Western Europe and North America, which created one of the largest migrant communities in the world.

Back in Kosovo, conditions for the remaining Albanians deteriorated as they were the subject of constant surveillance and harassment. Dr Julie Mertus, who was a member of Human Rights Watch, later reported that between the years 1989 and 1997, almost half the adult Albanian population in Kosovo was either arrested, interrogated, interned or remanded for no particular reason other than the fact they were not Serbs.

After nearly a decade of repression, the Albanians were no longer prepared to take a back seat and in 1966 they formed the Kosovo Liberation Army (KLA).

The KLA started off as a small guerilla organization that fought for independence from Serbian rule. Their initial attacks were aimed at the Serbian police, government officials and refugee centres in western Kosovo. Their aim was to provoke an open conflict in which they believed the West would be forced to intervene. Milosevic seized the opportunity and his regime started to plan a way of ridding Kosovo of Albanian culture once and for all – by acts of genocide.

THE KILLING STARTS

By 1997, the KLA's access to weapons was boosted by the eruption of civil war in neighbouring Albania. The country's armouries were raided by many different factions, and many of the automatic weapons found their way into the hands of the KLA.

The first major military assault by the KLA took place in September 1997, with the use of anti-tank weapons over a quite a large area of Kosovo. In February 1998, their attacks took on a more sinister tone when they started to attack Serb houses in the villages of Klina, Decani and Djakovica. They attacked a Serb refugee camp at Baboloc and ambushed several Serb policemen on the road between Glogovac and Srbica. Their actions provoked a major counter-offensive by Yugoslav security forces against the KLA strongholds, which resulted in one of the worst massacres in the history of Kosovo. Approximately 80 Albanians, including many women and children, were killed in the central Drenica region of Kosovo.

For two days the Serb police massacred the Albanians, either shooting them with shotguns or hitting them with other hard or sharp objects. Everywhere you could see the evidence of heinous carnage that had taken place. Bodies, many of which had been badly mutilated, lay on the ground and slumped across the thorny bushes that lined the roads.

Reprisal killings continued into 1998, including the massacre of the Deliaj clan in September of that year. After the massacre the bodies of 15 women, children and elderly members of the clan lay in grotesque positions among the rocks and streams of the gorge just below their village. Some had been shot at close range, others had been mutilated as they tried to escape the Serb forces. One of the cases of mutilation was a 30-year-old woman, Lumnije Deliaj, who was seven months pregnant. Her abdomen was slit open. Many of the houses had been burnt to the ground with the inhabitants still inside, too afraid to run outside for fear of being shot. Down a dirt track, just a few miles from the village lay the bodies of three elderly people, who had been shot in the head as they apparently came out to plead for their lives. However, the massacre that actually forced the West to get involved took place at the village of Racak on 16 January, 1999.

RACAK

In the early hours of 15 January, 1999, members of the Serb police force surrounded the village of Racak, in the district of Stimlje. They were searching for a group of terrorists from the KLA, who had killed a policeman, Svetislav Przic, five days earlier. They were notorious for having carried out multiple criminal acts of murder and torture and the security forces were eager to stop them doing any further damage.

The Serbs started by shelling the village in the early hours of morning, then stormed in and rounded up a group of around 40 men and youths. Most of them were severely beaten before being led down a steep path which went into a gully. The bodies of 45 ethnic Albanian civilians were later discovered outside the village by residents shortly after the government forces withdrew. The gully was filled with a mass of tangled bodies, there was blood everywhere and many corpses showed horrific signs of mutilation.

Following an international outcry, the Serbian government orchestrated a cover-up story by saying that Racak village was a base for KLA fighters. Appalled at what was happening in Kosovo, after the Racak massacre the international community, led by the USA, stepped up pressure on the Milosevic regime. They arranged a conference at the French chateau of Rambouillet to try and negotiate a peace settlement that would give Kosovo partial autonomy, not the full scale independence that the Albanians were demanding. The conference was a disaster, and the Serbs refused to sign any form of peace agreement. Instead, they withdrew to make their own plans to deal with the ethnic-Albanian problem. Their solution was 'Operation Horseshoe'.

The existence of the operation was immediately denied by the Yugoslav and Serbian governments, and by Milosevic himself, but it remains a subject of controversy right up to the current day. There is no doubt that there was some form of systematic ethnic cleansing, which produced the refugee crisis in Kosovo. It is estimated that a village a day was hit during 1998-99, targeting homes, shops and businesses owned by Albanians. Serb police used ruthless tactics to wipe out the villages neighbourhood by neighbourhood. The Albanians were literally ear-marked for destruction, solely because of their racial identity.

SUVA REKA

On 26 March, 1999, the Serb forces attacked the village of Suva Reka and killed 44 members of the Berisha family. Only two women and one child survived the massacre and one of them, Shyhrete Berisha, later testified at the trial of six former Serbian officials. Among the dead were 14 children, three babies and 14 women, including one who was nine months pregnant.

It all started when police stormed out of the local police station and started firing at six men standing in a courtyard outside their family home. Despite the fact that the men raised their arms in surrender, the police still shot them in cold blood. Other members of the family tried to run away, but they were stopped in front of a cafe not far from their house. The police forced the family inside the cafe, where they opened fire and threw two hand grenades inside the building.

Shyhrete Berisha was badly wounded, but she played dead as it appeared the police were firing at anything that moved. After about 30 minutes, the police threw the bodies into the back of a truck. Shyhrete and another two survivors managed to jump off the back of the truck without being noticed, and local Albanians helped them escape through the woods. A month later they all took refuge in Albania.

MEJA

On 30 April, 1999, an estimated 100 to 300 men and youths (the exact figures are still not known) are believed to have been executed at the village of Meja, northwest of Djakovica. Starting on 27 April, Serbian police and paramilitary units, together with soldiers of the Yugoslav army, forcibly expelled residents from the villages of Pecaj, Nivokaz, Dobrash, Sheremet, Jahoc, Ponashec, Racaj, Ramoc, Madanaj, Orizc and Cuska. The Serbs surrounded the villages, rounded up the inhabitants and forced them to walk towards Djakovica. During the course of the day many of the men and boys were taken away from the rest of the group. There are reports that the soldiers were seen holding literally hundreds of men at gunpoint. Those people who passed by later in the day reported having seen an 'enormous pile of bodies' at the side of the road.

Those who made it across the border into Albania, mainly women, children and the elderly, were severely traumatized and spoke of mass slaughter at the village of Meja. One witness claimed she saw 70 or more men squatting with their hands behind their heads in a small ditch that ran parallel with the road. Refugees that passed through Meja on that afternoon said there was blood and bodies everywhere, many lying face down and none of them were moving.

CLOSING DAYS OF THE WAR

In the closing days of the war, the grim and sordid details of mass slaughter appeared on the front pages of the world's newspapers. It was given the label of the 'Serbs Factory of Death' as more and more evidence came to light of the atrocities that had taken place. In Kosovo's capital of Prishtina, a beautiful 16th-century mosque was burnt down. Bulldozers had been used to flatten the rubble of many other mosques and buildings, leaving just the scars of war on the landscape. One elderly ethnic Albanian told a reporter,

'They tried to wipe out our Moslem history. You can erase our buildings but you cannot destroy our people.'

It appears that is exactly what the Serbs were trying to do: eradicate the Albanians from Kosovo. Vucitrn was another site of destruction, when the Serbs massacred about 70 men after being herded into courtyards. The women and children were robbed of their money and jewellery by masked paramilitaries, while listening to the screams of their menfolk being slaughtered. The only reminders of their families at the end of the day were the bloodstains on the grass and a pair of dentures embedded in the mud.

Ultimately, many displaced persons ended up in villages to the north-east of Vucitrn, such as Bajgore, Vesekovce, Kurillove and Sllakovce, which became overcrowded with the homeless, frightened Albanians. Several witnesses reported that they had to live with as many as 100 people to a single house and that others were forced to sleep out in the open air. On their travels to Albania the refugees had been subjected to cursing and threats from the Serb soldiers.

As the group of refugees passed through Vucitrn, seeing the bodies lying at the side of the road, they decided to tie a white cloth to their tractor, to show that they wanted to surrender. The soldiers simply ignored the symbol of surrender and started shooting and shelling the occupants of the tractor. A woman used a mattress to cover her children as they drove as fast as they could away from the village. As the refugees approached a warehouse, they saw a line of soldiers on the left hand side of the road. They stopped the refugees and told them to get out of their tractors, put their hands behind their heads and then to sit down on the road. The soldiers started cursing, kicking and beating them as they walked among the petrified families. One woman was beaten just because her child was crying.

There is no accurate record of just how many Albanians were killed during the Kosovo War, as new evidence is being discovered all the time. In 2001, the existence of a mass grave at Batajnica was uncovered, after the fall of the Milosevic regime in October 2000. As many as 1,100 bodies have been exhumed from this site alone, but it is believed their has been widespread tampering with the gravesites and destruction of evidence, in an attempt to cover the true extent of the atrocity. It is certain that genocidal massacres continued throughout the war, but then came the long, hard task of trying to find out who was responsible and bring them to justice.

Abuses in Darfur

————1983–present————

Since Sudan declared independence in 1956, it has been repeatedly torn apart by civil war. Since 1983 there has been ceaseless fighting between the largely Moslem, pro-government North and largely non-Moslem rebels in the South, making it the longest uninterrupted war in the history of the world. The death toll in Sudan is higher than the combined fatalities of Bosnia, Kosovo, Afghanistan, Chechnya, Somalia and Algeria and it is estimated that as many as two million Sudanese have died as a direct result of war.

The current crisis in Darfur is a continuation of a 15-year effort by Khartoum to quash potential political challenges and to expel rebels who are demanding greater regional independence and share of the power. Since the start of the rebel-insurgency in February 2003, the government of Sudan has persisted in using a military strategy that has violated the basic principles of international humanitarian and human rights law. It has failed to differentiate between military targets and civilian populations, the results of which have been dramatic. In just one year it is believed that as many as 750,000 people have been displaced in Darfur, with as many as 110,000 fleeing across the border into Chad. The severity of the crimes committed by Sudanese government forces and allied militias, the 'Janjaweed', amount to war crimes and crimes against humanity. On top of the forced displacement, they have committed murder, torture, pillage and rape on hundreds of thousands of civilians. Hundreds of villages have been destroyed, usually razed to the ground by fire, and all the villagers' personal belongings looted. Children have been abducted in large numbers and, even when they have fled their homes, the citizens are subjected to attacks by the militia as they pass through Janjaweed checkpoints dotted along the roads.

THE LATEST CONFLICT

The latest conflict in Darfur is deep-rooted, and there are key differences between the 2003–2004 conflict to prior bouts of fighting. The aggression started to have serious racial and ethnic undertones; a number of previously neutral ethnic groups became involved and it was hard for them to remain on the outside of the conflict. Basically, the hostilities were between the government and its militia and an insurgency was composed of two groups – the Sudan Liberation Army/ Movement (SLA/M) and the Justice and Equality

Movement (JEM). Initially the rebels consisted of three main ethnic groups – Zaghawa, Fur and Masaalit – but smaller groups of rebels joined in following attacks by the janjaweed militia on their communities. In addition, the militia were joined by some Arab and even non-Arab tribes in their fight against the rebels.

The SLA first emerged in 2003 and were originally called the Darfur Liberation Front. Its political demands included socio-economic development for the area, an end to tribal militia, and a share of power with the central government. Khartoum refused to cooperate with the SLA, who they considered to be little better than a group of bandits. In April 2003, the SLA surprised the government by launching an attack on El Fashir, which was the capital of North Darfur. They damaged several government-owned aircraft and helicopters and looted fuel and arms depots. The SLA captured a colonel in the Sudanese air force and made him give an interview on the Arab satellite TV news station, El Gezira. This was followed by another attack on Mellit, which is the second largest town in North Darfur, where again the SLA rebels raided government stocks. The conflict continued to escalate and the government were forced to make counter-attacks on the rebels, despite a cease-fire that was put in place in late 2002.

The government attacked villages and towns in North Darfur, and these attacks consisted of heavy aerial bombardment followed by ground attacks by the

Sudanese army and the Janjaweed militia. Following President Bashir's orders to 'annihilate the hirelings, traitors, agents and renegades', they launched major aerial bombing in the Zaghawa areas of Darfur, which caused thousands of civilians to flee into neighbouring Chad. Those who tried to stay in their homes were later forced to leave due to heavy military ground attacks. Although their initial plan was to destroy the bases of known rebels, the attacks got out of hand, especially when the Janjaweed militia were offered an incentive. They were given the opportunity to freely loot and capture the land of communities they had coveted for so long. They certainly took advantage of the conflict to loot, not confining their attacks to SLA or JEM troops or assets, but stepped over the line by targeting undefended villages.

As the war advanced, particularly after the collapse of cease-fire talks in 2003, the Janjaweed militia grew in size. The government, far from condemning the action, encouraged the Janjaweed in their activities. In fact, the destruction of water sources, burning of crops and theft of livestock were all key elements in the government's campaign. They realized that if they could cut off all food sources and water, that this would lead to inevitable forced displacement or even starvation – however, which under international laws this is a violation of humanitarian law.

The main target of aerial bombing in 2003 was the North Darfur state, which was the homeland of the

Zaghawa. Sudanese government aircraft, mainly Antonov planes, although MiGs and helicopters were also used, repeatedly bombed towns and villages at any time of day and night, without any prior warning. The attacks continued into 2004, with a disproportionate use of force in areas where there possibly could have been rebels present, although they were predominantly inhabited by defenceless civilians.

The bombing forced many people to leave their villages and move into the *wadis*, tree-lined riverbeds, that are dry except when there is heavy rain. They dug wells with their hands to access water under the riverbeds. However, even in the wadis they were not safe from attack and were continually being targeted by both air and ground assaults. It was obvious that the bombing of the wadis was part of the government's strategy to destroy the water supplies and other civilian institutions such as schools and hospitals.

The attacks spread to West and South Darfur, where Masaalit and Fur villages became the prime targets. At first, the attacks were carried out by armed Arab militia on either camels or horses and consisted mainly of theft of livestock and just verbal threats. However, as the months went by the attacks became worse, and by early 2004 they became more numerous and much more violent. Individuals have also reported that they were forced to pay the Janjaweed to allow them to return to their villages and farm their own land. However, once they return, their villages were attacked again or, in some cases, were already occupied by settlements of Arab nomads.

THE JANJAWEED

It is reported that the Sudanese government may have recruited as many as 20,000 Janjaweed militia to fight alongside their own army. Most of the Janjaweeed are believed to have come from Arab camel-herding tribes from North Darfur and Chad. Many of the tribesmen were attracted to the Janjaweed by the added incentive of looting. They have been described as wearing Sudanese government military uniforms, generally khaki in colour. Although they sometimes bear an insignia of a man on horseback, or a red patch on the shoulder, their ranks are generally broken up as regular government ranks, with the main leader taking the title of 'general'. They are armed with the latest military weapons, and although typically ride on camels or horses, they have often been seen travelling in Sudanese government vehicles.

Members of the Human Rights Watch have been told by credible sources that Janjaweed can be paid US$100 to US$400 as an enrolment fee, and that their relatives are guaranteed continued support should any member of the militia be killed in battle. They are also given identity cards and regular food supplies, stipends and communications equipment.

There have been numerous reports of rape by the

Janjaweed militia. One 18-year-old woman, the victim of a brutal racial attack, reported that the janjaweed had inserted a knife into her vagina saying, 'You get this because you are black'. Young boys who worked as shepherds have allegedly been abducted from Abu Gamra by the Janjaweed and were then subjected to sexual abuse and forced into domestic labour. In February 2004, residents of the town of Tawila were attacked; 67 were killed and 41 schoolgirls and female teachers were raped. Following the rape, the women were supposedly branded on the back of their hands to permanently stigmatize them.

There have also been an alarming number of abductions of both young girls and boys, although it is not possible to obtain an accurate number. It is estimated that the numbers are likely to be in their hundreds, ranging in age from infants to adolescents. A 20-year-old Zaghara woman named Mecca Hissab, was shot to death by the Janjaweed when she tried to stop them from taking her three-year-old son. Three shepherd boys from the village of Jirai, aged 10, 12 and 13, were all shot to death when they tried to stop the Janjaweed from stealing their animals. A 12-year-old girl from the same area also disappeared at the time of the attack and has not been seen since.

The primary target of the Janjaweed looting has been livestock – thousands of camels, cattle, sheep and goats belonging to Fur, Masaalit and Zaghawa villagers. Throughout the whole region of Darfur the native population rely heavily on their livestock for survival. Livestock are not only used for trade but also for family consumption, and the impact of the theft on the lives and livelihoods of millions of people cannot be stressed strongly enough. Without any compensation for their losses, thousands of families have already been rendered destitute. Any civilians attempting to stop the militia from stealing their stock or looting their homes risked death or serious injury.

NO SAFE REFUGE

Exhausted, terrified and hungry, and with nowhere to go, the refugees fled by their hundreds of thousands to neighbouring Chad, a largely semi-desert country and Africa's fifth-largest nation. However, like the Sudan, Chad has suffered from constant internal conflict. Poverty is rife and health and social conditions are inadequate, which is not helped by the influx of the refugees from Darfur. The refugees had a long and arduous journey of days, even weeks, travelling mainly at night to avoid attack. Deaths of their livestock and elderly family members have added to the general state of hopelessness felt by them. Hoping they would be safe once they crossed into Chad, the refugees didn't find the safe haven they had expected. The area was littered with landmines and other unexploded devices from Chad's own civil war in the 1970s. In some of the camps, up to 80 per cent of the refugees are children.

Their fathers stayed behind to salvage what they could of their belongings or are believed to be dead. Some of the men joined the rebel forces to try and overcome the militia.

Aid agencies are struggling to provide enough food, water and medical supplies, in what have been described as extremely difficult conditions. Disease is a problem and relief workers fear that the conditions will only get worse with the onset of the seasonal rains. Despite all these problems, the refugees' main fear is their own safety, because even across the border they are not safe from the ravages of the militia and their own government.

In an effort to protect the refugees from cross-border raids, UNHCR, the UN refugee agency, has moved more than 31,000 Sudanese homeless deeper into eastern Chad. The Chadian military are often in conflict with Janjaweed who slip across the border to further harass the refugees and steal their livestock.

PEACE AGREEMENT

In 2005, the Sudanese government and southern-based rebels signed a peace agreement to end their 21-year war. However, despite this agreement, Sudan's ruling party has failed to undertake the reforms that they promised to help end the human-rights abuses. There are concerns that the Sudanese government only entered into the peace agreement because it has already largely completed its programme of forced displacement. The UN fears that they will continue to manipulate humanitarian aid so that the refugees are forced to stay in the government-sponsored camps and be prevented from returning to their land and homes. Human Rights Watch have confirmed that the Janjaweed militia continued to control much of the rural area, imposing checkpoints and demands for payments on civilians trying to return to their land.

The UN called for an international commission of inquiry to establish the scale of the crimes against humanity in Darfur and the involvement of the Sudanese government in these atrocities. The US government eventually made a declaration of genocide after investigators had recorded the testimonies of over 1,136 refugees and displaced people from Darfur. The atrocities of Darfur have been described as 'one of the most forgotten and neglected humanitarian cases'.

Until the Sudanese government can feel the pain, not the profit, of its policy of violence and dispossession, it is feared that there will be no incentive to end the killing. There is certainly a definite need for international prosecutions to deter ongoing atrocities in Darfur. With attacks still being reported in the Darfur region, the UN has now authorized 20,000 troops to replace an under-equipped force of 7,000 African Union peacekeepers in Darfur. However, the Sudanese government, who has denied any part in the killings or any alliance with the Janjaweed, has refused to allow the peacekeepers into their country. This ongoing persecution of the innocent population of Darfur will be a long and difficult problem to solve.

Uganda's Atrocious War

—— 1988–present ——

*W*ith the wars in Iraq and Afghanistan capturing the media headlines, little attention has been given to the brutal atrocities that have been taking place in Uganda during the past 18 years. Uganda has always been thought of as one of the more successful African nations, and in most respects it is, but perhaps one of its greatest achievements is the fact that it has hidden its bloodthirsty war from the rest of the world for so long. The list of atrocities committed under the name of war is cannibalism, sex slavery, massacre, rape, torture and displacement.

COMPLEX WAR

The war in Uganda is a complex one that involves a brutal rebel group called the Lord's Resistance Army (LRA), which has abducted thousands of children and forced them to become either fighters or sex slaves. The rebels are led by Joseph Kony, whose group has become synonymous with torture, abductions and mass killings. The LRA's war was with the Ugandan government or the Allied Democratic Forces (ADF), whose undisciplined army has also committed crimes against civilians, the very people they are supposed to protect. As the war continues into its 19th year, an estimated 1.9 million Ugandans have been displaced and are still being ignored and unprotected from the abuses they receive at the hands of both the rebel and army forces.

LORD'S RESISTANCE ARMY

The LRA operates in the north from bases in southern Sudan. It is led by a former Catholic altar boy by the name of Joseph Kony, who seems to believe that his role in life is to cleanse the Acholi people. His army demands that Uganda be ruled according to the Bibical Ten Commandments, and Kony himself uses biblical references to explain why it is necessary to kill his own people. He told one of his captives, 'If the Acholi don't support us, they must be finished'. Kony sees himself as a spirit medium and makes up his own rules. He is thought to have as many as 60 wives, as he and his senior commanders take the pick of the girls they abduct. He has created an aura of fear and mysticism that seems to 'hypnotize' his rebels into following his strict rules and rituals. One young fighter who escaped from the LRA told a representative of the Humans Rights Watch, 'When you go to fight you make the sign of the cross first. If you fail to do this, you will be killed.'

The LRA has committed many serious abuses and atrocities, including the abduction, rape, maiming and killing of civilians, including many children. Many of the children and young adults were abducted for training as guerillas. Other children, mainly girls, were sold, traded or given as gifts to arms dealers in Sudan in exchange for weapons. The children were taken to a secret base where they were terrorized into virtual slavery either as guards, concubines or soldiers. They were beaten, raped and forced to march until they were exhausted, and many were compelled to participate in the killing of other children who had tried to escape. The LRA built up their numbers by the abduction of children, and in 1998 alone it is believed as many as 6,000 were taken and used as soldiers.

One young boy reported abuse at the hands of the LRA, when they falsely accused him of joining the government forces. They tied him down and told him not to cry or make any noise. Then a man sat on his chest while others held down his arms and legs. The boy pleaded with the rebels not to kill him, and as he cried one man picked up an axe and chopped off his left hand, then his right. After that he cut off his nose, his ears and his mouth with a knife. The young boy's ear was sent in a letter warning people against joining the ADF.

Tens of thousands of teenagers who are not prepared to take the risk of being abducted, either sleep out in the bushes or walk into urban centres to sleep in the grounds of hospitals or in the shelter of shop doorways. There is fear, however, that so many children sleeping in one place might be an easy pickings for the rebels.

On 25 July, 2002, 48 people were hacked to death near the town of Kitgum, which is in the far north of Uganda. Elderly people were reportedly killed with machetes and spears while babies were flung against trees. Ugandans were shocked by the brutality of the attack when they read the headlines the next day.

The LRA have been linked with Sudan because they allegedly support the Sudan People's Liberation Army, which is the rebel movement fighting against the Sudan government. Although Sudan officials deny this liaison, in February 2003 they agreed to let troops from Uganda enter its territory to attack the LRA rebels. The Ugandan army, who had been after the LRA for 18 years, asked the rebels to surrender or be defeated. By early 2003 there was growing optimism that the years of fighting could soon be over. Members of the LRA declared a cease-fire and said they wanted to hold talks with Uganda's president, Museveni. They agreed to stop all their ambushes, abductions and attacks, but this amnesty had little real effect. In June 2003, Joseph Kony told his fighters to destroy Catholic missions, kill priests and missionaries and brutally assault the nuns.

OPERATION IRON FIST

In March 2003, keen to distance itself from the accusations of supporting international terrorism, the Sudanese government agreed to assist in the fight against the LRA. Ugandan troops crossed into Sudan and launched large-scale raids against known LRA strongholds. An estimated 10,000 Ugandan troops were involved in the latest offensive, which became known as 'Operation Iron Fist'.

At first the Ugandans claimed success over the LRA, but their ebullience was to be short-lived when the rebels mounted a series of new attacks. Hundreds of Sudanese civilians were killed as the LRA were pushed further north by the Ugandan army. Far from knocking out the LRA forces, Uganda's 'Iron Fist' led to a new round of butchery and abductions.

Despite the gruesome results, the Ugandan government continued its operation, which – as Human Rights workers feared – has simply led to more bloodshed. The LRA attacked the Acholi-Pii and Maaji refugee camps, the Pabo IDP camp, and many villages and communities within the area. These attacks have resulted in the most horrific deaths, abductions and widespread displacement of civilians. In the attack on Acholi-Pii alone, it is believed that as many as 24,000 people were forced to leave the camp, and six teenage girls were taken away and never seen or heard of again.

Many of the abducted girls become pregnant and

give birth to their baby while in captivity. This makes it much harder for them to escape as they fear for the life of their infant, and those who do manage to get away, usually bear lifelong scars. It is believed that as many as 50 per cent of the girls who are abducted have contracted HIV (human immunodeficiency virus) and virtually 100 per cent have sexually transmitted infection as a result of sexual abuse.

Even though so-called 'protected camps' have been set up to try and help the victims of the Ugandan conflict, overcrowding and lack of facilities has led to widespread disease and poverty rather than protection from the LRA. There is little support for the victims of gender-based violence due to under-funding and lack of backing from the government.

AN END IN SIGHT

The fact that this conflict has been allowed to continue for 19 years is proof that there has been little positive action to create a lasting peace in Uganda. In October 2005, the International Criminal Court, which is based in The Hague, announced arrest warrants for Joseph Kony and four of his top associates. The charges included mutilation of civilians and the forced abduction of and sexual abuse of children. However, some Ugandans feared that this would only invite further conflict as the LRA members were certain to want avoid facing a trial.

In July 2006, representatives for the LRA took part in a series of peace talks with the Ugandan government in southern Sudan. Joseph Kony was not present at any of the meetings and was believed to be in hiding in the Congo to avoid prosecution for war crimes. The LRA tried to portray themselves as freedom fighters against President Museveni, but their ploy was useless as they had alienated themselves with the Ugandan people through their use of brutal tactics.

It is understandable that the Ugandan government is skeptical of the LRA's promises, given the fact that it has committed some of the worst humanitarian atrocities in the history of war, with devastating consequences. Nearly two million people have been run out of their homes and forced to live in overcrowded, squalid camps; tens of thousands have died, 30,000 children have been abducted, and hundreds of villages have been destroyed or abandoned.

The current peace talks are the closest the two sides have ever come to reaching a comprehensive agreement and Uganda now needs to know that the UN will be a supportive ally. The need to create incentives for both sides is paramount, so that the foundations can be laid for long-term reconstruction and reconciliation. It is feared that if this latest agreement breaks down, then peace will be a long time in coming to the people of Uganda.

Crimes in the Congo
————1998–2003————

*T*he war that took place between 1998 and 2003 in the Democratic Republic of Congo has been equalled to that of World War II. It is estimated that as many as 3.3 million people died as a result of the war, with the vast majority dying from starvation or disease due to the activities of the complex assortment of armed fighting forces operating in the country. Despite the fact that the Congo is an area rich in natural resources – diamonds, oil, uranium, gold, water, fertile land and exquisite wildlife – it became the object of a conflict that got completely out of hand and was dubbed 'Africa's first world war'. Despite the supposed cessation of hostilities in 2003, tensions are still high today.

It is the largest interstate war in the history of Africa and involves nine other African nations, as well as a further 20 armed groups. It is very difficult to understand the reasons for this conflict, due to the fact that there are so many players involved, but an easy way to explain it is that there are nine rebel groups in the Congo who are all fighting to overthrow governments in neighbouring countries. On top of that they all want a part of the region's riches. The internal conflicts were originally fuelled by ethnic struggles to gain power and riches for people that have never known either. Throughout the years of fighting the Congo became the subject of one of the worst human-rights situations in the world, leaving a trail of carnage, including massacre, rape, child abuse, kidnap and even canibalism.

MASSACRES

Tensions between the Hema and the Lendu tribes, who share fertile land close to the Ugandan border, have existed for many years. About 200 people died in brutal ethnic massacres in the early part of 2001 in the north-east of the Democratic Republic of Congo. After the bloodshed, vehicles went around the town parading severed heads that had been spiked on sticks.

The atrocities were not just limited to these two tribes, however. The Rwandan army and a Kigali-backed rebel groups have also been known to have carried out brutal and systematic massacres.

In May 2002, a massacre was carried out by the Rassemblement Congolais pour la Démocratie-Goma (RCD-G). The RCD relied on the military and political support of neighbouring Rwanda in its control of approximately 40 per cent of eastern Congo. The RCD soldiers entered the civilian neighbourhood of Mangobo and carried out indiscriminate killings of civilians, numerous rapes, beatings and widespread looting. They also arrested a large number of Congolese military and police who they suspected might be involved in a mutiny, which had taken control of the radio station and called for help in tracking down the Rwandans. These officers were executed on the nights of 14 and 15 May on the Tshopo bridge. They were ordered to lie down with their hands bound behind their backs and were then either shot or hacked to death with machetes, or had their throats slit. It is reported that many of the bodies were decapitated before being put into weighted-down plastic sacks and thrown over the side of bridge into the river. Other executions are known to have taken place at an abandoned brewery, the Bangboka Airport and the military barracks at Camp Ketele. Although members of the Human Rights Watch have been unable to identify the RCD officers implicated in these abuses, they stated that what had taken place amounted to war crimes.

Massacres continued throughout the Congo during 2003–2005. US officials are negotiating with Rwanda, Uganda, the Congo and Burundi to try and find a way of dealing with the armed rebel groups. Working in close coordination with the African Union, the EU and the UN, the US hopes to be able to reduce the amount of violence, which is estimated to be taking as many as 1,000 lives each day. Their ultimate goal is to try and bring stability and security back to the people of the Congo, something which they haven't experienced for a long time.

In April 2003, nearly 1,000 people were massacred in

the Ituri region of the Congo. The clashes between the Hema and Lendu tribes started out as a simple dispute over land but have since escalated into a far more volatile situation. When UN investigators were taken to the site of the massacre at Drodro, they saw about 20 mass graves with traces of fresh blood still visible. The victims bore the signs of tribal fighting with slashes from machetes, stab wounds and mutilation.

In May 2003, two rival groups – the Hema and Lendu tribes – fought for control in Ituri's largest town, Bunia. After the killing spree an eerie calm hung over Bunia, with dead bodies littering the now empty streets. The rebels had left behind their trademark as blood dripped from the machete slashes, the spear thrusts and bullet wounds. Other corpses had started to decay and were being eaten by packs of wild dogs. In the central marketplace, women's bodies littered the ground and a baby's body – a grim reminder – lay on the main street. Two priests had been killed while praying inside a church and the remains of a burning corpse lay on the UN compound's lawn.

The massacre began when the UN withdrew its troops in accordance with a recent peace agreement. The violence had been widely predicted and so it was no surprise when the Lendus took the town of Bunia, forcing 250,000 people to take flight. The remaining 12,000 pressed against the razor wire of the UN compound, screaming, as they tried to escape the machete-wielding militia. Women clutched their babies to their chests as they watched in horror as their families and neighbours were slayed. Many more bodies lay in front of the mud huts, which the militia had smashed to pieces. The death toll was approximately 350 people, and most of the bodies were later buried in simple, unmarked graves.

Two unarmed UN military observers were found dead about 65 km (40 miles) outside of the village. They had been mercilessly murdered and one had been disembowelled. The women, natives of Jordan and Malawi, were not even involved in the conflict – they had simply been sent there to gather information about the armed groups operating in Ituri.

Days after the massacre, the main Hema militia, the Union of Congolese Patriots (UPC) took control of Bunia. Their reputation was little better than the Lendu's, as their fighters are estimated to have massacred as many as 10,000 Lendus. Child fighters of the UPC went through Bunia, looting what they could from the remaining houses and off the corpses, showing no respect whatsoever.

In July 2005, 39 civilians were murdered in the village of Ntulumamba, a village in the south Kivu region of the Congo. The victims, mainly women and children, were locked inside their huts, which were then burnt to the ground. The rebels responsible were believed to be from Rwanda, who fled to the Congo when they were accused of taking part in the genocide that left some 800,000 Tutsis and moderate Hutus dead.

There is also considerable evidence that there were

many atrocities committed against women during the Congo War. Women have been reportedly tortured, genitally maimed, raped and killed – at times disembowelled to kill a foetus along with its mother. These are the type of atrocities that have taken place out of sight of UN peacekeepers. Mass rapes were often carried out to try and demoralize their enemies, and there are reports of women being buried alive after ramming sticks into their vaginas. In addition to the mental and physical injury suffered by women, there is also the risk of pregnancy and they are particularly vulnerable to contracting HIV because their bodies are open to infection. Women have also been abused in jails and forced into sexual slavery, including a number who have been victims of intimidation.

CANNIBALISM

Cannibalism has been added to the long list of atrocities that have allegedly been carried out by the tribal groups fighting in the Congo. Some of the bodies found at Bunia and other villages had been decapitated, others had their hearts, livers and lungs missing. It has been reported by witnesses that the rebels literally ripped out their victims' hearts and ate them while they were still warm. Militiamen have allegedly grilled their victims' bodies on spits over a fire, and two young girls were boiled alive while their mother watched on. Vital organs were said to have been cut off and used as magic charms to ward off evil spirits. In 2003, Zainabo Alfani told UN investigators that she had been forced to watch rebels kill and eat two of her children. She also said that in one corner of the camp she saw cooked flesh from bodies and another two bodies being grilled on a barbecue.

THE CURRENT SITUATION

Despite the fact that the UN peacekeeping mission has stepped up its efforts to combat armed rebel groups in the Congo, the insecurity and violence continue to torment the African civilians. Today it is estimated that there are still as many as 38,000 Congolese civilians dying each month, that is about 1,250 each day, either as a direct result of violence or preventable diseases and malnutrition.

For the first time in 40 years, 18 million Congolese went to the polls on 30 July, 2006. They voted for a new president and national assembly and, in general, the voting was a peaceful and well organized affair.

Congo's president, Joseph Kabila, was declared the winner of the elections by the Independent Electoral Commission of the Democratic Republic of Congo on 15 November, 2006, and following the results he called for calm. The final outcome was the culmination of a four-year transition process which was designed at bringing democracy to the troubled African nation after decades of dictatorship and war. However,

Kabila's rival, Jean-Pierre Bemba, released a statement saying that he was not prepared to accept the election result and his supporters disputed that the figures released were inaccurate. Election officials have rejected any claims of fraud and state the the polling was, in general, fair. The UN peacekeeping force stepped up its security for fear of renewed fighting, and it appears that the election results will do nothing to bring peace to the long-suffering people of the Congo.

CONGO REBEL CHARGED WITH WAR CRIMES

Thomas Lubanga, leader of the Union of Congolese Patriots (UPC) militia group, is the first person to be charged of war crimes at the International Criminal Court (ICC) in The Hague. The charges against him include recruitment of child soldiers, murder, torture and rape. The ICC was set up in 2002 to deal with war crimes and genocide worldwide. Lubanga was arrested in 2005 after nine Bangladeshi UN peacekeepers were killed in the volatile Ituri district. He is thought to be one of the most notorious warlords of the 21st century and, soldiers under his command, are accused not just of murder, torture and rape, but also of mutilation.

Although the ICC has also issued arrest warrants for leaders of Uganda's rebel Lord's Resistance Army, they are currently being given amnesty by the Ugandan government and so no action can be taken.

War Crimes in Chechnya

————1999–present————

*D*isturbing evidence has been gathered in Chechnya that proves that Russian and Chechen forces have committed major abuses, including war crimes, in their second campaign on an already war-torn republic. Since 2001 mass 'dumping sites' for human remains have been uncovered, adding to the already long list of human rights violations committed by the warring sides of the ongoing war. These violations include forced disappearances, mass hostage takings, rapes, massacres and mass killings.

Graffiti found on a wall in the city of Grozny, spells out what the citizens of Chechnya have been living through:

Welcome to Hell: Part Two!

These words sum up the atrocities that have taken place in Russia's supposed fight against terrorism, but it is the Chechen civilians who have borne the brunt of the Russian offensive in this war. Although both Russian and Chechen sides have been accused of resorting to unfair harsh methods during the conflict, it has, for a long time, been cleverly shielded from the eyes of the UN Commission on Human Rights.

CHECHNYA'S IMPORTANCE TO RUSSIA

Chechnya is not a separate country but a republic situated on the northern slopes of the Caucasus Mountains. It is strategically important to the Russian Federation for two reasons: its access routes to both the Black Sea and the Caspian Sea go through Chechnya, and vital oil and gas pipelines also run through Chechnya, connecting it with Kazakstan and Azerbaijan. With the dissolution of the Soviet Union in 1991, Chechnya declared its independence from Russia, which, as a result of ongoing differences, ultimately led to a civil war in 1993. Ethnic groups began stirring up trouble in their fight for more autonomy, and one of the more volatile groups were the Chechens. The Chechens had a long and bloody history of opposition to being governed by Moscow. By 1994, the relationship between the breakaway government in Chechnya and the Russian government had seriously deteriorated.

The First Chechen War started in 1994 when Russian forces entered Chechnya to try and restore constitutional order. What turned out to be a rather embarrassing and bloody conflict, ended in August 1996, with the Chechens claiming victory and independence, and the Russians also claiming victory and the retention of Chechnya as part of Russia. Clashes continued for a while until the 1996 Khasavyurt ceasefire agreement, causing the Russians to finally withdraw from Chechnya.

The 1997 election of a separatist president, Aslan Maskhadov, made an already volatile situation far worse. Even though Russia had accepted Chechnya's independence and the 1997 Moscow peace treaty had helped to dampen down the flames of animosity, a chilly relationship between the two nations continued. In May 1998, Valentin Vlasov, a personal envoy of Boris Yeltsin, was kidnapped, but he was later released on 13 November. It is reported that the Russian government paid as much as seven million dollars for his release. Tensions increased when in early 1999 President Maskhadov announced that Islamic Sharia law would be introduced into Chechnya in the course of the following three years.

ONSET OF WAR NUMBER TWO

Fighting broke out once again in August 1999 in the Russian area of Dagestan as guerilla forces began to filter through from neighbouring Chechnya. Following several clashes with Russian troops, the rebels managed to take control of several villages. The Russians gradually increased their military to 17,000 and started to carry out airstrikes against the rebels, forcing them to return to Chechnya. The Russians pursued the rebels with the intent of trying to end the separatist republic's existence, and this was to be the start of a ruthless military campaign. As the years went by the war turned from a rural guerrilla conflict into an urban campaign of terror.

ATROCITIES IN CHECHNYA

Right from the onset of the conflict, Russian troops have been accused of indiscriminately bombing and shelling civilian areas, causing heavy casualties of innocent, unarmed people. They have decided to ignore the Geneva Convention and have focused their attacks on the guerrillas without taking any safeguards to protect civilians. The Russian forces have used powerful surface-to-surface bombs on many of their raids, which have caused the deaths of literally hundreds of civilians. Their bombing campaign has turned many parts of Chechnya into nothing better than a wasteland, in particular the destruction of the capital Grozny. One of their missiles blew up in the courtyard of the only functioning maternity hospital in Grozny. The explosion killed 28 women and newborn babies and seven other people. In total, at least 143 people were killed in the attacks on the capital.

In February 2000, in an attempt to try and stop the

Chechen rebels, Russian forces bombed the village of Katyr-Yurt, despite the fact that the civilians were flying a white flag. As a result of the intense bombing and the arrival of a large number of fighters in the village, 20,000 refugees were forced to flee in desperation. It is thought that as many as 343 civilians were killed and there were reports of several women being raped.

For many Chechens, however, the constant bombing raids were only the beginning of the horrors they had to face. Once they came face to face with the Russian soldiers, they faced even greater dangers. There are reports of civilians being gunned down in the street and in their own yards while they waited for Russian troops to inspect their identity documents. These were not unavoidable casualties of war, these were plain and simple acts of murder.

MOSCOW THEATRE CRISIS

In October 2002, rebels took more than 700 people hostage in a Moscow theatre, demanding the end of Russian presence in Chechnya. The rebels threatened to execute their hostages if their demands were not met, and the Russians eventually ended the siege by storming the theatre. More than 100 of the hostages died as a result of the crippling knockout gas used by the Russian forces. What was even more horrifying was the fact that the Russians did not carry effective antidotes to the gas and concealed exactly what type of gas they had used to rescue workers, hampering them in their effort to save lives. Some of the victims were known to have choked on their vomit following the inhalation of gas, and many of the freed hostages were in a state of unconsciousness as they were loaded onto waiting buses and ambulances. Of the 41 militants who took part in the siege, 19 were known to have been women. Dressed in black, with their faces covered and explosives strapped to their waists, the women were known as the Chechen 'Black Widows'. It was the first time that Russian troops had used gas to resolve a hostage situation, and there is still an ongoing investigation into why they used such a toxic deterrent, knowing full well that many of the hostages would lose their lives. In fact, all but two of the fatalities among the hostages were caused by the adverse effects of the gas.

The following year saw a wave of lawsuits filed by former hostages and those who lost loved ones during and after the raid. Over 60 plaintiffs claimed millions of dollars in compensation for moral and material damages from the Moscow government.

BESLAN SCHOOL SIEGE

On 1 September, 2004, a group of militants took control of Beslan School Number One, which was attended by nearly 900 students. At about 9.20 a.m., on a hot and sunny day, a group of heavily armed men and women with machine guns, assault rifles, hand grenades and at least half a dozen bombs and detonators stormed through the school doors. On the other side of the building, another group of terrorists ran into a courtyard. It became chaotic as the shooting began, and many of the students ran towards the school gym. Many of the older students who were waiting outside when the shooting started escaped, but the younger children were unable to get away. More than 1,200 children, parents and teachers were herded into the gym. One of the fathers was killed straight away right in front of all the hostages, including his own two sons. The terrorists wired explosives all around the gym and threatened to detonate them if their demands were not met. At first, they allowed their captives access to water and toilets, but they were not given any food. However, as the day wore on, the terrorists cut off any privileges, making the whole situation far more tense and intolerable.

Outside the school, the whole town had gathered, desperate to find out what was going to happen to their children. The terrorists started to shoot at soldiers who had surrounded the school and also into the ceiling to further intimidate their captives. One of the terrorists told a teacher that they were simply 'fed up with the war in Chechnya'. He went on to explain that a Russian plane had killed his entire family and that he now wanted to kill, and didn't care if it was women and children. He told the teacher that the terrorists wanted the Russian president, Vladimir Putin, to announce the withdrawal of all troops from Chechnya.

As the days went by and the captives became more and more desperate, some of the children and adults started drinking their own urine. The situation became critical as hundreds of school children were suffering from severe dehydration. The townspeople demanded action, and the end to the horrific siege started with an explosion. After the explosion, there was a pile of dead children and when the screaming subsided, there was nothing but an eerie silence. Although survivors believe that the explosion was an accident, it was enough to instigate a stand-off.

The siege was eventually ended when the Alpha Group of OSNAZ, who were special forces troops within the KGB. It took nearly ten hours before all the shooting stopped and hundreds of wounded children were rushed to hospitals in any available vehicles. The final death toll was 331 civilians (176 of whom were children), 11 commandos and 31 militants.

LARGE-SCALE 'DISAPPEARANCES'

Another operation that has come to light during the Chechnya War is the arrest of large numbers of civilian men throughout Chechnya by the Russian authorities. These men, numbering well over 1,000, and occasionally women, have been taken to clandestine detention centres, leaving their relatives desperate to try and find their whereabouts. Some of the men were released after a few days when their families were able to bribe the Russian troops with money, weapons or ammunition. Those men that were able to return to their families consistently told of constant beatings, severe torture and even cases of rape against both men and women. One man said he had been hit with a heavy metal hammer which left him with severe back injuries. A second man told of broken ribs and that he had ongoing kidney problems as a result of the beatings.

Guards at these detention camps, or 'filtration points', treat the inmates cruelly because they know that these illegal camps are not registered anywhere and are unlikely to be traced. Because they are not sanctioned by law, no records are kept of who is being detained and where. If the bodies of these detainees are found, they usually bear the scars of torture and violent death. Sometimes the bodies have been blown up so that they cannot be identified.

As if this wasn't bad enough, there are now many people claiming that the Russians have set up a trade in corpses. Relatives have been known to pay as much as 100 to 3,000 dollars to have their relative's corpses returned to them for burial. The wealth of the family of the kidnapped or arrested person determines the ransom they are asked to pay. If the amount is not paid, the captive faces the 'death cave', or torture chamber. Those who die under torture are sold back to their families, knowing full well that they will pay because it is vital under the Chechen belief to have a traditional funeral and burial.

REFUGEE CRISIS

The number of people that have gone missing from Chechnya is reportedly as high as 10,000 and possibly as many as 15,000 being held in refugee camps. The conditions inside these camps are appalling with inadequate makeshift shelters and a shortage of food, clean water, heating and many other basic essentials. The shelters are either tents, railway carriages or empty truck containers, and many are forced to pay extortionate rents to try and avoid the overcrowding. Many refugees who run out of money are forced to return to the war zones, putting their lives at even further risk. Because of the constant looting and, as in the capital Grozny, complete destruction, many of the refugees do not actually have any homes to return to.

Russia is not permitting humanitarian organizations to operate freely and is virtually blocking any direct assistance for the refugees so desperately in need of help. There are limited medical supplies and the Chechen children are not permitted to attend school.

Although many of the refugees are unsure how long their welcome will last, the majority told interviewers that they would not return to their homes – or what is left of them – unless the Russian soldiers leave. The same thing was heard again and again, 'We are afraid for our male population, afraid we will have no husbands or sons'.

MASS GRAVES

The bodies of people who had been lost since the beginning of 2001 have started to turn up in mass graves. The first grave was uncovered on 25 February, 2001, at Khan-Kala, near Grozny, where there is a Russian military base. There were 200 corpses in the mass grave. Their arms and legs had been tied up and the majority were wearing blindfolds. Many of the corpses bore signs of mutilation, including stab wounds, broken limbs, flayed body parts, severed fingertips and ears cut off.

Reeling from the shock of the first discovery, the Chechen people had to face another at Roshni-Chu. This grave bore the body of a one-year-old baby. Since then more mass graves have been uncovered, revealing the atrocities that have taken place. Local people who discovered a grave in April 2002 in a mountain cave at Achkhoy-Martanovsky, reported that all the 100 bodies found there had been beheaded.

The discovery of these graves led to another gruesome detail; some of the bodies had had their internal organs removed. This opened the floodgates to speculation – what exactly had happened to these organs? There have been claims that the organs have been sold on the black market to be used in laboratories or as much sought-after transplants. Despite these allegations, as yet there is no organization to investigate these claims and get to the bottom of the missing organs.

WHAT IS LEFT OF CHECHNYA

The ongoing war has taken its toll on Chechnya and its people. Russian bombing has destroyed over 50,000 homes and out of the original 424 villages, 270 have been completely destroyed. Land mines and bombs have contaminated the agricultural lands of Chechnya, and threaten the future survival of a nation. Although Russia is trying to use the war against terrorism as an excuse for what is taking place in Chechnya, it is obvious that Putin is trying his hardest to cover up the atrocities that have really taken place. What is equally worrying, however, is the lack of a strong Western response to the continuing abuses of a people who are wounded by years of war.